Breaking Through — Women, Work and Careers

Breaking Through -
Women, Work and Careers

edited by Jocelynne A. Scutt

Artemis

Artemis Publishing Pty Ltd
PO Box 151
Market Street
Melbourne 3000 Victoria
fax: (03) 670 1252

First published 1992
Reprinted 1992
Copyright © Jocelynne A. Scutt 1992
Copyright in individual contributions
remains with the contributors.

All rights reserved. No part of this publication may be
reproduced, stored in a retrieval system, or transmitted
in any form or by any means, electronic, mechanical,
photocopying, recording or otherwise, without prior
written permission of the publisher.

National Library of Australia
Cataloguing-in-Publication entry:

Breaking through, women, work and careers.

  Includes index.
  ISBN 1 875658 00 9.

  1. Women – Employment – Australia – Biography. 2. Sex role in the work environment – Australia. I. Scutt, Jocelynne A., 1947– .

331.40922

Designed by Derrick I. Stone Design
Typeset in Goudy by Derrick I. Stone Design
Printed in Australia by The Book Printer

To Marjorie Josephine Needham Scutt

ACKNOWLEDGMENTS

I am appreciative of Carolyn Cartwright's work in administration, organisation, wordprocessing and proofreading of *Breaking Through*; Carla Taines in administration, organisation, editing and indexing; Derrick Stone for his work, including production design; Anne Thacker for reading and editing the manuscript; Lariane Fonseca for the cover photograph, 'Passionately Forward'; and Diarmuid Pigott for the background photograph of the Graces. The fine support of Di Graham, Kerry Heubel, Jennifer Aldred, Lesley Norris, Melanie Young, Renate Klein, Susan Hawthorne and Yvonne Carnahan sustains me as does, always, that of my family, Robin Joyce, Felicity Beth, Fleur Joyce, Kate McMullan and Bob McMullan.

In the compiling and writing of *Breaking Through* the ebulliance, enthusiasm and 'keeping-on' of the Women's Movement has been central.

The photographs of Patricia Brennan (Philip Le Mesurier), Gay Davidson (Bill Errington), Jocelynne A. Scutt (*Age*) and Carolyn Watts (ABC Radio 5AN Adelaide), are reprinted with permission.

Jocelynne A. Scutt
Melbourne 1992

CONTENTS

INTRODUCTION

Jocelynne A. Scutt   Dangerous Women   1

PART I   TELLING IT HOW IT IS

1 Jane Cafarella   Something of My Own   11

2 Louise Liddy-Corpus   Taking Control Now   21

3 Gay Davidson   Running Free – Then Confronting the Barriers   32

4 Carolyn Watts   No Well Lit Path   41

5 Shirley Stott Despoja   Fighting for Fair Shares   47

PART II   PUSHING THE MARGINS

6 Lisa Bellear   Keep Fighting, Keep Speaking Out   57

7 Janine Haines   A Sort of Crusade   64

8 Gracelyn Smallwood   Demanding More than a Great Vocabulary   71

9 Patricia Brennan   Not a Guided Tour   81

10 Irina Dunn   Careering Through Life   91

11 Greta Bird   Growing Up in Law School   101

PART III BREAKING THE BARRIERS

12 *Melba Marginson*   Not for the Money   115

13 *Jackie Huggins*   But You Couldn't Possibly ...!   124

14 *Sue Schmolke*   Genesis — Tennant Creek   131

15 *Dawn Rowan*   Beware, Oh Take Care   139

16 *Lariane Fonseca*   Hustling Pool   149

PART IV IN PRACTICE

17 *Jennifer Coate*   Slipping Through the Net   161

18 *Diane Fingleton*   Why am I Doing This?   171

19 *Irene Watson*   Surviving as a People   177

20 *Irene Moss*   Born in a Tomato Hothouse   187

21 *Fiona Tito*   Pieces in a Crazy Patchwork   197

22 *Beth Wilson*   Beyond the Legal Mystique   208

EPILOGUE

Jocelynne A. Scutt   Golden Girls and Good Women   217

INDEX   229

DANGEROUS WOMEN

Jocelynne A. Scutt

In 1948 in her book, *Anything But Love*, Elizabeth Hawes wrote:

> If economic necessity forces you to be productive outside your home after marriage, you will be taught how to pretend you aren't doing it. If you show any symptoms before marriage of going after a career other than that of facilitating your search for a man, you are peculiar and eccentric. If you go about saying you want and like to be a Worker, you'll be considered dangerous.

In *Breaking Through* the women writing of their work and careers might well be classed as 'dangerous women'. Each of them, whether beginning with work in a factory, commencing her career path as a secretary or teacher, or plunging straight from school into university, showed positive symptoms of going after a career as a matter unrelated to the search for a partner-in-marriage. Today, each of them goes about saying she wants and likes to be a Worker.

In the 1960s and 1970s when women of all ages embraced the sisterhood of the Women's Movement, there was a feeling amongst us that girls growing up, and young women, ought to be provided with a 'better' base upon which to build their lives. The implication was that women had somehow been 'wronged' in not being orientated or directed towards particular, defined or 'set' careers when six years old; that at school we *should have known* that when grown-up we *would be* a firefighter; or an astronaut; a traindriver or accountant; a farmer; or a lawyer, physicist or prime minister. Books were written drawing comparisons and distinctions between the growing-up of girls and that of boys. The message went abroad that the world was the way it was — with men in positions of power, men at the head of industry, men in parliament, as bankers, as media moguls — because girls had not been schooled in planning for a lifetime's work as treasurer or moonwalker.

Yet was (and is) this the problem? What of those men who do decide, as schoolboys, to become prime minister. And never make it. Does such a man then endure a lifetime of believing himself a failure? What of the schoolboy who determines he'll be a lawyer, then judge — and reaches his goal? A lifetime as a lawyer, and twenty years of it as a member of the judiciary, may well prove a recipe for boredom or stultification. How many psychiatrists and engineers, tradesmen and heads of department, feel 'locked in' at 35, or 47, or 52, or 55. How many, on retirement, look back upon a limited life, spent on doing what he thought he 'should'. How many, with the latitude given them by retirement look back, contemplating what their lives could have been had they not determined upon one path at an early age?

Women are disadvantaged in the job stakes. Government policies now recognise this disadvantage. Efforts are being made in the public and private sectors of paid employment to change this. Equal opportunity in employment and education, and affirmative action in public and private employment, are required through equal opportunity, affirmative action and anti-discrimination acts around Australia. Maternity leave is acknowledged by the Australian Industrial Relations Commission as an industrial issue, and New South Wales was the first state to introduce maternity leave legislation, passed in the early 1980s. Australia is a signatory to (and has ratified) the International Labour Organisation (ILO) Convention 156 which requires each member state to '... make it an aim of national policy to enable workers with family responsibilities to exercise their right to work, without discrimination ...' Programs have been introduced in the technical and further education sector to ensure that women who have been out of the paid workforce rearing children and caring for families have real opportunities to re-enter the paid workforce with new skills, or old skills renewed.

> **Women are disadvantaged in the job stakes.**

These initiatives are to be welcomed, must be persisted with, and taken further. At the same time, it is evident that the achievements of women, and the way in which women have organised work and careers, ought to be looked at afresh. Far from leading stultified lives, missing out on intellectual stimulation, job satisfaction, career paths and achievement, women have sometimes leapt obstacles at a single bound or, more often, surmounted them by persistent and consistent bounds–and by painstaking effort.

The private lives and paidwork lives of women intersect more closely than do the public and family lives of men. There is not the same dichotomising of experience: homeground versus paidwork. As a consequence, women lead more rounded lives. Because women are seen as having major responsibility for home and children, most women have had to organise their work and careers with this intersection in mind. Women have oftimes been obliged to leave a paidwork position to move elsewhere — interstate, to the country, or overseas — because the male 'head of the family' has determined to study at a foreign university, or his company or ambitions have dictated the move.

This means disruption for a woman. It means interrupting her career in the same way as having a child results in a woman placing her paidwork persona 'on the back burner'.

It is evident in the work and careers of each of the women in *Breaking Through* that being a woman has not barred the way to career fulfilment. Each has found an important centring of herself in the world, and in her work, through her existence as female. Each recognises that some steps she took were directly related to her perceived role as a woman, some to the real factors associated with being female (such as giving birth). Yet the fact of being a woman meant that each had latitudes she might not have had, or might not have been minded to make use of, if she had set herself on a definite career path at the age of six. All see that being female is a positive attribute. Being 'dangerous' has enhanced their work and careers.

Jane Austen began her career as writer in her parents' drawing-room. Or, to be more precise, her father's drawing-room: at the time, according to the law, the room, the house and everything in it belonged, solely, to her father. Until the *Matrimonial Property Acts* of the mid- to late nineteenth century and beyond, women were stripped of all ownership rights upon marriage. Even at betrothal women's property rights were truncated. As she wrote, Jane Austen pretended she was doing otherwise. When her writing was interrupted by the intrusion of outsiders, she hid it. It was not considered suitable for a woman to presume to authorship, much less be an author.

> **Being 'dangerous' has enhanced their work and careers.**

Yet women have been great writers. Women have expressed themselves through the years in letters, diaries, poetry, essays, the short story, drama, the novel. Women have also been great story-tellers, predating the troubadour tradition by centuries. As Lynne Spender writes in *Intruders on the Rights of Men — Women's Unpublished Heritage*:

> Whilst [some] societies kept alive their customs, ideology and knowledge through oral traditions, through dance, corroboree and ritual, we abandoned these methods and adopted *the printed word* as a means of storing our heritage and transmitting our culture.

She adds that now, as a consequence of using the printed word for so long as the medium of education and organisation, 'we have invested print with the status of recorder of our civilization and conveyor of our cultural truths'.

In the fourteenth century the Venetian writer, Christine de Pizan, published *The Book of the City of Ladies*. It was a response to the notion, firmly fixed in the literature of the time, that 'the behaviour of women is inclined to and full of every vice'. After thinking deeply about the proposition, Christine de Pizan rejected it. She examined her own character and conduct, and that of other women whose company she frequently kept—princesses, great ladies, women of the middle and lower classes. 'To the best of my knowledge,' she concluded:

> .. no matter how long I confronted or dissected the problem, I could not see or realise how [the] claims [of so many notable men] could be true when compared to the natural behaviour and character of women.

Widowed at 25, with three small children and no inheritance, at first she wrote from necessity. Christine de Pizan earned her living through writing on feminist and party politics.

In 'Telling It How It Is' five journalists write of their careers in writing and the media. Three of them — Jane Cafarella, Gay Davidson and Shirley Stott Despoja — were journalists from the outset. Louise Liddy-Corpus and Carolyn Watts worked in other fields before coming to the media. For Gay Davidson, 'university was a natural progression' from school in New Zealand. Her working life as a journalist began as a writer for *Canta*, the Christchurch student newspaper. As a student in an Opportunity C class at a school in New South Wales, Shirley Stott Despoja was able to practise in advance working as a journalist and broadcaster, as part of the school day. Jane Cafarella found her career through the vocational guidance department at her primary school — although she had to overcome a barrier: the careers booklet depicted no women as journalists. She began by editing the class magazine. Carolyn Watts gained a place with the Australian Broadcasting Corporation (ABC) after a varied career in a series of 'odd jobs'. This led her to work in various states. Louise Liddy-Corpus began at the ABC too: her opportunity to enter journalism arose when a trainee program for Kooris, Nungas, Murris and Aboriginal people generally was established.

Like Christine de Pizan, these women earn (or earned) their livings from their writing. Unlike Jane Austen, they did not have to hide their aspirations, although some were encouraged more than others. Some gained great inspiration — whether simply in writing, or in entering a male-dominated world, or persisting against odds imbued with anti-woman ideology. Shirley Stott Despoja and Jane Cafarella continue to work in the print media. Carolyn Watts works on in radio, currently taking 'time out' by studying for a higher degree in communications at the University of Chicago. Gay Davidson works as a journalist and public relations consultant. Louise Liddy-Corpus moved on to other work, in Darwin, with the Aboriginal Women's Resource Centre. Now back in communications, working in Australia Post, she sees barriers remaining for women in journalism. It may be that women have broken through with greater force in the print media than in radio and television. Having done so, this means that the same persistence will eventually force changes in those other worlds of writing.

Christine de Pizan recognised the political nature of the world in which she lived. She wrote of the politics of the public world of men, and the way women and women's achievements were downgraded and denied. Jane Austen recognised it too. She concentrated upon the politics of marriage and family relationships, and the intersection between the public world of economics and the private world of the marriage contract.

In 'Pushing the Margins', Lisa Bellear, Janine Haines, Gracelyn Smallwood, Patricia Brennan, Irina Dunn and Greta Bird write of their careers as workers in the world of politics inhabited mainly by men. Lisa Bellear's training is in social work, with a brief foray into local government politics. Her career is in the arena of university politics; she focuses on ensuring that Kooris, Nungas, Yamagee and Bardi people, Murris and their fellow Aborigines gain full access to higher education, and that the field is expanded to embrace broader notions of education. Greta Bird's career is in the university arena, too: her work has been as a law teacher, most recently in cross-cultural law. Gracelyn Smallwood works to change the politics of the health system so that Aboriginal people are not denied proper access and appropriate preventative medicine. Her aim is, similarly, to ensure that notions of medicine and health treatment are not narrowly focused on dominant 'white ways' which are incompatible with Aboriginal needs—and (it can be added) the real health needs of the whole population. The latter is the focus of Patricia Brennan's work as a doctor, a former missionary, and member of the Movement for the Ordination of Women (MOW). Janine Haines and Irina Dunn write of their work before, during and after federal politics: each held a seat in the Senate of the Australian parliament, Irina Dunn as an Independent, Janine Haines as a member (and later leader) of the Australian Democrats.

In *Sense and Sensibility* Jane Austen wrote of the contradictory way in which women are regarded: the sister who has 'sense' marries for love — without property; she who is classed as 'sensitive' simply must marry wealth — her delicate life will be blighted without all that money can buy. Men are generally regarded as having more 'sense' than women; men begin, remain in and end their careers with more money. Women continue to earn, on average, a maximum of 83 percent of male pay; if part-time paid workers are included, the average descends to 69 cents. Yet this does not deter women.

Just as Christine de Pizan understood the political nature of the relations between the sexes and thus (no doubt) why she earned less than her male counterparts, in 'Breaking the Barriers' women who work in Women's Movement politics recognise the obstacles — yet refuse to give in. Melba Marginson began her political work in the Philippines, and continues it in Australia, particularly in support of women who have been

Women continue to earn, on average, a maximum of 83 percent of male pay.

'bought' into marriage, and too frequently battered, abused and even killed by the purchaser. In Queensland and Canberra, Jackie Huggins has worked for Aboriginal Rights, Land Rights and the Women's Movement. For her (like the others) money's not the motivator: change, rights, justice are. So too for Sue Schmolke who began her career by studying commerce — and quickly moved into other fields, eventually finding herself the Convenor of the Women's Advisory Council in the Northern Territory. Dawn Rowan's work has been centred upon the women's refuge or women's shelter movement in South Australia. Like Lariane Fonseca (whose career spans Queensland, South Australia, London, Victoria), she moved into the women's health movement.

Law is central to women's position in the world. It has been (and remains) a significant means of keeping women 'in their place'. At the same time, law can be used to fight back against disadvantage, to overturn oppression, and to benefit the powerless. Jane Austen recognised marriage law as vital to women's economic survival. Christine de Pizan's work shows a clear appreciation of the centrality of law to power and exploitation. She was particularly conscious of the way law is practised, and methods for keeping women out:

> ... tell me still, if you please, why women do not plead law cases in the courts of justice, are unfamiliar with legal disputes and do not hand down judgments? For these men say that it is because of some woman (whom I don't know) who governed unwisely from the seat of justice.

'My daughter,' replies the wise one, 'everything told about this woman is frivolous and contrived out of deception.' She continues:

> ... if anyone maintained that women do not possess enough understanding to learn the laws, the opposite is obvious from the proof afforded by experience, which is manifest and has been manifested in many women ... who have been very great philosophers and have mastered fields far more complicated, subtle, and lofty than written laws and man-made institutions ...

The women who have written of their careers 'In Practice' bear out the wise woman's words and the plea of Christine de Pizan that women be enabled to enter the legal profession. Jennifer Coate began her career as a teacher then, like Diane Fingleton (who began as a secretary), qualified in law. She worked as a sole practitioner in her own firm and is now taking a new direction. Diane Fingleton, like Fiona Tito, worked in government for a time (Diane Fingleton as a ministerial advisor, Fiona Tito as ministerial advisor, and as public servant). Diane Fingleton is now in practice as a suburban solicitor. Irene Watson worked in the media, then qualified as a lawyer as a direct result of her political activism in the Land Rights Movement: she wanted to understand the legalistic arguments used against the justice of Land Rights. Fiona Tito, like Irene Moss, went from school to law school. Irene Moss has grown up with a dual understanding: what it is to be a woman in law, and what it is to be a person of minority ethnic background working for justice. And, after working in a factory, Beth Wilson returned to study to qualify for university entrance, then worked her way through law and librarianship, and now sits as a member of a tribunal determining the rights of litigants.

Each of the women in *Breaking Through* has combined her work and career with a strong appreciation of the rights of women—and of the wrongs of a world which too often ignores those rights. They have come to their careers from different ethnic and racial backgrounds and geographical locations. Yet each is firm in her recognition of the importance of work to the development of her ideas, to her economic independence, and to her recognition of herself as a political being. These women are Workers. And if they are 'dangerous women' (as Elizabeth Hawes assures us they are), we can demand only there should be more of them.

PART I
Telling It How It Is

SOMETHING OF MY OWN

Jane Cafarella

Jane Cafarella is a cartoonist and journalist with the Age in Melbourne. She began her career with Standard Newspapers in Cheltenham, where she held a cadetship. Her cartoons have been shown in a number of exhibitions, including the Amnesty International Exhibition, at the Fringe Festival and at the Comedy Festival — Australian Comic Art (Jester Press) Exhibition. The Victorian State Library has 11 of her cartoons. Jane Cafarella also works as a freelance cartoonist for other groups. For the last two years she has written for 'Accent Age' and in 1991 became 'Accent' Editor.

'Always have something of your own.' Of all the things my mother told me, this was the most memorable. Although at times I wished I could forget it, like a beetroot stain on a white cotton shirt it seeped into my brain and would not come out. While other mothers wanted good husbands for their daughters, my mother's aspirations for me were much higher. She wanted my happiness to be the result of my own achievements, not somebody else's. It was not that she did not see being a wife and mother as an achievement. She saw it as the icing on the cake. The cake you had to make yourself.

That 'something of my own' has sustained me when others have let me down.

What exactly I would have of my own, I did not know. Being a good all-rounder at school, there was no obvious choice. I envied those who excelled in one particular area, as their path was chosen for them. Eventually, I chose the thing I liked to do best: writing.

Perhaps if I had been faced with the choices open to girls today it would have been even more difficult, but then standing in the Wellington Primary

School Library (in Mulgrave) in Grade 5 looking at the booklets about potential careers, one alone appealed: a little orange booklet on journalism, with pictures of serious young men in 1950s suits, sitting at desks and looking important.

As far as I remember, there were no women in the booklet. However, this did not deter me as much as the other options: teaching and nursing. I was sick of school and a life ruled by bells, so teaching was out. As for nursing, I had spent enough time in hospital to know what nurses did. As an outpatient at the Royal Children's Hospital, I had a crush on my doctor, but this inspired me to consider marrying one, not becoming one. Luckily, I recovered both my health and my senses.

My grandparents were voracious readers of newspapers, but a newspaper strayed into our home only if it was for wrapping the bean peelings and tea leaves. My mother read literature and encouraged me to read books. My father read *Popular Mechanics*. The sole book I saw him read was *The Rise and Fall of the Third Reich* and his progress on this depended on his bowels rather than his brain.

The only politics ever discussed was the politics of my parents' relationship. Like an emotional chess game with a bevy of supporters and observers, each move was analysed carefully. And like Fern in *Charlotte's Web*, who sat in Homer's barn and listened and observed the animals, I was a silent witness, accepted if not included. I was instinctively on the side of the White Queen, but the Black King inevitably won. In the game of life the Queen, with dependent children and no reliable job or car, could barely move one space at a time, while the King came and went as he pleased.

> I was a silent witness, accepted if not included.

At home, I played umpire in a game I didn't understand. At school, the rules were clearer, and winning was easier. My mother delighted in my progress and that of my sister. My father's delight came from pointing out what was lost, rather than gained. If I got a 9 $1/2$ out of 10 for a test, his response was: 'Why didn't you get 10?' It was meant as a joke, but it made me want to cry.

If my mother inspired me to achieve, my father's two youngest sisters provided an early model of what achievement could bring. While their elder brothers and sisters lamented their lack of family, children and, therefore, purpose in life, I admired the fact that, unburdened by family responsibilities, they seemed able to please themselves rather than others.

I visited my aunt Tess, the elder of the two, while she was studying at the Melbourne University library. The smell of books and heavy air of contemplation intrigued me. When the same aunt returned after two years overseas, I inhaled the smell of success. This was no longer my aunt, but a royal princess for whom banners had been hung and a feast prepared. Like Scheherazade, in the *Arabian Nights*, she told tales of adventure. She played guitar and sang haunting folksongs, spoke several languages, laughed and wore a red dress. She was handsome and independent and I wanted to be like her.

I began school at Mentone Primary and ended up at Mentone Girls High School, six schools and 12 years later. (We always kept one move ahead of the debt collectors.) The result was that I remember people by type (bully, teacher's pet, wimp) rather than by name.

I could already read when I started school at the age of six, as my mother had given us our pre-school education at home. My sister, being shy, had thrown the banana sandwich at the kindergarten teacher and pulled all the buttons off my mother's cardigan in her efforts to resist pre-school, and as we were only 18 months apart in age, her resistance won me my freedom too.

Starting school must have been hard for me as, suffering from chronic lymphodemia of the right leg, I had one leg bigger than the other, and I also took six tablets daily for childhood epilepsy. However, I have only one memory of crying on the way home because a boy had taunted me with: 'That girl's got one fat leg and one skinny leg.' My mother told me to say simply that yes, that was true, and there was nothing that could be done about it. I did, and it must have worked because I don't remember being a victim. I was expected to be strong, and so I was. So much so that I befriended another girl who had a deformed hand and tried to be strong for her too.

I was expected to be strong, and so I was.

In Form 1 at Lyndale High School in Dandenong I was part of an experimental 'integrated studies' class, where the only formal subjects studied were maths and Indonesian. Here I had my first taste of journalism. We took turns to edit the class magazine, which I did for some time, when there were no other takers. This involved including the creative outpourings of the people you liked, while chucking out those of the people you didn't.

We were also encouraged to write a 'book' each. This was the era where putting seven adjectives before each noun was considered creative. I offered my convoluted tale, positively psychedelic with 'colour', of 'The Rose and the Dagger' and sat back, waiting for the bouquets to fall. The only thing that fell was my pride. When my best friend's simple little tale of a girl and her family was hailed as the winner I was devastated. It was my first important lesson that writing about what you know and what has meaning for you is often what means most to others.

When we moved to a flat in Highett, I attended Moorabbin High School for two tortured terms. Tortured because by this time, my sister had run away to Sydney to be found weeks later and was now in the Convent of the Good Shepherd in St Kilda (who took her only after pleas from my mother to save her from Winlaton).

The White Queen and the Black King had found my sister a useful pawn and she had declared checkmate. Now my role as the Good Girl was as official as was hers as the Bad Girl.

SOMETHING OF MY OWN

Guiltily my parents turned up at the convent every weekend laden with goodies, myself included. However, I was the one goody that made my sister sick. She threw juice at me one day, and I don't remember visiting much after that. By the time she came out to work at a chemist shop, my parents had separated. She became engaged the following year and married and we have seldom seen each other since.

Looking back on that year is like looking through the water window at the National Gallery of Victoria. I remember crying, or wanting to cry. At school, I felt like a geriatric who had been mistakenly placed with teenagers. The things that interested my peers seemed trivial to one who had the weight of the world on her shoulders. One afternoon when we were preparing for the school dance, 'Daddy Cool' was playing. The teacher urged me to dance. 'I can't,' I replied. It was true. I was too old.

The one ray of light was my correspondence with the author Alan Marshall, to whom I had written after reading *I Can Jump Puddles* when I was about 11-years-old. We maintained contact until his death. Like millions of other children throughout the world I was inspired by him. I met him once when I was about 14, but mostly communicated by mail. Later, I interviewed him for work. In one of his last interviews, to publicise a 'collected works', he confided that his publishers obviously thought he was on his last leg (he only had one by then). Why else would they want to cash in on his collected works? He was right.

In Form 3, I found myself at Mentone Girls High School with the people I had known in prep. Strangely, they were still in the same cliques and the labels put on them then had stuck.

It was a girls' school, with a good academic reputation which my mother hoped would encourage my brains to outstrip my hormones. Little did she know. At Moorabbin High school there had been genuine academic competition between the boys and the girls, and lively classroom debate. Here, the girls in the leading social set were bored and surly, with their skirts far higher than their aspirations. Did I have a boyfriend and did I 'do it' were the first questions they asked. I failed on both counts.

I enjoyed maths but, having chosen journalism as my career, I was steered towards French, of which I knew nothing. Indonesian had been my only foray into foreign languages. The most practical thing I learnt was typing, which was compulsory in Form 3.

In my HSC year, two women, Jessie Jans, my English expression teacher, and Pat Cerni, my English lit. teacher, provided the spark to ignite my mind. As I had taken only four subjects (my fifth choice clashing with everything else) I had a lot of spare time, which I was keen to spend with Ivan Hutchinson and his midday movie, my best friend and the cream cake specials from the local cake shop. However, Mrs Jans in particular encouraged me to read outside the curriculum so, when Ivan wasn't around, I read.

By this stage my hormones had left my brain cells for dead and I had what

I wanted almost as badly as HSC — a boyfriend. He had a job, a car and was good looking and arrogant — everything a 17-year-old schoolgirl could wish for. However, he did encourage me in something other than gymnastics in his Volkswagen. He cut out Philip Adams' articles for me and referred me to the Learning Exchange, a non-profit paper designed to link people and ideas, and which invited volunteers to help write and produce it.

My English expression and literature marks got me a university entrance. I chose instead to go to the Royal Melbourne Institute of Technology (RMIT) while applying for cadetships. I didn't finish the course: I was too busy doing the real thing. When I am old and wearing purple, I'll go back.

When Bill Hoey at the *Herald* asked me about my family, I candidly told him that my parents had divorced. 'And how did that affect you?' he asked. I was tempted to tell him the truth — that I had been relieved. Instead I told him it had not affected me. He looked sceptical and, judging by the test he set for me, must have considered me a bad risk. It was the end of the Whitlam era — I had swotted diligently about local politics and was prepared for anything except what he asked. 'Hmmm,' he said. 'Cafarella — that's Italian, isn't it? What's the situation in Italy?'

Italy? Italy! I would have been lucky to find it on a map let alone give a political diagnosis. I was ushered out with a 'Don't ring us, we'll ring you' farewell. Similarly at the *Age*, I failed to make an impression. The local paper, *Standard Newspapers*, finally accepted me after receiving the umpteenth letter since I had first written to them in Form 3. I think they decided it was easier to let me write for them, rather than to them.

Grounded after an operation, I wrote a play (about our family dynamics) for a Fellowship of Australian Writers competition. I had meant to change the names, but somehow it didn't ring true, so I left them. When the letter arrived saying I had won a prize, my mother was elated. My heart sank as she settled contentedly back to read the works of her progeny. She made me promise never to write anything about her again. This is the first time I have broken that promise (sorry Mum).

> because it seemed natural, I provided a funny picture with many other stories I submitted

Writing about other people was safer. For my first story for *Standard News* I wrote about leaving school and included one of my funny drawings. It was terrible, but Murray Smith, the editor-in-chief, published it. Then, because it seemed natural, I provided a funny picture with many other stories I submitted and most were published, for better or worse.

My cartooning was an evolutionary process. Like a leopard which, after millions of years, finds itself perfectly adapted to its environment, so I have found myself perfectly adapted to the role of cartoonist. It began, I think, with the urge to fill spaces, to put one's mark on the blank wall of life.

My father also liked to fill blank spaces. He drew on our white laminex table (my mother just wiped it off), on the inside of my school textbooks—on anything. Mostly he drew what he planned to build (inspired by the latest issue of *Popular Mechanics*), or he drew people. My mother spent her youth making perfect copies of ballerinas and nudes (an interest which she has since taken up again) and encouraged my interest in drawing as well as writing. She also has a strong sense of the ridiculous, which I have inherited.

When I was nine with the mumps, a friend gave me a whole box of Disney comic books. They were the old-fashioned sort; beautiful strong colours on shiny paper. I devoured them and when I'd finished, began copying the drawings into a notebook. Progressing to copies of Charles Schultz's 'Peanuts' characters, I made frontispieces for my high school books. However, high school 'art' didn't interest me. It was too prescribed and, to me, it seemed that you didn't have to be good at drawing to do well at it—just good at doing what you were told.

Sometimes drawing was easier than writing. When I was banned from the City of Chelsea for describing the mayoral ball too accurately, I responded to the deluge of angry letters with a cartoon of me, as Cinderella, being booted out of the town hall at midnight. Murray was courageous in his support of me.

> Sometimes drawing was easier than writing.

When the *Herald and Weekly Times* took over the *Standard News*, Dallas Swinstead was appointed to pull us all into line. One of the first decrees: the graffiti wallpapering the office (including many of my cartoons) was to come down. One of the next: I would be paid $10 per cartoon (a $10 rise). A ceiling of $50 was applied soon after, as I was threatening to send the company broke. My pay came down again and the graffiti went up again.

When I wanted to join the *Herald*, Dallas referred me to the chief-of-staff, Bruce Baskett, as a cartoonist rather than a journalist. But the chief doubted I was fast enough to meet the tough *Herald* deadlines. So, for two and a half years, as a general and local government reporter for the *Herald*, I didn't put cartoon pen to paper.

After five years at *Standard*, the *Herald* engulfed me in a fog of awe and ignorance. While I was good at getting quirky human-interest stories which the *Herald* loved, when it came to analysing the issues, well, I wrote about them but seldom thought about them.

One of the best and worst things about the *Herald* was the speed. How I envied the *Age* reporters who could sit back and listen to the whole day's hearings at an inquiry and pick the best angle. While they listened and pondered, I darted in and out trying to catch editions with snatches of meaningless, disconnected comments from early boring witnesses. Inevitably, the crucial evidence of 'Miss X' would be heard while I was kneeling prayerlike by a red phone down a hallway, notebook on knee, chanting to the copy-takers: 'That's C for Charlie, A for Apple, D for

David.' One of the legacies of the *Herald* was camel knees and an elephant hide.

I interviewed a bereaved family and was expected to phone the story through immediately from their living-room. Somehow I couldn't bring myself to do my 'A for Apple' routine in front of the weeping mother. I pleaded for time. 'Fine, if you can get back before the deadline,' the chief said. I phoned the story from a booth on the Geelong Freeway. By the time we got back, the edition was out and the story was on the front-page, as damp and fragile as a newborn baby. My baby.

Another time I was to interview the bereaved family of dare-devil motorcyclist Dale Buggins who had shot and killed himself at the Marco Polo Hotel in Flemington. I managed to get into the hotel and found myself wandering around the rooms, some of them open and being cleaned by the housemaids.

Neither I nor the *Herald* had the right to intrude into their grief.

Perhaps one of them had been Dale Buggins' room. But there was nothing to indicate it: no bloodstained sheets or shotguns. Downstairs in the foyer, making my phone call, some of the Buggins family waited with their luggage, staring at me with accusing, shocked eyes. Somehow, I couldn't go up to them and ask how they felt. I knew how they felt, and that neither I nor the *Herald* had the right to intrude into their grief. So I stared back at them and their luggage as I told the chief-of-staff that they had already left.

That first year at the *Herald* I wrote so many sob stories that my colleagues nominated a box of tissues as my end-of-year award. My naivety and shock at the real world of metropolitan journalism, after my cosy five years on a local paper, came through in many stories. Even reporting Moomba with a jaded photographer did not tarnish it for me. 'Not another bloody Moomba,' he said. For me, as for many of the children there, it was my first. However, I spent most of those two and a half years alternating between states of terror and excitement.

By this time I had been married several years. I did it at the age of 20 because I fell in love with his father putting the rubbish tins out on the right night. Compared to my family, they seemed so normal. And with hindsight, I see now that I needed a legitimate reason to leave home. Also, my first husband was the first man I felt truly comfortable with. I basked in the warmth and acceptance of his family. But comfort soon gave way to boredom and fear that one day I would wake up and find out that it would be too late to do all the things I had been putting off because he wasn't ready or didn't want to. I left him almost seven years later for someone else.

At the same time, I left the *Herald* for a new local paper, the *Western Times*, to much horror. Nobody left a metropolitan daily to go back to a local paper!

The *Western Times* was more of a boon to me than I to it. Its relationship with some advertisers suffered as a result of my cartoons. My work as a cartoonist threatened to make me redundant as a journalist. 'Nobody needs to read the story,' said the sub-editor when I did a cartoon about a weight loss business in which the only weight the clients lost was from their hip pocket. It showed me that a picture really did say a thousand words — a cartoon, perhaps two thousand.

Then I met Carolyn Bond, a local financial counsellor who had a file full of great stories and a zeal for justice that attracted me. We teamed up for a consumer column. On the strength of this I got a six-month job at the Ministry of Consumer Affairs translating the new *Credit Act* into plain English, the equivalent of turning straw into gold. My vision for publicity for the new act included television ads, something like 'Life. Be in it.' ('Credit. Don't be in it.') with matching pamphlets and posters. I didn't imagine using my cartoons — I wanted the real thing. But as their budget did not stretch as far as *my* imagination, we finished up with pamphlets featuring the rough cartoons I had done as examples.

This led the Financial Counsellors' Association of Victoria to ask me to illustrate and edit their training manual. (You try drawing 50 cartoons about credit!) By the project's end my knowledge of credit and my cartoons had improved dramatically. I had to become quicker; my line relaxed and became more spontaneous.

I began getting freelance work. The Ministry of Consumer Affairs asked me to illustrate their training manual — another 50 cartoons on credit. Carolyn and I were planning to go overseas, but at the last minute I had to trade my pack and ticket for a cot and pram, thus embarking on an unexpected and totally new career.

Motherhood was initially a relief. How wonderful not to have to perform. As a mother, staying home is a virtue, not a cop out. However such virtues, I found, did not come naturally.

'You do so many things with him,' said my mother admiringly as I tore round to playgroups and pantomimes. But I did it for me. I'd do the dishes, make the bed and then think, now what? While I did not miss having to perform, I did miss my audience.

After boredom came anger. I found while the Madonna was on the pedestal it was fine, but when she came down to earth she could not get the pram up the steps to the bank; while her money was welcome at the supermarket, her pram was not; and while motherhood was regarded as an essential service, it was considered boring dinner-table talk.

So I went back into paidwork. I had three jobs to choose from, and while I was deciding, my partner decided that the grass was greener elsewhere.

Meanwhile, my new job at the Premier's Department was not working out. The supervisor had been a graphic designer turned administrator and publicity officer. I came along, took over publicity and drew cartoons too. Her sugary tones developed a sour edge.

My son was only 16 months old. As he came down with every virus at the crèche so did I. Also, the previous occupant of my office had been carted off to hospital: the air conditioning system had spread a Pandora's Box of viruses and plagues, and her absenteeism proved contagious.

My son had an accident and had to have plastic surgery at the Children's Hospital; I took eight days off to nurse him and my guilt. On returning I was told that even if he had died, I was only entitled to three days off. I had sold my labour, not my soul. I rang Colin Duck at the now defunct *Sunday Press*, got a part-time job and gave two weeks' notice. My supervisor gave me the warmest send off.

I had sold my labour, not my soul.

Working for the *Sunday Press* was like infiltrating enemy lines. My lefty friends were delighted. No more preaching to the converted. I wrote left-wing stories which appeared intact with right wing headings. About the same time, a friend mentioned that there was some part-time sub-editing work at the *Age*. I had never subbed but I did not let this stop me. I rang up Bob Millington (now 'News Diary') the chief night sub-editor. He'd been a friend of my adventurous aunt for many years and considered himself a de facto member of my family. 'Ah, Cafarella,' he said. 'Lovely family! Yes, come in.' When I did, Millo was at the other office, 'The Golden Age'.

The first week at the *Age* was torture. I had forgotten the most basic things. After nearly 18 months of churning out mashed banana, I was incapable of churning out anything else. I lost confidence and became incompetent. My boss (Millo's successor), mistaking my lack of confidence for lack of application, gave me a stern lecture, which resulted in six months of seething before I gathered the courage to tell him that he had misjudged me. In anger, I wrote a story for 'Accent' about motherhood which Rosemary West, then editor, published. It was the second of my 'Accent' stories. The first was published a year before about the difficulty I had in keeping my own name on my driver's licence on marriage.

The *Age* subs' room, arranged like a refectory with a 'top table' for those designing the pages, and a 'down table' for those subbing the stories, was male dominated. The subs were masters of the English language who were daily confronted and affronted by the hurried offerings of good and bad reporters, and were understandably, well, pissed off. The *Age*, being a writers' paper, gave little credit or status to subs, so like chooks they had their own hierarchy. After the first edition, we would gather at the bar in the men's locker room (officially known as the Age Locker Room Club, unofficially as The Bog Bar), to witch-hunt and peck.

I was good at caption writing so I was often given the pictures of babies and mothers or human-interest items. This proved great training for cartoon caption writing.

Rosemary West then began commissioning me. She would send me night time messages via computer asking me to illustrate a particular story. I would call the story up on the computer, do a rough drawing at my break, get her approval, then do the final drawing at home. A courier would pick it up in the morning. It was the only time I ever did a draft. Usually I draw it first off. If it doesn't work, start again from scratch, otherwise the line looks too contrived.

When the two 'Accent' reporters each left to have babies, I was chosen to replace them. I couldn't believe my good fortune. With a brilliant mind, a relentless thirst for truth and the ruthless pursuit of justice, particularly for women, Rosemary proved inspirational. She is a tall poppy who, unlike some, does not overshadow others, but nurtures them so that around her there grows a field of other sturdy poppies.

For Rosemary, our collaboration proved somewhat frustrating, if rewarding. As a journalist, there is nothing more daunting than a blank piece of paper (or VDT screen). As a cartoonist, there is nothing more irresistible. Which probably explains why I draw when I'm supposed to write, and write when I'm supposed to draw. 'That's very nice, Jane' she would say of my unsolicited cartoons: 'But where's the story?'

The urge to fill space meant that even opening the mail is inspiring. I drew my comments on the press releases, putting Rosemary in a dilemma by turning what she previously perceived to be junk into 'works of art'.

As for real drawing, such as still life with fruit, forget it. I can't draw for nuts. My 6-year-old has woken up to this. 'Can you draw that?' he challenges sceptically when we are reading a picture book. 'No.' I sigh.

Recently, I was doing some cartoons at my parents' place in Maldon to be faxed to the *Age*. My son found a pile of half-finished rejects, and finished them off for me — complete with captions. It took a trained eye to tell the difference and I had trouble explaining why mine were published and his were not. 'It's the joke,' I explained. 'What joke?' he said. After all, there was no mention of bottoms, which is the only thing that inspires humour in a 6-year-old.

Many people, particularly women, must learn to be risk-takers. To risk failure as well as success. This is one of the great lessons of journalism. Deadline pressure means that it can never be your absolute best work, just the best at the time. The other lesson is that both success and failure are fleeting — today's news is tomorrow's fish and chips. Such pressure means letting go of crippling perfectionism that can stop you from having a go.

women must learn to be risk-takers

For women who are trying to scale the hurdle of high expectation handicapped by low self-esteem, this can seem insurmountable. Talent may be one thing, but it will be undiscovered if the person who possesses it does not have the confidence to risk trying. This is the most valuable encouragement I have received: to keep trying.

TAKING CONTROL NOW

Louise Liddy-Corpus

Born in Darwin in 1949, Louise Liddy-Corpus has worked in public relations and journalism, and in equal opportunity. She has spirit ancestors, but her main Dreaming is a particular waterfall in Nangiumerri lands. She writes: 'I am a waterfall. I was a waterfall before I came into the human form and when I die I will go back to that waterfall.'

I was born in Darwin. My mother is from the west coast of the Northern Territory, the Daly River, and my father from Broome on the west coast of Western Australia. Broome is built on the land of the Yaoro and Bardi people. I am descendant of the Yaoro people and probably also the Bardi. My skin name is Na'amitj, which is the female version of Namatjira, so Albert Namatjira is my brother.

Like the South Sea Islanders kidnapped to work in the Australian cane fields ('Blackbirding') Asians were shanghaied, sold, and brought to Australia to work the pearl-diving industry. My great-grandfather was brought to Australia from a little village called Vigan in the far north of the Philippines. My father is of Filipino, English and Aboriginal descent.

One of my cousin's father is Japanese, interned during the Second World War. My Auntie Lina, married to Matsumato, a Japanese man, was interned with her children. Dad's brother, Pinky Corpus, was allowed by the Australian authorities to be responsible for them, as their chaperone or monitor. Little did they know he was also part Japanese. Through my mother I am part Chinese, part Irish and part Aboriginal, and I have four Aboriginal ancestral groups going right down to the Gurindji people, who were in the walk out against Lord Vesty during the 1960s.

My parents dumped me. I cannot claim I was one of the stolen kids. I went to Darwin Primary School, and then Nightcliff. When I began, there was only one government school, 'normal' school. There was a Catholic school down the road, and then there was an Aboriginal school on the Bagot reserve compound, the other side of the barbed-wire fence from the mission. While I was learning fractions, the Reserve School girls in the same grade were years behind.

The institution in which I was raised was run initially along an age and gender dormitory system overseen by a kind, unmarried white woman, Miss Shankleton (Laelie). In the early 1960s the Home moved into a new compound which had a cottage system in which each individual cottage was run autonomously although coming under the general jurisdiction of the male (married) superintendent.

I lived at the mission. The savage white couple in charge of my cottage belted me constantly. Every time I had a migraine headache I was accused of trying to get out of work, although I wasn't. Brought up in that system from birth, we took pride in our chores. I got sick and tired of running away to my parents and their relatives, and being brought back to the mission home by police. It never ever dawned on me to run away to welfare. Later I went to the former superintendent of the home, who organised through welfare for me to be placed elsewhere, so I went to school in New South Wales.

I had an older brother who was adopted. My younger brother was in the institution with me. My mother was stolen when she was six-years-old. With the Second World War, the Methodist Overseas Mission brought everyone from Croker Island to Otway in southern New South Wales near Wollongong. There, my mother was impregnated at 10. The Methodist mission people put up her age. She lived out the rest of her life assuming an increased age. She tried to tell me she was 19 when she had me but she was only 15. She had my older brother when she was 11.

I attended Paramatta High School. I didn't like it, though probably created a lot of the problems myself. I was stupid. I got so angry and just bashed, instead of trying to reason. A whitefella, Phillip, got hit by a softball bat, his nose swelling enormously. He sat on a suitcase with his legs wide open, making light of his predicament: 'Louise, I've got a nose like you now I've got an Aboriginal nose.' I went bang, smash, 'I haven't got a big nose'. Conscious of coming from a society of many nationalities in all colours and shapes, I was constantly reminded I was different. Some friend would say, in winter, when everyone was wearing stockings, gloves and beret: 'Gee, you wouldn't know that you were brown from behind.' Constantly telling me that I was not quite one of them, they seemed preoccupied with colour. I reacted violently.

> **By the end of first term I had bashed up everyone bashable.**

By the end of first term I had bashed up everyone bashable. Everybody else ran away. I came home with my schoolbooks and ripped right through them all with my biro, screaming, ranting and raving and demanding to go home. My foster father asked if I would like to try another school. No, but I didn't want to return to the violence of Retta Dixon homes. My foster father encouraged me. I went to Greystanes. Half the teachers were Jews, including the principal. The other half were white Australians. I got on with all the Jews, and with very few of the others. I still fought and argued with teachers but began to settle down.

I had all the encouragement possible — so much so that I felt I was cocktail Black. The emphasis was that it was great I was in high school: there was only one other Aboriginal in high school in New South Wales going for the Intermediate Certificate. The school psychologist came to look me over. At Nightcliff Primary School I had come within the top five in grade seven. When I went south I became quite dumb, just scraping through. It wasn't until university, getting distinctions for almost every assignment I lazily submitted, that I realised how difficult it was at 14, changing from a child into a woman, going from a town of 13 000 people to a town where the white people were all crazy — I mean, had you heard of the Beatles? Then there was the Viet Nam war, and learning new concepts like time. Before, at the mission, at school, everything was delivered, and it just happened.

I tried for the School Certificate and failed, so went to work in the Commonwealth Bank clearing department. I wanted to be a teller out there with the public. Not many women were working as tellers at the time. My concept of a bank was the local branch down the road where they knew the local people, and I had visions of eventually working in the Commonwealth Bank in Darwin. In Sydney, they really couldn't place me in a branch because being an Aboriginal I might offend the customers. But in the clearing department I had a wonderful boss, Alison Reid. Most of the women were fantastic.

> I wanted to be a teller out there with the public.

The clearing branch was tucked away from the average businessman in the street (as they were in those days). Workers who had physical and mental impairments were not able to become permanent members. I was, because I didn't have any disabilities, although as an Aboriginal my permanency could have been contested.

My supervisor fought for equal rights for women in the bank. Alison Reid supervised 100 or so women. A bloke on our floor, who had never ever received a promotion, was earning more than she.

Alison was in the union. We got along well, not just because I was Black. She said if you were an Australian you should be paid for the work you do, and just because you were a woman you shouldn't receive three-quarters of the pay. When I joined in 1966, they had just started allowing married women to continue working for the Commonwealth Bank. During my time they also allowed married pregnant women to continue. Alison fought for all that.

My first promotion in the Commonwealth Bank came after only 18 months. They gave you points, assessing you every three or six months on appearance, punctuality, ability to get on with your co-workers, ability to take orders. Six months after the initial promotion I got the second. Women in the bank were upset, saying it was only because I was an Aboriginal. I knew it wasn't, because it was one area where my foster parents and the church or the mission didn't have any control. I persevered for about 9 months, then went to the PMG processing money orders. I played basketball and went to the foundation dances in Sydney, weaning myself away from the security offered by my foster parents. I looked for Aboriginal groups and wanted to connect with them. I rented a flat, got away from my foster parents, then moved back home to Darwin.

I was not scared that I would not get another job. I knew I had marketable skills even if it was cleaning. When I was 14, in 1963, I had spent three days a week off from school, ironing clothes at the RAAF base. One day I'd be playing basketball as intensively as 14-year-old girls can muster in the tropics, in bare feet on a cement court. Next day, blisters galore with my feet bandaged up, I'd be merrily ironing away. I was paid excellent money. I tried to tell them at the Saturday job that I was being paid £1 for a day's work at these other places, and they really only had to pay me 10s, but they wouldn't have it, so I was earning £4, a lot in 1963. In 1966 at the Commonwealth Bank I earned $36 fortnightly. As a cleaner and ironer I had earned just as much.

I was 21 when I returned to Darwin. I had to wait until I was 21 because I was confused about my citizenship rights. It was not until the 1967 referendum that Aborigines became Australian citizens.

At home, I met a bloke, fell in love and resigned from the PMG. Earlier, at the bank, I had applied for transfers to Darwin, never getting past the manager of the floor. Banks then allowed two-year transfers only. They guessed that sooner or later I would stay in Darwin and didn't like the idea of providing permanent accommodation for me, I think.

When I walked into the Commonwealth Bank in Darwin, telling them I had worked in the bank down south, I got a job instantly. The resistance was in the south. I worked on ledgers, work I had never done. I remained for a year, returning south in 1971. In 1972 the Aboriginal tent embassy was set up in Canberra. There was an explosion of pride in being Aboriginal.

In Sydney in 1972 I went back to the PMG, to the mail exchange in Redfern, finishing at 5.30 am. I was earning fantastic money and was able to breakfast in a restaurant every morning in King's Cross, feeling so liberated. Then I toddled off to the Wayside Chapel and the bus. We collected food from the hospitals, then kids from the homes, and took them to the park for a three-course meal of cereals, hot tucker, and fruit. We'd then drop the kids back, to go to school with a full belly.

In 1963, when I was ironing clothes at the RAAF base, Australia asked all the primary school kids in Papua New Guinea what they wanted to be trained as and began putting them into high school on a study path enabling them to become doctors, lawyers and engineers. It wasn't until two years after New Guinea got independence in 1975 that the Australian government came up with a program for training us: NESA (the National Employment Strategy for Aboriginals).

I went into NESA in 1980. Until then I worked in a variety of jobs, constantly backwards and forwards from Redfern to Darwin. I went for jobs I hadn't been trained for. Because I was up-front about it people believed I had all sorts of skills. For six months I worked in a one-off course for chronically unemployed Aboriginals, showing them how they should present themselves for interviews. I didn't have an idea myself. Out of that course 100% became employed, but in short-term jobs. I wasn't able to sell the work ethic or, if I was, the jobs weren't there. Government departments, Aboriginal organisations and white business people used the NESA scheme to exceed staff ceilings or gain free labour, and I had Aboriginal people in the class who had been bank robbers, rapists, and mixed race, and who really hated being forced into an Aboriginal identity. I had to bear the brunt. At the other extreme were shy, innocent, young girls from the suburbs of Darwin or remote little towns out in the scrub. People from all walks of life were lumped under the umbrella 'Aboriginal'. Blokes sat under the palm tree outside the classroom with a flagon of wine and a packet of cigarettes, walking in when they wanted to. It was hard for me because I didn't know how to get around it. I knew my brief — to get them into the paid workforce. The blokes who were 'coloured' weren't Aboriginals. They knew I was a 'Black power bitch'. Sitting outside the classroom, they poked their fingers up, swearing at me. Today they realise only too well just where they are in Australian society and why they have never been able to get a job, and have stopped resisting being Black. They are mates of mine now.

Today they realise only too well just where they are in Australian society and have stopped resisting being Black.

The ringleader was the bloke I was with when Mum died. I had gone to the pub to get something to smoke because mum was dying, and I needed it. I ended up with no money left for grog. He had a couple of dollars for beers, and between us we had a merry old time. He is a diehard alcoholic. He teaches me a lot. I said to him one day: 'There is no such thing as an alcoholic—anyone can overcome if they want to.' He giggled and I realised I didn't know what the fuck I was talking about. I presumed it was possible. How could I be so naive as to say anyone could give up grog, just a matter of making up your mind.

Years before, in 1980, I went to see Mum because I had to bury my little brother by myself. I'd sent her an urgent telegram: 'Wally is dead. Am bringing the body home. If you are able to assist I would appreciate it. If not,

I'll understand.' I prepaid her reply. Back came the message: 'Unable to assist. Kind regards.' I stupidly thought Wally's death would have affected my mother. Concerned for her to know there was no blame attached, I wanted to make sure she was all right. So I went to Townsville, off my usual track. She said: 'Can't you get it through your fucking head I don't want fucking Abos coming around.' She was half-Aboriginal. So I thought right, you bitch, I'll stay in Townsville and get into your home by hook or by crook.

I got a job at the Australian Broadcasting Commission (ABC) fronting a drive-time program, interviewing people like Ian Sinclair and Gareth Evans. I had had ideas of becoming a journalist. When I was working with the Commonwealth Bank in Darwin in 1971 I was offered a job as a cadet journalist, on the basis of some of my writing, with the *Northern Territory News*. My boyfriend, a policeman, said the paper was anti-cop. Being my first lover, there was no way I would endanger that so I chose to work in the bank. When I approached the ABC wanting to be a journalist, the manager thought the editor of the newsroom was racist, and that there would be problems. He was not wrong. He got me into public affairs as a program officer, the 'poor cousin' of journalists. You're not quite a journalist unless registered with the Australian Journalists' Association (AJA), and there is a lot of resentment about public affairs program officers doing the work. No one explained to me that because three quarters of my duties were reporting I could gain admission to the AJA. You only find out these things later. Then you share it with everybody to make sure they know. I was supposed to be getting trained, but had ideas and wanted to share the vision of broadcasting for indigenous Australians. I went to the Torres Straits for a weekend doing a documentary for a dance duo. I told the Torres Strait people of my hidden agenda: to get a media steering committee established. The ADC was there at the same time, opening new offices. An invitation was sent to residents of Thursday Island for the official opening, then came another opening for the community. A lot of the native people on Thursday Island had status in their areas of employment. The ADC sent invitations for attendance to their white spouses, not the indigenous people. Irrespective of sex and status, invitations were sent in their spouses' names. The indigenous spouses, some being people of great importance, were angry. They wanted the invitations in their own right. With the ABC equipment, I taped the demonstration. That's how I sold media to the people and got an interim committee set up on the Torres Straits. From there the regional manager of Townsville ABC carried on the process. He had status and the means of getting it to fruition.

My Mum's daughter to the white man she'd married told me that every day Mum turned on the ABC, listening to me. There is a song by Perry Como called 'Forever and Ever'. As a child, I thought it was 'sweet violets forever' not 'let bygones be bygones forever'. On the radio I'd say: 'I just discovered what these words are. I always thought they were "violets sweet violets", and maybe it was because my Mum's name is Violet. But anyway here it is, Perry

Como, "Let Bygones Be Bygones".' I flirted with my mother over the airwaves. I would say: 'Oh it's my Mum's birthday today, Happy Birthday Mum.' Then my older brother Eric died. It took me a year to go around to tell her. I was so scared. I thought she would carry on like she did before. Mum's daughter drove me back into the city. I asked her: 'Does Mum know I'm on the radio? Does she ever listen?' 'What do you think,' she reckons. 'Every bloody day!' So in her own quiet way she was there constantly sticky-beaking into my life. She would never ever give me any credit for it. She'd say: 'Oh yes, and what are you around for now?' 'Mum, Eric died.' She was a bitch, but she made it obvious until the day she died that that was the way she wanted it. It was devastating but I understand now. I love her but it doesn't make any difference.

I was at the ABC until 1982. When my NESA traineeship was finished, I emerged with skills but wasn't marketable, not even with the ABC because they were not required by the Commonwealth Employment Service (CES) to provide me with qualifications. I was accepted by James Cook University, but at the same time got a job being assistant producer on 'Class of '82' with Janet Bell. She had fantastic humour, and was lovely. Later, I was offered a job with the Aboriginal Development Corporation (ADC) with Charles Perkins, in public relations. Going to Canberra some months ahead to settle in, I couldn't get over the Blacks there. They spoke differently. I came from a street level politics community and they were talking at government level, so I thought fuck this, and went back to Townsville and university.

I finally got to university because Australians woke up to themselves that people may not conveniently fit into the anglo-saxon/celtic background. I was a woman, so I got in on that. I was mature age, I got in on that. I was a Black and I got in on that. I came under three categories able to go to university without the academic qualifications. . .

I did well. It was a culture shock again, coping, but exciting because of the universality of equality there more than any other part of my life, with your marks and your politics. Not game enough to take four subjects, I studied Australian political science, European history and English, with distinctions in all of them. English helped me compose the structured essays which was important for me. A friend suggested I do European history: 'It gives you a background to the parliamentary system we have in Australia. It complements Australian political science.' I wasn't keen but my European history lecturer captivated me. He got up at the podium, adjusted his glasses, leaned over the rostrum with both hands forward, like a praying mantis: 'We are going to find out what the world owes the European.' I sat up, and I sat up all year long.

I discovered the upper Daly land claim was on. I had to go home.

Later in the year I went home for holidays and discovered the upper Daly land claim was on. I had to go home. Our land claim is still going on.

On the dole waiting for the claim to go through I was appointed regional co-ordinator for the top end of the Northern Territory for the Aboriginal Women's Task Force, the first government enquiry into the views of Aboriginal women. This was on 'Wage Pause' money. I was there for about twelve months.

Part of the problem when I was at university was the difficulty of adjusting from a wage to study allowance. It took ages to get my first cheque. Cheques were lost. I'd chase them for months. So when I discovered the public service had scholarships for Aboriginal public servants to go to university on full pay, I determined to join. And lo and behold, my first job was with the Public Service Board administering the very program. I was responsible for the implementation of the Aboriginal and Torres Strait Islander areas of EEO, working with Dr Gail Radford. I could have got the Canberra job permanently; I had a contract for six months to be reviewed at the end of three. But I wanted to be at home because of the land claim, so worked at DAA for two years, in the Darwin office in public relations. I had a drunk, white, male boss who was never at work. He signed in of a morning, returned to sign at lunchtime, then came back and signed off again at day's end. His wage was far superior to mine, and I was doing his job, my job — and working 17-hour days. The regional manager would daily come out: 'Where's so and so?' I'd shrug my shoulders: 'I don't know, do you?'

I couldn't continue working in that environment so went to Canberra. DAA was one of the last government departments to get the EEO plan approved; it was knocked back by the Public Service Board. A woman from Darwin, Veronica Teppitt, now deceased, was running the Aboriginal section of EEO in the Public Service Board. All she could do was make recommendations. The board made the decision. Our plan had fantastic goals and ambitions for disabled people and people of foreign non-English speaking backgrounds. But for women and even more so for Aboriginal and Torres Strait Islanders it lacked ambition. The only way I would get the plan approved was to ask the Black people what they wanted. So I called staff meetings.

I started from base one: 'Do you fellows know what EEO is or not? Okay EEO stands for equal employment opportunity. Do you know what that means?' No. Then I had to explain the different groups, and the way selection panels operate. I got a bloke who was ex-CES and who had come in to work on developing the AEDP (the Aboriginal Employment Development Program), Danny Rose, in with me for credibility. Danny was an executive. I said: 'You people tell me what your problem is, and I'll write it down and then Danny will assist me. We've got to convert so that you are protected, so that your gripe is not seen as you being a problem.' That was the total sum of Danny's involvement. But his support was vital.

I realised a journalist could work in public relations. I wanted to be a journalist. When the tent embassy was destroyed, I had knocked back a journalist cadetship in Darwin. I was writing for *Meanjin*, the Aboriginal edition in 1977, the DAA journal in 1973 and *Simply Living*. I had done exhibitions of posters, and been writing Black poetry since about 13, and illustrated my poetry for a women's festival at Bondi in 1977. After Cyclone Tracy I explored universal poetry. Any woman could identify with it, about the cyclone, about love. I wrote a poem about being a mother, which I am not. A journalist was deeply offended, saying I had no right to write it because I wasn't a mother. Until she realised I had written it, she thought it was brilliant.

Some work, I want people to know without question is mine, like my version of the Australian National Anthem:

I love my sunburnt people, a race of friendly smiles
I love our cheeky dimples and quiet expressive eyes,
I love our bond of unity, I love our native life,
But most of all, I love us, our skin the colour's right.

I hate the crowded cities the white man built around,
I hate the way they want to grind Blacks into the ground.
I hate their independence, not sharing love nor strife,
But most of all I hate the way they're always fucking right.

Other work I chuck away like old clothes. Once the job is done it is done.

I started on poetry because I was filled with so much rage about my mother. I had spent my life trying to become her friend. She remained loyal to her disowning of me. When she died I was so angry, I cried for many months.

Role models in my early years were few. All the people of authority were white. But the contribution of the white female missionaries has been treated with contempt and that saddens me because they were my mothers. They did it for love, the love of god. Their example is not a role model for me, but I suffered pain when they died.

When Miss Shankleton, or Laelie as we called her, died, my pain came from knowing she had suffered for the dozens of us there. We were part of a family she didn't set out to create, but she happened to be in a certain place at an historical time that led to the creation of the family of Retta Dixon kids. It was the most wonderful, harmonious, happy and contented group of funeral wakers. We were satisfied with her input into our lives.

Then there was Aunty Spohn, my favourite missionary, a good lieutenant to Laelie. I was too influenced by her. She was intense and almost unbending; fair, but authoritative. She took us kids on toe to toe and lip to lip, never backing down. I would like to be able to negotiate and withdraw when

> **We were satisfied with her input into our lives.**

appropriate. She never did teach me to withdraw. She taught me never to back down. I am not sure that was a good stance to acquire—never backing down, never dodging, taking confrontation head on.

It wasn't until the tent embassy that I found Blacks I could look at with admiration and appreciation, starting with Bobbi Sykes. In overcoming the odds and surviving, people like Pat Turner and Bobbi are admirable. Pat is one of the quiet achievers, an Alice Springs woman working for the Department of Prime Minister and Cabinet, engineering transformations within the Aboriginal affairs bureaucracy. She has an amazing capacity to work around stumbling blocks; she doesn't take things front on but she never backs down.

> Many Aboriginal women in the Northern Territory make me humble.

Many Aboriginal women in the Northern Territory make me humble. I see women like Tjululuk (Bridget), my aunty at Nauiyu Nambiyi which used to be the Daly River Catholic mission and her daughter Ungunmerr (Geraldine). Tjululuk takes in a lot of other children, fulfilling a traditional role of being responsible for the children in our clan. Miriam Rose, principal of the local school, has dignity and poise. Daly River art is the best Aboriginal art in Australia, totally different from any art anywhere. Miriam's work has long been recognised. She is a good athlete and painter. The church is decorated with her art. She has taught women how to use oils and canvas and acrylics. Miriam Rose's Aboriginal name is Ungunmerr, the same as Geraldine. She was the first Aboriginal woman to become president of a community. Because she is highly educated and experienced, a lot of pressure is on her to perform as a role model. She had to flee from Darwin because of the pressure and return to the Daly. So Miriam is one of my role models, as is Aunty Netta who grew up with my Mum, giving me many hours of her time answering a lot of questions I needed to ask. She comes across as a pushover, but is tough underneath. Seeing how she survives makes me want to emulate her. She has gone through her own personal hell and back, yet she creates a happy environment. She doesn't try to take over other people's problems but assists in solving them, like running people to and from court, and taking them shopping.

When I met Margaret Reynolds I thought she was too good to be true. Then I met her mother. Margaret has little ways of making everything you say important. One of the reasons I admired Margaret Reynolds was that she was the first Australian politician to fly an Aboriginal flag in a formal ceremony. People who are real role models are those who inspire others to contribute. Miriam Rose and Senator Margaret Reynolds are people like that.

Geraldine Willessee is a special friend of mine. She is a Broome connection, part-Filipino, part-Irish. She was actively involved in supporting the struggle of Aboriginals in accessing the media and sharing the knowledge. This is my goal, too, and I feel a sense of achievement through Aboriginal media groups, the Torres Strait Island Media Association, and the Townsville Aboriginal and Islander Media Association.

At DAA I saw the effects of those early efforts when I moved into the broadcasting area. I was involved in the BRACS program (Broadcasting for Remote Aboriginal Communities Services), introduced as a prelude to the Bicentenary. The Torres Strait Island people talked about seceding from Australia, so a decision was made to connect the satellite system, TV and radio on the Torres Straits, bringing Australian communications there to undermine the isolation and the secession away from Australia. Torres Strait Islanders articulated precisely what they wanted, what sort of people should be in their media.

Now I am working on a novel, *Gravel Patch*, and I also want to write a book on my father. I need a computer and I need a typewriter. I am living on $100 a fortnight and saving $825. I feel good about it.

> we shouldn't have to be grateful because some white was kind enough to invest that extra mile

My dream is to be able to live in a little cottage and write, because it takes my fancy and I have the time and the financial wherewithal to do just that. I know now after four years out of work what I don't want in my life. One is being grateful to white women who refuse to understand that we can do it, and take our jobs from us; and white men too. As citizens, we shouldn't have to be grateful because some white was kind enough to invest that extra mile. We should be taking control now.

RUNNING FREE — THEN CONFRONTING THE BARRIERS

Gay Davidson

Gay Davidson is a journalist in Canberra, having had a recent four-year stint in public/government relations. She was born in Christchurch, New Zealand, where she began her career. She has been married twice and had two daughters, one of whom died in 1984.

Gay has had a few 'female firsts' — as a political correspondent and head of bureau in the Federal Press Gallery, and president of the National Press Club — and has been very involved in community issues and organisations.

I can still see Rose Kaine on the start of the bitumen at our farmgate in her lisle stockings, cleaning dust off her shoes before trudging another half mile to the tram stop. She was 14-years-old, the eldest girl in a large family, off to work sewing uniforms. A bit down the road, the Kerrs lived — until Deborah woke up to Laurie's goings-on with his young daughters. God knows how she had the courage in 1947 to divorce him on the grounds of incest. Further on there was Mrs Harvey who barred me from her house after I spoke derisively at school, aged seven, about her requiring her kids to refer politely to BTMs (bums were very rude, so were dunnies). Gary Wheeler kept a pig farm and was always very jolly by 10 am because he'd been around the city hotels collecting swill and having a couple with all the night porters. Opposite were the Richards who kindly let me use their piano for practice — until I said 'No' to his groping. Mind you, I horrified them too: Mrs Richards reported to my mother that she'd heard me and two other little girls prancing home from school chanting, 'My mother's a bloody old bitch, my mother's a bloody old bitch.'

At the tramstop was a nice neighbour who allowed everyone to park bikes against his frontyard trees, and Campbell's general store where I was delighted once to witness utter shock when Mrs Shearer lowered herself heavily on to a sack of flour and said: 'Aaah, I haven't sat on my bum all day.' Nearby stood a house with SCAB painted large across the front during the 1951 waterfront strike. The family inside didn't dare remove it for two years. Opposite, the Cross' named their daughter Victoria. She dealt with that at 16, marrying a Mr Matthews and living to regret her haste. He turned out to be another jolly soul before lunch-time, driving a delivery dray for Ballins' Brewery, and taking full advantage of the daily free quota. Further on past Aranui Primary School was Patello's poultry farm. We kids would go there after school to watch the mothers sitting in a row, generally with a roll y'r own hanging out, plucking chooks. Mrs Pounsford fascinated me. She didn't miss a beat as she plucked and smoked, and never bothered about the lice moving in and out of her hairline.

I kept contact with that semi-rural neighbourhood on the outskirts of Christchurch, and years later knew who was getting married and why. But at eight I was removed from the local school, sent off to a High Anglican school in town, then later to the selective government girls' school. The sisters from the Community of the Sacred Name were women with a strong authoritarian streak, absolutely certain that a vocation or career was essential for any sensible, self-respecting gel and so were the high school teachers (most of whom had been pupils at Christchurch Girls High School (CGHS), gone to Canterbury University and returned). Mother Teresa was a wise old lady. She was the one I turned to in panic the night before I first married at 21. Help, I don't think I want to do this, let me come to the convent. She firmly refused, saying I'd never cop the restrictions.

My mother, orphaned in Cork at 11, emigrating to New Zealand at 14 and into domestic service, preferred to think I would go into business: me owning a millinery shop. My father (English, good second-rank public schools for the boys, finishing schools for the girls) assumed I'd go to university and into a profession. I didn't think about it. I worked hard at school and at home, enjoyed reading, radio and the 500 acres of Drainage Board Farm and personal playground next door.

At nine I remember a funeral mass for a child who took a candle to bed to read comics. I was furious when school closed early one year because of the first polio epidemic, precluding me from being the Virgin Mary in the nativity play. One kid returned the next year with a calliper. Another succumbed completely. At home our cow, Ol' Doll, regularly had milk fever with every calf, which had to be hauled out by Father and the vet. Finally Father and a couple of blokes dug a big hole. Father fired his service revolver, then threw it in the pit with her. Then there was the Ballantynes' fire.

Though the department store was only three storeys high, 41 died (42 according to the ambulancemen who counted a pregnant woman's baby). Some said the death toll would have been lower if the girls in upper floor workrooms had been hustled out at the same time as the retail floors and their customers. Many jumped to their deaths before the firemen could get the ladders in place.

Second year of high school, Juliet and Pauline, the girl I'd been sitting next to, murdered Pauline's mother upon discovering that there hadn't been a marriage, and Pauline was illegitimate. The trials were pretty sensational, although they didn't get at the diaries which were widely rumoured to indicate that Juliet's mother was next, the pair having discovered an extra-marital relationship. Not long after, a lad known to my family was charged with murdering a 17-year-old girl he'd plied with coffee laced with cantharides, obtained when he was working at Kempthorne Prossors' chemical plant during the holidays. He knew the dosage for mares. It was a terrible death for the poor girl, burned from the inside out. I still have a very posed photograph of him and me aged two and coyly kissing.

CGHS, as well as being a selective school for the whole province, was also an area school for the square mile of the inner city. Some girls smoked behind the bike sheds and were into knowing boys, and could be a bit of nuisance to me as a prefect. But I went through school in the top stream with the daughters of doctors, lawyers, farmers, vicars and academics, and a milksop lot we were. It wasn't until my fifth and last year, the scholarship year after matriculation, that we rebelled against anything. Miss Waller said: 'Girls, I have to go to a meeting, I'm putting you on your honour to carry on working quietly.' There was a spontaneous revolution. As one, we took out our lunches and began toasting sandwiches over the fire.

> I went through school in the top stream

University was a natural progression. I'd done most of the first year arts subjects work in my last year at school. I'd saved up for and bought a 1936 Singer sportscar learning to sew as well (since I couldn't afford to buy clothes, too). I had a great time: Father introduced me to scotch when I was 16 so I didn't get into trouble at parties — nobody could afford spirits, I turned up my nose at beer, and I didn't need a lift home. I had a proposal and a copy of *Escoffier's Modern Cookery* from a nice bloke who worked at the Co-op (communist) bookshop. I appreciated the book but the honourable intentions scared me off to a worse situation, a Jewish boy whose overwhelming mother thought I'd be the making of her lad. So when I happened across an elderly (at least 44) artist who was only interested in school girls in serge tunics, black stockings and suspenders, I felt socially secure again, and began working out how to leave home the following year.

The first thing was money. Then my parents dropped a bombshell: they were leaving me and Christchurch, off to Waimate in South Canterbury. I could get a boarding allowance, but that wasn't enough to flat on my own. Working in refrigerator temperatures on the pea belt at Birdseye six days a week, 10 hours a day, I was getting a lot more than waitressing or wardsmaiding but the boys driving the pea trucks were getting almost twice as much. My father was half-owner of a garage so I got myself some training, experience, a heavy traffic driving licence, and presented myself to the pea trucks subcontractor. He invited me to lift the tailgate off one of his monsters. At 5 ft 1/2 in. I couldn't reach. I said I was offering myself as a competent driver, not as the driver's mate, but he just laughed and said goodbye. It was the first time anyone had ever suggested I couldn't do something because I was a girl. By chance I was offered a job by friends of the Jewish mother. They had opened a coffee bar/restaurant and were aiming to get a liquor licence (there was only one in Christchurch at the time). I began cooking from 9.00 am till 7.00 pm (the family looking after the evening shift).

Cash for the next year was still a worry, until I had a brainwave. My aging artist friend kept himself in cheap red and smokes by working the odd night in something called the reading room at the *Christchurch Press*. I talked to the chief-of-staff (who turned out to be the father of one of the boys I'd known since high school dances). Jim Caffin started off huffing and puffing about how he couldn't employ women in the reading room: knock-off time was 2 am, well after public transport, and they'd have to provide taxis for any women! Then he began telling me about journalists' pay, from £20 at the top to £5 for first-year cadets. Utterly in the dark about what journalism meant, so acting totally on the goosebumps, I asked if I could be a journalist. I did have the sense to say: 'Not the women's pages.' Roly Cant the editor looked surprised to see me but courteously asked me about my schools, education and work experience. He seemed to like the bit about my father having been a runner (delivery contractor) for the *Christchurch Star*, and my spending Saturday mornings biking around the suburbs, chatting with the customers and collecting their money. Jim dismissed me with a wave of his pipe: 'Start at 2.00 on Monday, but you'd better be here at 1.30 pm to read the paper first.' I was the first female cadet the *Press* had taken on since the War.

> I was the first female the *Press* had taken on since the War.

It took a fortnight before people began using four letter words in front of me, and two days before I was charged with working the 64-line switchboard between 5 and 6 pm, while Phyllis 'the switch' had dinner (usually with the assistant chief-of-staff, who didn't drink). Everyone else was at 'The Dom' across the alley. The Dominion had a clientele from the *Press* and the *Star*, Trades Hall, plus detectives and lawyers, and several ladies from the NZBC Symphony Orchestra whenever it was in town. I wasn't allowed to know all these interesting people until I was 21. By then I had after-hours privileges in three other pubs. Between my family, school, university and first few months on the *Press* I knew an amazingly diverse range of citizens: and I also learned early that politics permeates every part of life, from the bird fanciers' annual show to the Anglican Synod. I never doubted that the job to go for was political correspondent.

On my first day at Court, the Magistrate was outraged at my appearance in a dress, buttoned to the neck but without sleeves. A few months later Government House expressed extreme displeasure when I didn't wear a hat and gloves to an investiture. I quickly found my male colleagues could curry favour with the cops by swapping dirty stories or salacious gossip. My best bet was a latest sport result or cricket score. I also learned fast when answering female voices on newsroom phones to say: 'He's out on a job' not 'He's at the Dom/on dinner/no one's seen him for hours.' I learned the hard way not to trust colleagues. One about to leave for Australia casually asked me if I'd known the girls in the Hulme-Parker murder case. Yes, of course, we were in the same class, I'd visited Pauline in prison on a number of occasions, she was studying as well as sewing mailbags. A version appeared in the Melbourne *Truth* a month later, attributed to a 19-year-old Christchurch newspaper woman. I was sent to coventry and told the publication had put paid to intended early releases from detention at Queen's pleasure.

Jim Caffin was the best chief-of-staff for whom I ever worked. He wouldn't upset his time book to fit in with university lectures, he had a disdain for journalists with, or trying to acquire, a degree, there was no formal cadet training— but he gave real guidance on building on sources and resources, and how to tell a story. There were no bylines, apart from the political correspondent, and certainly no 'I' anywhere in the paper— it took years after before I could bring myself to use the first person singular. When Jim had a day off (and so hadn't allocated the work) he expected to discern who had written what in the next day's paper; he encouraged individual observation and writing styles.

In those days there was no automatic progression through the grades after the four-year cadetship, resulting in fairly high mobility among younger journalists. My first promotion, after 16 months, came when I landed a job on a weekly in Wellington. Ten months later I moved on to another in Auckland, but it wasn't just for the money. I'd been sacked because the women's editor discovered me in bed with Hillary Naylor, a young sub-editor on the *Dominion*, whom I married a few months later. She felt it necessary to tell the editor. I was three months short of 21; he informed me he was in *loco parentis* and couldn't take responsibility for such a wayward gel. The Journalists' Association president was keen to make a case of it but I welshed, thinking of my parents in country town Waimate, population about 2000. After a year in Auckland, Naylor (called Nails) was offered a job back in Wellington in the press gallery. I'd have given my eye teeth for the opportunity, but he decided instead to go to university. So I negotiated a job on the *Christchurch Star* (afternoon paper, mainly day hours), dropping back my wage. There were a number of weeks when dinner before payday was based on faggot (the butcher's home-made black pudding).

After a few months I tried for another grading and a rise. The editor didn't attempt to deny my work justified it, just said I was getting enough for a girl, and there were men with families before me. He'd think about it. A few days later came a reasonable face-saver: a dictation and read-back test (all cadets were supposed to have done shorthand before getting graded). I'd only picked up a few Greggs outlines, had worked out a fair number of my own, including words from other languages covering whole phrases in English, and I had a good ear for other people's personal language. I got the upgrading.

Later, in 1962, the NZBC advertised for journalists — it was the introduction of television, and the old New Zealand Broadcasting Service, an outrider from the Government Tourist Bureau and government propaganda arm, was being made independent and celebrating the event with its very own news service. I applied and was the only woman journalist offered a job. The *Christchurch Star* refused my resignation. Jock Mathieson, a Labour frontbencher and former publisher of the *Star*, and family friend was enlisted to warn me of the horrors of working in a public-service bureaucracy. But as my mother would say, I wouldn't be said to.

I stuck there nearly six years, learning about radio and TV journalism, and about man's inhumanity to man and woman. When I joined the Christchurch NZBC newsroom there were just two of us. We worked hard. Until we acquired more staff, I did seven days a week, mainly because I had all the local knowledge. My superior had done provincial journalism in New Zealand, then gone to Australia, returning for this job. We were intensely competitive and created an impossible work situation. The end started over a pub lunch followed by the monthly meeting of the Lyttelton Road Tunnel Authority, a jolly bunch who usually ended up with a few sherbets. I arrived back around 5.00 pm and was met with: 'You're drunk — go home.' In fact the authority meeting had gone on longer than usual, I wasn't, and I typed out a couple of competent stories before leaving. But the wheels had been set in motion. Suspended, I announced I was fighting, and I did, backed by the New Zealand Journalists' Association (NZJA), the Public Service Association and a friendly lawyer (for free!). After reinstatement I stuck around for six months, until Nails acquired an MA in political science and a Commonwealth Scholarship for PhD study at the Australian National University (ANU). I gladly phoned Bob Ferris, then chief sub-editor at the *Canberra Times* and an old journalist mate, to arrange a job. This was late 1967 and I was 28 years old. It was not easy to leave a city, a whole country I knew and where I worked well and easily, leaping into the unknown again. But it was time to go.

Accepting a C grade after being the highest paid woman news journalist in New Zealand was galling, but I copped it. After coming to Canberra, I swapped the political scientist for the economist, Ken Davidson, then working for the *Australian*, and for the past 16 years for the *Age*, and worked my way up in the *Canberra Times*, leaving the public service round for Political Correspondent in 1974. Around Budget '85 I came across a speech by Henry Bosch of the National Companies and Securities Commission (NCSC) saying heretical things about Australia's White Knights of the entrepreneurial world being nasty corporate raiders, pointing out that in many countries loopholes available here were being or had been closed. For six weeks I kept bringing it to Ken's attention. Finally, although it wasn't strictly my field, I wrote it myself as my weekly column. The day it appeared, there were excited calls and a few ready followers. Over the next 18 months I wrote at least a dozen columns describing how corporate raiders, usually aided by their bankers and some other major financial institutions, accessed debt to avoid paying tax, explaining what this meant to productive investment, the economy and the long suffering PAYE taxpayer, and why the Treasurer was suffering from delusions of adequacy in refusing to face up to some pretty obvious changes to the taxation regime. The *Canberra Times* assigned me to be the parliamentary news sub-editor in May 1987 — no more columns or news space. For the third time I resigned from the *Canberra Times*.

For the third time I resigned from the *Canberra Times*.

The other two resignations were over the births of our daughters in 1970 and 1971. The first a few days before the birth, the second the day after (I delivered several weeks early). Ken was furious over what he regarded as my weakness in copping the editor's dictum, but there was literally nothing I could do about it. The Australian Journalists' Association (AJA) appeared to regard it as perfectly reasonable. It was a fellow AJA member of staff who brought the second resignation letter into Royal Canberra Hospital for me to sign. Each time I'd several weeks leave owing and simply wanted an additional few weeks leave without pay to give me three months off. Instead, there wasn't even an understanding that there would be a job for me to come back to (in fact there was, after my intended three months). Even the tax office didn't believe the situation, and required full tax instead of the normal 5 percent on severance pay.

Early in 1973, I was finally up to B grade (replacing a male A) on the public service round and the next year jumped to A1, following David Solomon as political correspondent. I suspect the downturn in advertising revenues in the June quarter of 1974, and the *Canberra Times*' traditional role as milch cow to Broadway (the Sydney centre of the Fairfax Press), had something to do with their not poaching some well-known senior male journalist at an over-award salary and expenses, but I was delighted with the opportunity, the first woman Political Correspondent and head of bureau in any press gallery in Australia or New Zealand. The late Ian Fitchett, then the doyen of the gallery, commented when he heard about it: 'What's wrong with [David] Solomon, letting a bloody sheila get his job'!

In fact there was little overt sexism in the gallery or Parliament House generally (and Fitch became a good friend, too). A few parliamentarians were not comfortable with women at work— Malcolm Fraser was one. I did my bit to remove one very basic barrier when Shirley, the teleprinter operator next door in the Australian Broadcasting Commission (now Corporation) broke her leg. Our two offices were the closest to the gallery gentlemen's. The nearest ladies' were either about 30 metres away in the new wing, or down two flights of stairs. When I came across Shirley grimly setting off on a long hop, I immediately offered to inspect first and stand guard. I and (at my urging) others in my office also used the facility. After a few days I explained to the Sergeant-at-Arms what was happening. He was delighted—there weren't enough lavatories for all the Members, Senators, Officials and Gentlemen and very few were women or ladies. In the end the gallery lav became unisex— the word used was Toilet.

What set me apart a bit from the real 'heavies' in the gallery was not sex or even the size of my paper's circulation. Rather, it was the inherited problem of the relationships between the major papers' and my paper's readerships and government ministers. There were no personal votes in those days for any minister in giving anything to the national capital's newspaper. Frankly, I've always thought they were stupid not to recognise it as a vehicle for getting messages through to the public service. However, not favoured with leaks from Parliament House, I maintained and improved my contacts in the public service and the ANU, and was not afraid to be first in writing about an issue which might become important on the political agenda.

David Solomon, as political commentator for Radio 2GB, had been part of the late Brian White's 4–6 pm talkshow. He persuaded Brian to pass that 'rat' (extra-curricula paying job) on to me, although in 1974 in Australia it was unheard of for women to be regarded as sounding authoritative on radio in current affairs. It worked well, and boosted my confidence. Radio 2GB and I both got good feedback, encouraging them to think of women as 'strong' talent on air, and assisting my efforts to make contact with New South Wales politicians on both sides. Brian Johns (now of SBS) was generous too. He gave me advice about having a disciplined approach to the job, warning me against the fairly common practice of political correspondents' taking over other staff members' major stories (it's no way to achieve a close-knit and enthusiastically working team). He advised that when a rival broke real political news, whether it was initially treated as a major story or not, it mustn't be ignored.

> Radio 2GB and I both got good feedback, encouraging them to think of women as 'strong' talent on air.

Leaving Parliament House in the early 1980s to be leader writer and national political commentator, I became more comfortable about campaigning (in the pamphleteering sense). I went into top gear on education funding in the interests of the government schools system. I also lobbied ministers and wrote about the need for more and much stronger preventive action on children's health. That was prompted in 1984 by our younger daughter dying at 13 of sub-acute sclerosing panencephalitis— that name's a real eye-glazer but the invariably fatal condition and dreadful, slow death arose from her not being immunised against measles. She, her sister and I were all briefly laid low with measles during the 1975 election campaign. At the time I suffered worst. Kiri apparently recovered completely, but she turned out to be one of up to 20 children in Australia each year who ultimately die of the disease. About seven years after apparently recovering from measles, the virus starts replicating in the brain (where it has lain dormant) and affects the whole body. It was too terrible not to try to warn all parents, especially when I was in a privileged position with media, political and bureaucratic access. There are still measles outbreaks, and the health and education bureaucracies are still not working together sufficiently to ensure all kids get all the various childhood shots. But the situation has improved on what it was before the Bicentennial Measles Campaign.

I've had plenty of practice at bereavements and major family health disasters, although none prepared me for that one. I thought I was grieving throughout the 14 months from diagnosis to death when I was simply being busy–busy, looking after Kiri, keeping up a hospitable household (so we weren't isolated in either a friends or work sense), and continuing to work three days a week initially, then four. I traded leave owing to maintain income. In the 1950s the journalist at the *Christchurch Press* who covered the Hulme–Parker case had a breakdown when it was over, and was given a year's leave on full pay before returning to a gentle regime. When I returned full-time, two weeks after the funeral, the general manager was disparaging about my having turned up at a stop-work meeting a few days previously.

There are different rules for men and women and there's little thanks for trying to change them — particularly for the benefit of women and kids. Some men have just as strong a sense of social justice as the women who try to put it into practice, but they tend to think of targeted populations, are impatient with individuals, and blind to it as a concept applying to their colleagues and families. Both my daughters displayed a strong sense of fairness and backbones of steel from an early age, so I have no fears for Tui. No doubt she'll encounter some discomfitures similar to mine, and I hope she wakes up sooner rather than later to the fact that it's more satisfying to have a hand in guiding social policy than in being an underpaid and stressed social worker. I'm sure she'll have her interesting times, personal satisfactions, work and fun, too, and what more can you wish for the next generation?

NO WELL LIT PATH

Carolyn Watts

Born in a farming community in WA, Carolyn Watts came to her career as a broadcast journalist late in life, having travelled, studied and done 'odd jobs' after leaving school in 1972. She has worked in all aspects of radio — as a journalist, producer and presenter of music, current affairs, and lifestyle programs.

Before travelling to the University of Chicago to take up her William Benton Fellowship for Broadcast Journalists, Carolyn Watts presented an afternoon current affairs program in Adelaide.

One of those fortunates whose parents and siblings did not suffer the delusion that girls couldn't do everything, I was born into a family of eight children. Living on a farm in Western Australia, my early life was spent enjoying the simple things of nature. As a youngster, to me a career was something into which boys and men were forced to fit. A woman could enjoy the best in life provided for by a man's earnings, and could also write, play music, be creative without being constrained. When I listened to the wireless and heard a woman's voice, I pictured her as doing this for enjoyment, in her spare time. As a young adult the concept of career was one that felt inhibiting and alien. Only in recent years has the thought of pursuing a career fitted into my life.

My mother was a nurse before marrying; at school she'd studied typing and Latin. One of my strongest memories of her influence on my schooling is in the words 'no daughter of mine will study typing or domestic science, and as for Latin, it's a dead language and should stay dead'. Her influence was that of a mentor, determined I should be and do whatever I chose. This philosophy didn't apply to my personal life. I often found myself gated for the smallest of reasons it seemed. Her choice saw the girls in our family privately educated at a convent with a plethora of good role models. Jokes abound about convent education, but I'll always be grateful I was surrounded by images of women saints, not to mention the Virgin Mary, a powerful influence on my belief that women are at least the equal of, and in many cases superior to, men. Not all teachers appreciated my strong will and rebellious spirit, but the headmistress was somehow able to see the value of my strong convictions, and reinforced my beliefs and my right to hold them.

> my belief that women are at least the equal of, and in many cases superior to, men

Soon after leaving school I went to Europe. In England I worked as an occasional nanny. In Europe I did the odd bit of translation and interpreting, and for a time was a ski instructor to several children. Paidwork was a way of supporting myself in my travels. It wasn't until I joined the Australian Broadcasting Corporation (ABC) many years later, that I realised work could provide great personal reward and fill a social need.

I first went to university in Italy, ostensibly to study Italian art history. I couldn't tell you much about it, but I could tell you the joys of heading into the Tuscan hills with a bunch of other students, laden with wine, cheese and bread, for a day of studying that turned into a lazy afternoon in the sun. When I returned to Western Australia I attempted philosophy and languages, but the studies lacked the spark I expected. It wasn't until I discovered it was possible to study something as alive and relevant as journalism that I found my niche in tertiary education. We did news collection and presentation for a half-hour bulletin once a week. Here was real excitement. I strove to get to the bottom of questions I'd wondered about but never had the possibility of asking the responsible ministers. Now interviewees wanted to speak to me: knowing that if they didn't talk their opposite number would be only too happy. I listen to some of the early tapes now and I sound fearful and timid. The first day I worked on public radio as a paid employee presenting a half hour program, I emerged panic stricken and white from the studio ... one of the elderly volunteers took me aside, sat me down, and gave me a 'nice cup of tea, dear'. Pieta O'Shaugnessy, a remarkable woman, was the co-ordinator of programs at 6NR. It was she who offered me the job there. Currently in England, she's no doubt encouraging more would-be broadcasters through her insistence that it's all up to you, you can make whatever you like of your life, you just need to choose your course.

I found semiotics, a study of language, its meanings and its motivations. The spark was there, that reason to learn for the joy of learning. My mentors were both men. Men who'd call themselves feminists (a title over which we had much hot debate). One took particular care over questions about journalistic ethics and responsibilities. When I got my first job he congratulated me, saying I shouldn't stay too long in the mainstream of the industry as it could be soul-destroying. When I had to cut news stories that might have spanned several months, into stories of less than a minute of radio time with '30-second grabs' of voice on tape, I learned what he meant. Filling hourly news bulletins is fondly called 'feeding the beast', and it takes a particular kind of journalist to do this task well. With a two-hour program come different stresses but many minutes to delve into each of the day's nine interviews.

I stumbled into journalism. A creative writing course at Curtin University lacked vitality. I changed course literally and metaphorically. In journalism, I studied all aspects of print and radio, and was offered a paid position as producer/presenter of a current affairs program on public radio as soon as I had finished my degree. After six months at Radio 6NR, I joined the ABC Radio Newsroom in Perth. Even there, the concept of journalism as a career wasn't clear. It seemed to offer the possibility of travel as well as earning a living. But there seemed to be so many reasons not to pursue this course: the different news values I seemed to hold from my chief-of-staff at the time; the horror of having a burly sub-editor take me to task over some apparently insignificant point. **I loved the challenge.** The short-term hassles sometimes got on top of me and were the unrecognised source of silly arguments at home. But all changed with my move to Hobart. I was offered the job of presenter/journalist of a new drive-time news and current affairs program. I loved the challenge. Here I first experienced the 'family' world you can find in an organisation. About six months into my program the prospect of this enjoyable task as a long-term possibility first occurred to me.

While I was in Hobart my father became quite ill. I questioned the value of working so far away from this man I loved so much and might not have for much longer. After some unsuccessful applications, I was appointed as producer at the ABC metropolitan station in Perth and eventually moved to produce a morning program presented by Des Guilfoyle. He has been one of my primary mentors, teaching me that it is possible to work as a dedicated and committed journalist within a bureaucracy.

It takes a while to understand how a bureaucracy works. I often received helpful advice from a woman who produced spoken word programs so I could understand and confront what otherwise have been frustrating bureaucratic procedures. I'll never be as bureaucratically informed as she, yet I was able to see the structures underlying the otherwise apparently arbitrary decisions that are made.

Many new-style role models existed for me, as the late 1980s seemed to be filled with women in positions formerly held by men. More of these women were outside work than within. Sharryn Jackson, now assistant secretary of the Miscellaneous Workers Union in Western Australia, was a great friend and worked as the Women's Officer at the Trades and Labour Council (TLC). A cheerful, fiery, intelligent woman, she was also a well of compassion. Long debates with her helped sort out particular issues I saw as personal limitations. Sharryn's perspective taught me that the personal is political, especially where different story priorities were seen by myself and my sub-editor. The realisation that the troubles I often encountered were those being met throughout the world by women moving into a male work sphere gave me the energy and determination not to get stuck. Sharryn often provided the impetus to fight hard on an issue I'd otherwise have grudgingly put down to experience. From her I learned that with change comes discomfort, and nothing is easily won. Heather Foumaini, now a freelance journalist based in London, was a wonderful influence because she never seemed to take the ABC seriously. Heather was one of those strong women whom most of the male managers seemed to find threatening and whom other women found supportive. She had a laugh that shrugged off the drudgery.

I've never seen myself as a career woman. Nonetheless many of my colleagues and managers have seen me as ambitious. From the outside it looks like I've made some determined moves in the transition from current affairs producer on public radio to current affairs presenter on ABC metropolitan stations. From my side of the fence it's been a run of luck on the career side largely brought about by my personal circumstances. My earliest change came through wanting to be closer to my father, who is now as hardy as his vegetable garden. The other major factor was my lover of ten years, also a journalist. That he had a daughter in Perth made him less willing to move with me. I suppose if I were a hard-nosed career woman I'd have ended the relationship. But I'd have given up my job before doing that. If he had been transferred I'd have found another job wherever he needed to go, maybe leaving the security of the ABC. As it was that didn't arise, but I'd given it quite some thought. My career was a supplement to the relationship in good times and, at tough times, a stabilising reminder of my capabilities in other areas.

The importance of paidwork insinuated itself slowly, in stages. After I left school I worked both in Perth and Europe, but at short-term jobs chosen because they required nothing much of me. Paidwork was a means to an end over several years and different jobs.

I didn't develop an appreciation of the rewards of paidwork, other than the monetary ones, until I first worked on public radio. I've always said that if I wasn't getting paid for my job I'd volunteer to do it. These days I'd sometimes prefer to be a volunteer and be able to take the spring day to potter in the garden rather than face another day of angst about something at work. But the task itself is always rewarding.

Because I don't see my career as a structured and well-lit path, I still find I have to embroider the future as I see it for myself in the ABC. I've leapt over barriers to get to where I am now. In my early days, I saw these as insurmountable, but little by little, I've learned to use the bureaucratic formulae to my own advantage, instead of being at their whim. Probably the person who helped me most to recognise that my career in the ABC would be whatever I made of it, was a charming, middle-aged broadcaster, with whom I had a discussion early in the newsroom phase of my career. He told me that he had waited 16 years to get out of the clerical side of the ABC and onto the wireless. (Not unheard of in a large organisation such as ours.) He was an excellent broadcaster. He explained it was necessary to wait for what you want. This was not the path I would travel. I haven't waited and I've got pretty much what I've wanted. Some managers have found my being a journalist disturbing. When I'm hell-bent on a story, I work at a pretty high rate, expecting others to do the same. I can't count the times I've been advised to lower my standards for the sake of industrial harmony. One manager was a journalist himself, and it made a nice change to be congratulated for the speed and quality of my work rather than castigated for not 'fitting in' with people who worked at a slower pace.

Mine is an odd job: I put myself and my beliefs on the line each day. Sometimes people, generally disgruntled elderly men, telephone, saying 'this outrageous feminist has to go'. Just as many older women and younger men call to congratulate me for not taking nonsense. It's good to check whether the disgruntled chaps are representative of the mainstream of our listeners: the ratings prove them to be peripheral. The responses I get from women who phone in are generally positive, even when they're calling with a complaint. Most are reassured to see a woman of my age take on such a public profile.

Most interviewees don't think twice about my being a woman. Fellow workers seem not to notice my being a woman; at least they don't comment on it often. The occasional man likes to 'help out': a woman 'might need a man's guidance'. It doesn't take them long to realise that I don't appreciate patronising assistance. But in fairness there aren't many. Some male support staff still seem to find it difficult to take clear instructions without a sluggish or surly response, but I put that down to their perception that their position is subservient, rather than to disdain for working with a woman. Many women have been supportive; some have been nasty. In the media, there are always knives, but many women choose not to wield them. When they do, I generally read it as a personal concern they have at seeing another woman get to places they are still telling people they haven't got to 'because they are a woman'.

> **Many women have been supportive; some have been nasty.**

I enjoy radio but my personality thrives on change and challenge. If I am broadcasting at 65, it will follow several career changes. These will be decided by different opportunities and the prospective pleasure of the next option. Now, the greatest pleasure in my work is 'talk-back'. A generous aspect of radio, it allows people to be just who they are and say just what they think.

It's been a few short years since I finished my journalism degree, and I've presented metropolitan radio in five Australian states. Yet it's not the little wins at the ABC that I've seen as my main achievements. It's the personal changes, the stages from school to now. My perspective is different, broader and clearer. I've achieved a lot to get past the initial frustrations, and to trust my friends' advice enough to push through the hard times.

I want to live a good full life and work at something that makes me happy and that I believe to be productive. I've never seen myself as heading in a particular direction. If ambition is achieving the things that make my every day life feel worthwhile at the same time as earning a living, then I'm ambitious. I'd like to try motherhood. Perhaps that's the ultimate ambition for me, to be a mother and still work at the job I love. My work is eminently suited to mothering and earning a living part-time.

I have been influenced by admirable women, and admirable women are many. Equal Opportunity Commissioner in Victoria, Moira Rayner has strength and eloquence when addressing issues on radio as well as being successful in her field. Dr Robyn Rowland, social psychologist from Deakin University, pushes the edge of the gender gap. Diana Warnock, broadcaster in Western Australia, is admirable for her professionalism and tenacity. A stayer, Pru Goward of the ABC is an exceptional journalist whose standards are uncompromising. Jane Singleton, in public relations and no longer a broadcaster, is dedicated to her profession, and to her conscience. I once had the good fortune to 'produce' Dr Carmen Lawrence, now premier of Western Australia. An outstanding intellect, her clarity and compassion are obvious to even the most cynical of journalists.

Brought up to believe I could do anything I wanted and achieve anything I put my mind to, I believed this was so for all women. I thought we were the lucky sex, able to choose marriage, career, or both. Years of travelling gave me insights into the conditions of women's existence which militate against following the heart's desire. This insight was borne out by my studies. I continue to argue with my siblings as to my claim that one's potential depends on how you are brought up, when you were brought up and where, rather than on individual character traits.

Ultimately I desire to live in a rural community, or at least have a property in the country. I dream of work on the land, fully equipped with the latest technology, so I can write and sell stories to city newspapers from this rural retreat. So far only a dream, and sometimes dreams are there only to broaden my perceptions and widen my scope wherever I am. I reflect on my good fortune at having been born into a time when so many other women showed us by example that our dreams could come true. Sometimes I succeed, sometimes I fail, but I try.

FIGHTING FOR FAIR SHARES

Shirley Stott Despoja

Shirley Stott Despoja began her career in journalism writing for a church newspaper, the Anglican, *in Sydney. She joined the* Adelaide Advertiser *in 1960 as the only woman journalist in general reporting. Shirley Stott Despoja was the first arts editor for the* Advertiser *and held that position for a number of years. She also wrote a column, 'Saturday Serve' which had a large following. She is currently literary editor with the* Advertiser.

To Flora

For a few years, Clive James' life and mine ran parallel. It was not the glamorous part of his life. He went from Kogarah Primary to a class for bright boys at Hurstville. I went from Kogarah Primary to a class for bright girls at Hurstville. They were called Opportunity C classes. James has made light of his Opportunity, but the female opportunists at Hurstville made the most of theirs, correctly divining they would need what help they could get for the long haul ahead.

Freed from most of the upper primary curriculum, or having covered it (we were not told things in those days), we pretended to be journalists and broadcasters (with a fake microphone), wrote and presented our own plays, held class debates and read what we chose. Our class of about 30 girls — from very poor to comfortably middle-class homes — had a golden opportunity. No boys demanded the lion's share of the teacher's attention. The natural leaders took a natural lead and those less inclined got a chance to discover whether they might like to try their hand at leading. We learnt a lot about what we thought was Aboriginal culture. We made plays from a book of

Aboriginal legends. If it was not the real thing, we learnt some respect for a culture not our own. One 11-year-old pursued her passion for Spanish history. We went to symphony concerts and plays though the parents of some of us might never have done so.

Try as I might to be blasé, like James, about the Opportunity C class, it was a formative experience. That particular type of pre-secondary schooling for children who performed well in school IQ tests at nine years and six months began to be frowned on not long after I went on St George Girls High School, Kogarah. It saddened me then and it does now that this kind of special education was stigmatised as elitist, something to do with intellectual snobbery. Bright girls need all the help they can get: in the late 1940s all the messages were to become good wives and mothers. Somehow the message didn't get through to Hurstville Opportunity C girls, busy enjoying their creativity and being as intellectual as they chose.

We didn't talk much about being wives and mothers at St George, either, but the onset of puberty and examinations crowded out many of the good things of our years at Hurstville. There was a half-hearted attempt to teach us cooking and because I wanted to do art I had to take on sewing, but our pursuits were mainly academic and, if we could escape the attentions of one sadistic maths teacher, enjoyable.

I won a Commonwealth Scholarship, but it wouldn't have taken the child of a Rockdale widow to university. A Soldiers' Children's Education Scheme scholarship did, however, because it paid for books as well as fees. Mum went to work in a factory; I went to read philosophy at Sydney University. Lecturers still wore gowns in those days. They all seemed remote and unapproachable. The university was probably in its dullest period in history. Gone were the ex-service people on Repat. scholarships whose relative maturity had made the university a heady place in the immediate post-war years. The political clubs were in the doldrums. The most populous club was the Evangelical Union. My school friends headed for the EU in droves. They became strangers to me. I debated, and acted with SUDS (the Sydney University Drama Society), attracting some attention, but did not know how to follow it up. The problem was that all the girls from North Shore homes and private schools spoke in a code I couldn't crack. The men might have been from another planet. I went home each night, a hell of a long haul, too, to a little Rockdale house with autumn-toned wall-to-wall.

I took to acting with a Rockdale drama group and my studies began to wobble. My confidence crashed from the dizzy heights of Hurstville Opportunity C to the misery of drinking coffee at Manning House with Evangelical Union worthies, while watching the real people I wanted to meet as they remained oblivious of my presence. The girls with breasts shaped by Maidenform cones seemed to have no difficulty getting the attention of tutors and lecturers. One of them, in a queue waiting for the Fisher Library to open, refused noisily to contribute a coin towards a collection for the first Aboriginal scholarship. I was shocked, but admired her dark green twinset and short rope of pearls. My essays got good marks; my nerve failed at examinations.

A good student counsellor might have sorted me out. There was none. I was sick a lot. I was a working-class kid out of my environment. It was not a happy time. It has made me a lifelong opponent of university fees which more than anything keep working-class kids, and girls in particular, out of tertiary education. When I see today's university campuses, with their mix of young people of all classes and races, I feel cheated by my university experience. As I see fees creeping in and the growing conservatism of political groups on campuses, I think we are going back, though I pray not so far as the early 1950s, to something society will regret.

> I was a working-class kid out of my environment.

A social and political awareness was dawning, but it had no means of expression. I took my first chance to get out of the university in the hope of learning something I obviously needed to learn, which was simply unavailable at Sydney University then (though things improved shortly after, it seems). I became a sub-editor on the *Anglican* newspaper and found journalism. For six months I worked ridiculous hours, longer than I needed to, just to be around the press which was on the *Anglican* premises. I wrote my first published reviews: of a jazz mass and a recording of Noel Coward songs. I was introduced to bishops as 'our young atheist on the staff'. This was much to my taste. I was taught to check facts, punctuation, by having the *Oxford Concise* thrown at me (or very close to me) when I made a mistake. I took myself away from the *Anglican*, its very right and most reverends, from its formal style pinched from the *Times* of London, its intellectual snobbery which I found endearing for a while, its obsessions and eccentricities, and found a job on the *Canberra Times*.

Behind the *Canberra Times*, in Mort Street, Braddon, was a large paddock where orange-berried cotoneasters grew unchecked. I picked them at the end of my shift, nearly midnight, and took them back to my hostel to fill the copper jug I bought with my first spare cash. This was Canberra in the late 1950s. Golden poplars grew where now there is a man-made lake. Walking from one building to the next could take half an hour, across paddocks. It was a country town without the cohesion. It was beautiful. But most of all it lacked menace.

Others spoke of missing Sydney or Melbourne and couldn't wait to organise a ride at weekends. I could only think that never again would I have to face the train to Rockdale late at night, watching the drunk in the corner of the carriage to see whether he was planning to move closer, to speak to me, to flash; praying all the while the conductor would walk through the carriage or another woman get on at a station. In Canberra I got an inkling of what had been controlling my life, the threat of male violence, simply by feeling its absence in this lovely place. There had never been a murder in Canberra, I was told. Well, there had been an 'axe incident', but that was a domestic: it didn't quite rate as murder.

I had never written a news story before Canberra. But my confidence had returned. I wrote up police rounds, theatre reviews, interviews; reporting lectures, courts. The incest case I covered didn't upset my notions of a non-violent town. That little girl, who looks so angelic in her white dress in court, the police told me, knows what's what; she isn't so innocent. I was astonished by the questions she was asked, about towels and semen, and fascinated by the legal palaver. I assumed the cops knew what they were talking about.

My politics remained unfocused on parties. I handed out leaflets for a female Liberal candidate, to the derision of my friends. 'I'd do the same for a woman in Labor,' I said. Oh ha, ha. My friends laughed at my scarlet face. The Irish lefties were a clan that had no place for me anyway; boozers, mateyness. I got better at my job and decided I wanted a turn at the important round the fellas did. The editor, a huge man loved by all except me (my legs turned to jelly in his presence), was so angry his face, some feet above mine, turned red and then white. 'No, you won't take that away from the men,' he said. It wasn't a glass ceiling I had hit. It was the gender barrier, solid as rock. I stopped feeling, as I had done for some time, like the cat who had found the cream. The cream was turning sour, anyway.

> It was the gender barrier, solid as a rock.

A romantic night by the Cotter River, expected by me to be a night of sweet words and held hands, became a near rape. A man's hand came through my window at the hostel as I was reading in bed at 2 am after the late shift at work. A man in the group I was acting with made a move when his wife's back was turned. My underwear was pinched from the laundry by the hostel pervert. I began to think about, as well as report, what was happening in the courts. I had gone as far as I would go at the office. It was time to move on. They gave me a sequined handbag as a goodbye present.

All my life I have been running from male violence, which makes me different from other women only in so far as I was paid just enough in my job to make fleeing a possibility. In Canberra, and for a long time afterwards, I did not articulate this even to myself. I had known at university that my crush on a young man was influenced by the fact he was going to be a minister of religion. I felt I would be safe with him. What a lot I had to learn. In Canberra the gender barrier and violence began to fit together like a hinged tool.

The *Adelaide Advertiser* offered me a C grade and a promise of no 'women's page work'. My mother had moved to Adelaide by this time, as had my married eldest sister. It seemed the place to go. Adelaide in September 1960 looked shaven and pale; its wide streets a little dusty and dull. I had a few pangs about leaving Canberra's beauty, but the job was what it promised to be. I was the only woman on general reporting. They had tried others who somehow hadn't fitted in. This I was given to understand had something to do with sitting on desks and 'flaunting it' while making telephone calls; with sometimes crying when they made mistakes or didn't like assignments. I never found out whether this was fact or myth, but I was aware of passing tests that had little to do with my capabilities as a writer and reporter. I had grown up with two older brothers as well as two sisters; brothers who were my idols, so I knew the sort of behaviour that brothers required to call me 'matey'. It worked, and I was mad about my job.

After the late shift I went to parties with my male colleagues. The mateship continued outside the office. It was years before I found that honorary mateship, like an honorary degree, is fake, conveys nothing worth having but a comfortable illusion. I felt I had found a safe place, an easy place to get around in, no need to catch trains. No one seemed to resent me though I was upgraded quickly. Looking back I realise that, being the only female on general reporting duties, I was a pet not a threat.

> honorary mateship, like an honorary degree, is fake, conveys nothing worth having but a comfortable illusion

What is it that makes us journalists? No job offers quicker psychic return for effort. The adrenalin runs. I am addicted to the fear of not being able to perform, of not finding the good intro, let alone the satisfying ending. Your last story (performance) is that by which you are judged. Failure is disgrace. What people say after they've read you, like theatre reviews, causes either elation or despair. There is the barrier between you and readers (audience), the sub-editor (director), who either meddles causing acute resentment and embarrassment, or saves you from making a fool of yourself. When you are up and running, with your style worn like a second skin and perhaps a little learning worn lightly, sub-editors, who for some reason always think they know better, are a menace. Still, there is not one of us who doesn't have a sub to thank for something that might have occasioned the indefensible defamation case or a red face.

My aim as a writer-journalist is to speak in my own write/right, in a political or personal column. Particularly in the personal column, the line blurs between craft and art. I plunder my life's experiences for columns with a short life expectancy. I have often felt like a caterpillar eating the very leaf it stands on, waiting for the last munch, when the source of life and sustenance is consumed, and it drops into the void. I can't imagine writing without a degree of terror.

Journalists take risks. There is no point in having a bit of space unless one fills it with something worth reading. No one worth reading has one eye on the audience waiting for a sign of love. If you please yourself, you will please someone other than yourself, provided you have skills; if you write just to please others, you will convince nobody.

But of course you don't own the space. It belongs to Mr Murdoch or Mr Fairfax most likely, and your tenure is insecure. If you think of that, you are done for. Nonetheless, getting something in the paper of which your editor does not approve (it will be phrased thus: 'I am thinking of *your* credibility in this matter') may take hours of soul-destroying argument; energy that could be used in your creativity. Be good on your feet, I can only counsel; have the best arguments at the ready, and let them be such that they flatter the intelligence and superior understanding that your editor may or may not have. Write so well that your work cannot be refused easily, whatever its message. Write what you believe, if you have the opportunity, and beware of censorship by osmosis (that is, saying only what you know your boss will find acceptable or what you *think* your boss finds acceptable). This is the most insidious form of censorship, rife in Australia, where the media monopoly does not present a vast array of opinions from which a writer can select a set nearest to her own when offering her work.

Interlude

Oh sisters. What a time to ask me about my brilliant career. I am in the middle of the worst possible scenario. A work-related incident occurred. I sought an acknowledgment of what happened and an apology. When that wasn't forthcoming, I started a worker's compensation case which became bogged down in appeals; the expense threatened what little I have in the way of assets: namely Villa Soursob, the once happy location of events in my weekly column, 'Saturday Serve'. That column has disappeared, I am told, forever. It was more than a column to me, of course. It was my way of communicating with women — and men — a two-way discourse that is perhaps best managed in writing by someone as deaf as I am.

A lot of my readers were deaf, too, or partly isolated in other ways. They have shared my dismay at what has happened to me and the loss of the column. But they find themselves as I do, without much recourse. If what had happened to me had happened elsewhere, a newspaper might have championed my cause. When the power of the fourth estate is against you, you are in trouble. Some of my colleagues, similarly abused, support me; a few are busy consolidating their alliance with the powerful. I watch them, the collaborators, knowing that if the problem were removed tomorrow, they would revert to being nice people. They will say they didn't know what was going on. They will forget. The strategy includes, as Primo Levi said, a war on memory.

When I had the power of the Press behind me, I took risks which didn't seem so risky at the time. I made some enemies: the usual ones that don't like what you write, and some more substantial ones, who didn't like my win over the Australian Bureau of Statistics whose attempt to make me reveal information I thought prejudiced my personal safety ended in a court battle. It was only borrowed power that I had.

I can remember standing on a green lino tile in the passage leading to the *Advertiser* staff canteen, and thinking I had it all. The green tile is of no significance except that it is still there, 30 years on, and I visit it to forgive and feel pity for the girl I was then. Girl nothing. I was 23; three years older than my daughter is now, she who accepts the pain of looking realistically at the world, who has 'The Knowledge', of how women are controlled or done in. She is the toughest fighter I know. I am not bragging about my daughter. To take any credit for her is to take credit from her staunch brave self. I only say that if I had a different kind of daughter I wouldn't be here now, writing this, or anything else.

It was the early 1960s. I had a job I loved, the prospect of working in London, and a man I was going to marry who would banish all my fears.

The job in London was mine, but someone at the *Advertiser* forgot to tell me. The boyfriend took off for a while and when he returned marriage was off the agenda. My family found out I was sleeping with him. They gave me the choice: him or them; my sexual activity outside marriage was killing my mother. I chose my family and sex, which meant I had to marry. I became another man's fiancée. Without realising I had a choice, I gave up London.

The marriage was an inter-cultural disaster. He took off for Canberra. I followed, rapidly going deaf. And scared as hell. I had removed the last bit of power (my financial independence through my job) from my life. After five years over which I will draw a veil, as they say, I turned up my new hearing aid, left my husband and went back to Adelaide as the *Advertiser*'s first arts editor.

> **The marriage was an inter-cultural disaster.**

The Song of the Serpent: 'If I could hear as well as see, no man or beast would pass by me.' I decided they would not pass unreckoned with, anyway. The job, in the most volatile area I had encountered, threw up plenty of men to challenge, and a good few beasts. An arts official who didn't like what I wrote about his job performance complained that I was a 'disappointed lady'. The voyeurs in the office got their fill questioning me about that sexual slur. I was writing so well on the politics of the arts that I survived this and other kinds of put-downs. With childcare a continual problem and expense, I didn't have time to watch my back. A local monthly paper reported that the kinds of things said about Shirley Despoja in the Adelaide Festival Centre (the hub of arts activity then) could not be repeated in their columns. Attempts to do me in failed only because the *Advertiser* was getting the sort of copy it wanted from me, but when the Festival Centre hit the paper's most sensitive nerve by withdrawing a bit of weekly advertising, it was time for me, after six years, to accept a sideways move to being literary editor again without a fuss.

It finally occurred to me that despite my obvious value to the paper, any male cadet had a better chance of promotion than I. Politically my mind was catching up with what I had internalised for so long. I wrote what was going on, what was being done to women. Through blood-on-the-carpet arguing with the editor and co., I got a lot of it in the paper, testing the limits sometimes, ignoring them most of the time. Shirl had come out. The best years followed. The bloody battles were at least productive. I never reckoned a cost, except, perhaps, to my children. Deafness isolated me. Even if I had thought of networking, I wasn't sure I approved of it. Wasn't that the boys' game? I was wrong. It is the power game, and one that must be played to ensure survival if not for today, then for further down the track.

My column, 'Saturday Serve', was a success. Women identified with me in my battles with The Man who is Glad He is Not Married to Me, a real person who became a useful device. I was also writing about a little cottage in suburbia, with kids and cats and soursobs smothering the garden; about flu in winter and sunsets and Christmas, and 'Eastenders' on the telly when the Bureau of Statistics called demanding answers to questions about whether I lived alone, smoked, had rattles in my chest. There was a gentle side which threatened no one; and there was a fierce side, a reckoning of what was happening in the world and to women in particular. The message was getting across in ways that people who disliked it couldn't quite put their finger on.

Postlude

I am writing, now, not what I want to write, but awaiting my resurrection. I sing a modified version of the 'Song of the Serpent': 'If I could hear as well as see, no woman would pass, unawakened to the true nature of power and why women must, *must*, fight for a share of it and win.' And in the words of Voltaire (it pleases me to subvert the words of men): 'I am cultivating my own anger.'

I am no longer running.

Scene: A morning editorial conference

Shirley: Apart from a sketch of Madonna, an edition of today's paper contained only one image of women, only one photograph of two women in the whole news area. What kind of message is this sending to our readers, and to women in particular?

Response: The picture on page three is of an aeroplane. Some people think of planes as female. And look at this [several pages of department store advertisements for sweaters and blouses worn by women]. What nonsense you speak ...

Other conference members: Oh Shir—ley!

Lone supporter (?), male: I happen to agree with Shirley, but let's get on to something important...

PART II
Pushing the Margins

KEEP FIGHTING, KEEP SPEAKING OUT

Lisa Bellear

Lisa Bellear is a founding member of Ilbijeri Aboriginal Theatre Co-op Ltd in Victoria and president of the Aboriginal Affairs Policy Committee of the Victorian Branch of the Australian Labor Party (ALP). She has been, for a number of years, a member of the Victorian Aborigines Advancement League Inc., a member of the Victorian Aboriginal Education Association Inc., Higher Education Sub-Committee and vice- president of the Melbourne Aboriginal Education Association Inc. Lisa Bellear is a radio broadcaster with Radio 3CR, on the 'Not Another Koori Show' and works as Aboriginal Liaison Officer with the University of Melbourne.

Since the invasion, one in six Aboriginal children has been removed from their natural family. I was one of those victims. Because of the support and love of some close friends who are more like family, I can now call myself a survivor.

Anger and sadness and loss have occurred throughout my life, yet I tend to keep to myself much of what I have experienced. I've never gone in for crying much, although I've been told it's good for the soul. And I guess there are issues that even close friends find difficult to understand, so to make life easier for all I leave a lot unsaid. This is particularly so when it comes to talking about my life, prior to November 1986 when I finally had the courage, through the help of my dear friend who is more like my sister, Destiny Deacon, to find out who my real family was.

Australia has a responsibility to redress the injustices that have been (and in many respects are still being) committed against the indigenous population of this country. It is through sharing these experiences, however painful or distasteful, that we as a country can begin to grow together, and work for a better future for all Australians.

In Victoria, the average life expectancy of a Koori male is 42, and 46 for a Koori female. So much more needs to be done. Building of bridges must be a united effort by all people of all political persuasions, if justice is not only seen to be done, but is done.

For this reason I am prepared to pen some parts of my life, although it brings me much sadness. I still cannot understand why Aboriginal people have suffered so much at the hands of the dominant culture.

> I still cannot understand why Aboriginal people have suffered so much at the hands of the dominant culture.

When I first had the courage to go to the Department of Community Services Victoria adoption information service with my friend Destiny, I was given my old file. Occasionally I am capable of pulling it out from its hiding place. I go through it and still cannot believe that the file is about me, about my life. I can't even use my adoptive name, it makes me so very sad. I was made a ward of the state, then adopted into a white family. I tried to survive. It inspired me to fight for social justice and become keenly involved in the media.

In 1960 my mother Binks Bellear, whose tribe is Nunuccal, left the North Coast of New South Wales. She came to Melbourne and was fortunate to obtain work with the Post Master General's Department (PMG, now Australia Post). My mother lived in a boarding house in Lygon Street, Carlton. Although the exact details remain sketchy, she met my father Stanko Kvesic, who was at the time a heavyweight boxer from Croatia. I was born on 2 May 1961.

Not long after, my mother became so ill that she returned home; it was expected she would get well and come back to Melbourne for me, or I would be sent up to the North Coast, to her. My father Stanko told me he went to Queensland to earn more money. Through this period I was cared for by Berry Street Babies Home in East Melbourne.

At this time, if a child were placed in Berry Street, a parent had to pay for the child's keep as well as sign an agreement that if the payment fell in arrears of one month or more, the child automatically became a ward of the state. Another even more sinister policy was in operation: the government's active assimilationist program, where Aboriginal children were at an alarming rate being adopted or fostered into non-Aboriginal families or institutions.

My mother, on realising how ill she was, wrote a will to Berry Street requesting that if she died I was to be cared for by my grandmother who at the time was raising my mother's eight brothers and sisters in northern New South Wales. The administrator at Berry Street replied in writing, stating that I could be sent to my grandmother if two airfares were provided, along with adequate winter clothing; in addition the letter said that my mother's will was not a legally binding document as it had not been witnessed by a justice of the peace. Not long after, before my mother could comply with the demand, she died.

Meanwhile my Uncle Bob and Aunty Kay Bellear came down from Sydney to try to find me. They were only teenagers and did not receive any co-operation from the Social Welfare Department. When I finally did meet with my nan, Sadie Bellear, she showed me the receipts from the post office: she had kept up the payments at Berry Street. I was made a state ward nonetheless and not long afterwards adopted.

The happiest times of my life up until I met my family were at boarding school at Sacred Heart in Ballarat East, although I was always getting into trouble for giving cheek to the nuns, swearing or hanging out with the smokers. (I never smoked.)

According to my adoptive mother, I was sent to boarding school because there I would receive a better education. The real reason was I was being sexually abused by my adoptive father. Although she knew of this, nothing was ever said. When I had the courage to confront her with it, years later, my adoptive mother said she didn't go to the police because my adoptive father might have ended up in gaol—and where would that leave her. I didn't pursue it further because she had suffered enough from him, through domestic and other family violence. I know what it's like to hurt and I couldn't deliberately go on, and say: 'But why? How could you?' A lot has changed, with publicity given to incest, and I am glad that now young children are taught to speak out and learn what is good touching and what is bad touching, and whom they should tell if they feel uncomfortable.

Throughout my teenage years I had a fairly destructive attitude towards myself.

Throughout my teenage years I had a fairly destructive attitude towards myself. I liked lighting fires and at fifteen I lit the shed at home, where old newspapers were stored. The shed was about fifteen feet from my bedroom. However the fire was quickly extinguished. I wanted to see what would happen if I blew on some still smouldering newspapers. The fire began again. This time I returned to my bedroom, and went to sleep. The shed burnt down. But the fire brigade arrived, so the room where I slept was saved. I remember thinking Thomas Edison was 15 when he burnt down his first shed, and he sure made a contribution to the world.

I mucked up again at the end of Year 10, getting sprung for being light-fingered. Because I was at a private school, the police were not involved. However I was asked not to return. I contemplated running away or killing myself. But I had a longing for security; so although I didn't want to return to the white adoptive family, I didn't know where else to go or to whom I could turn. Sure enough, I got the biggest flogging with a metal pipe. I was given the ultimatum of going on the dole or attending yet another new school to complete Years 11 and 12. I chose the latter.

In my isolation I enjoyed reading books and newspapers. In particular *Who's Who in Australia*, and newspapers, and watching television. I can't remember the exact year or incident when I began to take an interest in Susan Ryan and her political career in federal parliament; however I do recall her speaking out on issues: Aboriginal people, women and education. I began to focus my energy into a more positive mode. I told myself that if I stuck at school, attended university, I would be able to work for Susan Ryan in Canberra.

According to my file I was either Chinese-Malay or possibly Polynesian. I was told my great-great grandmother was a Polynesian princess. At one stage my adoptive parents even contemplated moving to New Zealand so I could be closer to my supposedly Polynesian heritage. I was given books about Hawaii but I never felt that the images I saw looked like me. I didn't have anyone or any Black people I could talk to, or about the racism I experienced, I couldn't talk with my adoptive family about being called a boong, abo, it didn't make sense. The only Black people I saw were on television or the occasional article in the newspaper. As a direct result of having to rely on the mainstream media for my understanding of Aboriginal people and the issues that faced them, my views were severely clouded to the point where I could have been called a racist.

When I began to feel more comfortable mixing with the Koori community with the encouragement of Destiny's family, I felt ashamed I had been so gullible in not challenging the negative images of Aboriginal people in the media.

My earliest fond memories of identifying with Kooris occurred back in January 1972 when the Aboriginal tent embassy was set up on the lawns of Parliament in Canberra. On the television I remember seeing Black people and their supporters being bashed for standing up for what they believed in. There was Gary Foley, Bobbi Sykes (now Dr Roberta Sykes) and the guy with the wild hair called Sol Bellear. I'd go to my bedroom and think about what I had seen.

> My earliest fond memories of identifying with Kooris occurred when the Aboriginal tent embassy was set up on the lawns of Parliament in Canberra.

I didn't even know that Sol Bellear was my mum's younger brother; it was my uncle who was speaking out on how the indigenous people of Australia deserve to be treated with dignity and respect. When I look back at the old documentary footage, I see many of my family that have been and of course still are active. Like my uncle Bob, a barrister who worked on the Royal Commission into Aboriginal Deaths in Custody.

While the idea of working for Susan Ryan motivated me to stay at school,

I then had to figure out which course to study at university. I was constantly representing my various schools at athletics, swimming and field events, so aiming to be a physical education teacher seemed to make sense. However the prerequisites were maths and science and I was hopeless in this area, so I had to re-think what to do. I passed Year 12 much to the surprise of my school, the Catholic Regional College in Camperdown (Victoria). My form teacher commented they didn't think I would pass. Although my marks weren't the best, because I was determined not to study all the time, I was relieved to open the letter and see my results.

Relief of passing gave way to frustration, not knowing the next step. I didn't have anyone to talk to about careers and most importantly career options. I took myself off to the library and looked up a guide on employment and education. I figured out I liked people, so how about youth work or social work.

I was admitted into the youth work course at the old Coburg State College. I was also accepted into the social work course at the Phillip Institute of Technology in Bundoora, however, because I kept moving around, I didn't know this. I started the youth work course and lasted a year. For some reason I was determined to do the social work course. I told one student at Coburg about my plans to become a social worker, and within a few days most of the students in the course stopped talking to me. I had committed the grave act of wanting to become a social worker.

> I was determined to do the social work course.

I was only 19 at the time, and have since worked through why I wanted to become a social worker. The main reason was to ascertain how someone in the 'helping professions' could remove a child from their natural family. I wanted to see if it was the course or the individual. But one thing is for sure, I am happy that I obtained my Bachelor of social work from the University of Melbourne in 1986.

After graduating from the university, I applied for several positions, including a social work job with the Department of Community Services Victoria. To my surprise it was the University of Melbourne that gave me my first job opportunity as the Aboriginal Liaison Officer.

Primarily the job was to recruit Aboriginal and Torres Strait Islanders to study and/or work on campus, through the Universities Aboriginal Student Admission Scheme and the Aboriginal Employment Strategy. It was also to provide appropriate support mechanisms and links with the Koori community locally and Australia wide. In 1988 the university became the first tertiary institution with DEET co-sponsorship to initiate an Aboriginal Recruitment and Career Development Strategy. As a consequence, an Aboriginal Employment Co-ordinator was employed, and I can now focus more on student related issues.

Often people wonder how someone like me can work at an institution like the University of Melbourne. I sometimes wonder myself. Yes the place has its moments, but I have always been encouraged to maintain and develop my creativity, plus most people (and that includes men in grey suits) are capable of laughing at my jokes, so that makes it okay. There's plenty of laughter in the office. Without humour, I don't think I would still be working here or alive or continue to be willing to share my spirit and energy with non-Aboriginal Australians.

In 1988 I became the first Koori to be elected to local government in Victoria: Collingwood City Council. I stood for local council because I felt that the ordinary citizens making up a large percentage of the municipality were not being adequately represented. I'm not saying that middle-class home owners are not capable of representing the unemployed Kooris, working-class, people from non-English speaking backgrounds, and people who live in housing commission accommodation, it's just perhaps they needed to get out more and realise that the world does not revolve around and solely depend on the business community for direction.

> I became the first Koori to be elected to local government in Victoria

I was constantly surprised by the number of people who asked me whether I had resigned from my position as Aboriginal Liaison Officer with the University of Melbourne, so I could pursue councilling on a full-time basis. How did they think our household would survive, especially since a councillor receives only an honorarium, and our rent for a two-bedroom house was $150 per week.

Being a councillor was a valuable experience, however, my well-being and spirit began to suffer. The turning point came after I attended the first Indigenous Women's Conference in Adelaide in July 1989. There's nothing like women being together to rejuvenate the spirit and enable a woman to come back fighting. I made the difficult decision of resigning from the Collingwood City Council, and was criticised for doing so. Some people said it would be an end to a potential promising political career. But though it was a difficult decision, I made the right choice for me. I don't have regrets and I would encourage Kooris and other marginalised groups to stand for local government.

Over the years I've had to figure out my priorities and where to place my energy. No one person can create a world which is fair, equitable and free of racism and sexism. Many people have their theories, their world view and there is usually a healthy degree of scepticism thrown in. I wish the 'sceptics', or 'cynics', would convert their energies into encouraging people who believe that change for the good is possible: not to lose hope, and to keep fighting and keep speaking out.

Every so often I have to take time out, travel around and listen to other people's views, especially our Elders. I love to travel and meet up with different Kooris, Nungas, Murris, Wongais, Torres Strait Islanders and South

Sea Islanders, and even non-Aboriginal people. I enjoy a good yarn and listening to what different people believe in, though I may not agree with all I hear. I am then able to share these meetings and stories with other people.

I have to be optimistic, I have to believe that we as a nation can come to terms with Australia being a Black person's country. That we can create a future where Australia can be recognised as a country that treats its indigenous population with respect and dignity. That issues such as Aboriginal Deaths in Custody, unemployment, infant mortality, lack of education opportunities (culturally relevant in particular), poor housing, low self-esteem and Aboriginal child removal and racism will cease.

> I have to believe that we as a nation can come to terms with Australia being a Black person's country.

To me, the creative arts is the most powerful of all mediums which can be used as a vehicle to educate all Australians. Through the arts—theatre, writing, acting, painting, photography, playwrights—Australia can come to terms with its appalling treatment of Aboriginal and Torres Strait Islanders and South Sea Islanders (including Blackbirding). Through Aboriginal and Islander artists being properly supported, financially and in other ways, so they can express their ideas and project a vision of not only what was, but what may be, or more aptly what should be.

Many people have enabled me to live and be proud of being Koori. One day you will all be thanked: Aunty Fay Carter, Aunty Merle Jackomos, Aunty Liz Hoffman, Aunty Iris Lovett, Eleanor Harding, Janina Harding, Johnny Harding, Christine Gillespie, Dr Eve Fesl, Virginia Fraser, Michael Mansell, Paul Morgan, Kylie Belling and Eva Johnson.

A SORT OF CRUSADE

Janine Haines

Janine Haines was the first Australian woman to lead a major political party. As a parliamentary member of the Australian Democrats she was deputy leader to Don Chipp, succeeding him to the leadership in 1986. Janine Haines trained as a teacher. She currently works as a freelance journalist, a political commentator and public speaker.

I didn't 'decide' to be a career woman because it simply never occurred to me at any stage in my life not to be a career woman. I'd grown up in a family where for the first eight or nine years of my life my parents lived and worked out of the same residence. My father was a country policemen in the days when the police station and the residence were the same building. Both he and my mother, who was not then in the paid workforce, were around the place all day— or at least it seemed that way to me.

Then we moved to the city and my father changed jobs. His work in the Commonwealth Public Service took him outside the home during normal working hours. My mother did a teacher training course and so she, too, worked outside the home. Thus I lived in a family where it was considered perfectly normal for both parents to go to work and hence for both parents to share the housework at the weekends and when they got home from their paid occupation.

Neither of my parents ever complained about the work they did so I assumed they both enjoyed it. As a child I recognised the importance paidwork would have in my life. I simply recognised, or thought I recognised, that work was something every adult male and female did: they worked in the paid workforce and then they shared, as parents, the housework and the raising of the children. It wasn't until I was in my late teens that I realised this was not the norm; rather it was quite an odd way for a couple to behave in the 1950s. But by then the idea of having a career was already entrenched.

My education was pretty much dictated by the schools I attended as well as the ease with which I took to schoolwork and the total (though unspoken) belief, held by both my parents, that education was essential; that every child, regardless of gender, should pursue education as far as possible. My parents were apparently told by an education department psychologist who visited my primary school that I would have no trouble with schoolwork right up to fifth year high school (leaving honours) which, in the early 1960s, was usually done only by students wanting to go on to university.

Neither of my parents had been to university but neither questioned the fact that I would—if that was what I wanted. When I went to the local high school, the IQ test results meant I went into the A stream. My memory of it all is that apart from doing the homework set, I didn't do a bit of extra study. Nobody told me I was clever and I tended to assume that anyone who didn't do well simply wasn't trying.

I came to my senses at university. I spectacularly failed several subjects in first year because I spent more time in the refectory playing bridge than I did in the Barr Smith library. Continuing with university work even after failing some subjects in my first year was never in doubt. University was, as far as I could see, something everyone did if they had the ability and wanted to do it.

I enjoyed school. My mother was a school teacher and I had a great deal of respect for the teachers at my school. From as far back as I can remember in secondary school, I wanted to be a teacher.

The Education Department in those days paid your way through university, gave you another year's teacher training and then popped you into a school somewhere. I saw it as interesting work and a stable occupation. At no stage did I consider that it would be something temporary.

Indeed, even when we had children, which was several years after I married, I didn't consider this would lead to a significant break in my career. After I had been home for about six weeks following the birth of our first child, both Ian and I were anxious for me to get back to work. It was driving me crackers being at home alone all day with nobody to talk to and no one to deal with other than a little girl, about 20 inches long, who cried most of the time. I returned to teaching part-time. Two years or so later, after our second child was born, I added to the part-time teaching some part-time postgraduate work at Adelaide University. The children went to childcare and we shared the housework and child-raising as we shared the income earning.

I had had no experience of discrimination for the first 21 years of my life, having had parents who shared everything. I had no notion of women being regarded as a different and lesser class of people by the vast majority of others out there in the world.

When I went to secondary school, IQ tests meant students went into classes according to their scores. The classes in the school I attended were single-sex classes for the first three years of high school, although the school itself was co-educational. There was no conflict for me between social and academic success. There was no problem with doing well in maths or chemistry or English or history because that was no threat to your social existence. There were no pressures to behave like a 'real girl' in case you upset the new boy in your life. I believe this is the best school situation for both boys and girls and cannot understand why more state schools don't operate this way.

I simply do not remember, until I was in my early thirties, anybody saying to me that a girl or a woman or a mother or a wife shouldn't do this, that or something else. So I just did things. What I wanted to do was what I did. Which didn't alter my awareness that other women were discriminated against. But I tended to think that those people were strange for saying what they did about what women could do rather than that I was strange for doing and being what I was.

> **I simply do not remember anybody saying to me that a girl shouldn't do this, so I just did things.**

When I left university and went teaching I suddenly discovered discrimination. In those days, in the middle 1960s, women in the teaching profession, as in most other areas of work, were paid considerably less than their male colleagues regardless of their qualifications or experience. When women married we had to resign from the permanent teaching force and become temporary assistants. The pressure directed at male teachers to go into a superannuation scheme was never applied to female teachers. There was the assumption that women would marry, leave the profession and live for ever (happily or otherwise) with a man who would look after them.

When I returned to university part-time, I was married and I had children and I was also working part-time and there were a number of other women in a similar position—as were several men. It was some time before we became aware of it, but the women in the course were apparently known around that faculty as 'The Mad Housewives'. The men who were studying part-time and working part-time were regarded as serious in their endeavours. The full-time students were also taken seriously whether they were male or female, but those of us who were married women with children and were doing post-graduate work were regarded as 'playing' with our studies. This made me angry.

In the meantime, I had had some considerable trouble finding affordable childcare because there wasn't any government-provided care at the time. The private childcare centre to which I sent the children was good but expensive. Ultimately we enrolled the children in the prep. class of a private school once they were both old enough, because it was cheaper.

JANINE HAINES

No one in the family thought it was odd that I wanted to work outside the home after I had children. My mother was my major role model and I had plenty of support and encouragement from my family in whatever I wanted to do. That continued when I decided that entering parliament was the only way I could do something to correct what by then I had realised was an unequal existence for women in the workforce and elsewhere. (When we applied for a home loan, my salary and future earning capacity was ignored — indeed dismissed as being of no relevance.)

> My mother was my major role model.

My husband and my family were strongly supportive. Nobody said it wasn't the right thing for me to do, to leave home every few weeks going to Canberra, leaving Ian at home to deal with his job, the children and the house. At least, no one in my family said it was the wrong thing to do.

Each role in my work-life gave me an opportunity to provide other people with information and to do it in a form that was as understandable and relevant to them as possible. So for me, becoming a member of parliament was simply an exercise in teaching — and this applies similarly to my current occupation as a political columnist and speaker.

Once I joined a political party, I gained a mentor. A male member of state parliament encouraged me to do what I wanted to do, believed in me and gave me plenty of support. In the Democrats, as in any other political party or any business or union, it's helpful to have the support and encouragement and guidance of somebody who's 'been there and done that' and who is influential within the organisation of course. There were the usual groundless stories about an affair.

If I modelled myself as a member of parliament on anyone at all it was probably him. Robin Millhouse was a man of considerable principle; somebody who believed in saying what he believed was right and didn't worry too much about who might be shocked or offended. Now Justice Millhouse, Robin Millhouse was Attorney-General under the short-lived Hall Liberal government in the late 1960s and was responsible for, among other reformist legislation, the *Abortion Law Reform Act* 1969. In the early 1970s he resigned from the Liberal Party which he regarded as too conservative and helped form the Liberal Movement which, in 1977, became the Australian Democrats. I joined the Liberal Movement in 1974 because I believed any group of politicians who were prepared to put their careers on the line for a principle which I also supported deserved support.

Robin Millhouse's behaviour as a member of parliament during the time I was acting as his unpaid assistant from 1975 to 1977 was exemplary. I didn't always agree with what he did, but to me it was more important that he did what he did believing in what he did rather than because some political party or a pressure group told him to do it.

In my early years as a teacher I was an unconscious feminist partly because I was not familiar with the word — having always had a tendency to operate in my own little world. I challenged a lot of other people's preconceived notions in my own way —but mainly by just doing what I wanted to do without worrying whether other people were also doing it.

Feminism became an issue for me in the mid-1970s, although I was not aware of any ideology pushing me at that stage. Once I went into parliament I realised just how ignored women's issues were by male politicians and other groups of decision makers in the community. I hadn't realised just how entrenched the male agenda was until 1978 when I first took my seat as a Senator.

The issue of equal pay had been addressed if not fully dealt with; the position of married women in the public sector was fairly secure in most states; but there was still plenty of discrimination in pay and advancement opportunities—and there still are, despite the *Sex Discrimination Act* of 1984 and affirmative action legislation and the states' equal opportunity and anti-discrimination acts.

I went into parliament on a sort of crusade to level the playing field. The media and much of the electorate found me an odd entity. The most frequent question I was asked in the early years was: 'How does the family cope?' I'm prepared to bet that no man, no matter how old he was or how long he had been married or how young his children were has ever been asked that question!

> I went into Parliament on a sort of crusade to level the playing field.

There were dire predictions of divorce and the children becoming wards of the state, or worse, because it was just not 'normal' for a woman of 32 with two young children and a husband to go into federal parliament.

I was one of only seven women in the parliament in those days. That was a record, and they were all in the Senate. Indeed even now most of the women in federal parliament are in the Senate. It's safer for the men — large numbers of women in the House mean that sooner or later one of them will want to be Prime Minister, for heaven's sake, and that threat is too much for most of the men to even contemplate.

Other women in the parliament tend not to support female colleagues outside their own political party. This is perfectly understandable and should really be no more a matter for comment, much less criticism, than whether men support each other. It is much more important to see whether women in the parliament get support from women in their own party. I recall (Liberal) Senator Chris Puplick saying to (Labor) Senator Margaret Reynolds, when she was Minister for Local Government, that she was there 'because of her chromosomes not because of her neurones'. It was left to me to make a strong public objection to that —her own male Labor Party colleagues let it go.

The attitude of some conservative women that there are no longer any barriers for women, and that their own success proves this, makes me angry.

Successful women need to go out into the community to encourage other women—and warn them of the problems.

Senator Bronwyn Bishop's claim that she won her New South Wales' Senate seat on merit is breathtaking in its arrogance and ignorance. She was elected to the Senate in 1987 and was the first woman the New South Wales Division of the Liberal Party sent to Canberra. Surely she can't be serious in implying that she was the first woman of talent in the 86 years following federation to seek preselection from her party?

Too many successful women have an attitude toward women's issues whereby they grandstand on issues such as pornography when they are in opposition, but keep their mouths shut when they are in government — as, by and large, the Labor women do. Liberal–National Party women are unsupportive of any legislative measures aimed at helping women enter the paid workforce. They hated the *Sex Discrimination Act* and went berserk over the affirmative action legislation. Worse, they didn't bother to let facts get in the way of a good argument! Their ideological commitment to the so-called free enterprise system meant they opposed government intervention and opposed government-funded childcare centres, rape crisis centres and women's shelters. This may also be partly due to their becoming surrogate males to achieve credibility and success.

This has not been my own experience. I have had strong support from both men and women in the Australian Democrats as well as within my family. Ian went out of his way not to make my job more difficult than it had to be. He was certainly more patient than I would have been had our positions been reversed. He never complained about my frequent absences or the early morning and late night media phone calls.

One or two of my male colleagues within the parliamentary wing were less than supportive after I defeated them in the Democrats' leadership ballot in 1986, but I sorted them out in the long run. Don Chipp, on the other hand, was enormously supportive as was Senator Michael Macklin both before and after he became my deputy leader. Staff will make or break any executive and my staff were superb. I knew I could rely on them absolutely. It is a pity more men in senior positions don't recognise how crucial is the support of staff and family members..

My daughters are in fairly traditional female occupations. One is a hairdresser, the other works for a bank. That is their right and if I have taught them nothing else, I have taught them that they are real people; that 'just' and 'only' are never to be used about themselves and their achievements or those of other women; and that they owe it to themselves to do their best at whatever they choose.

All my working life I have derived a great deal of pleasure from teaching and encouraging people to think and to challenge their own ideas as well as other people's. I couldn't survive intellectually or emotionally without the contact of other people and the chance to learn and teach.

Being a role model has been equally important. I spend a lot of time talking to groups of young women as well as older women about choices and challenges and about the right women have to be ambitious and to reach for whatever goals they want. I intend to continue putting a case for fairness and equity; for real choices for women and men; for long-term national planning; for grasping opportunities as an individual.

Losing the 1990 election was probably my worst experience, but I don't believe in regrets or dwelling on defeats. My philosophy is that you pick up the pieces, put them back together again and look for a new horizon to conquer.

I'm an open and giving person and set myself very high standards. I won't ever retire from my commitment to women or educating until the Goddess closes her little black book on me and finally shuts me up. When that happens I hope that what I have done with and during my life will inspire some of the next generation as so many women from the past and present have inspired me.

Note: On abortion law reform, see N. Blewett and D. Jensch, *Playford to Dunstan*, 1971, pp. 188-9.

DEMANDING MORE THAN A GREAT VOCABULARY

Gracelyn Smallwood

A registered nurse and midwife, with a diploma in mental health and degree of Master of science, Gracelyn Smallwood was born in Queensland on 25 November 1951. She has worked as a registered nurse, a tutor and lecturer in Aboriginal health, and as an AIDS educator, as well as being honorary consultant to many organisations, councils and committees. From September to November 1990 she was consultant on Aboriginal health to the Queensland Minister for Health. In April 1991 she was awarded a fellowship from the National Health and Medical Research Council (NHMRC) to undertake a PhD.

To my husband Joseph, and children Christopher, Dorothy and Alfred

One of 19 children, mother had 13, father the remainder through two relationships, I was born in Townsville, Northern Queensland, in the 1950s. Life in Northern Queensland in the 1950s and 1960s was difficult for Aborigines and Islanders. I was fortunate in having a large supportive family, especially my eldest sister, Dorothy. She encouraged me to get a good education and even sacrificed her own education so I could go to school while she stayed home to help with the family business.

My father, a Birrigubba man, was born in Ayr and sent to Palm Island where he was raised by the only paternal grandparents known to me, Eric and Bessie Lymburner. (His real parents were Percy and Nora Smallwood, whom I never knew.) Palm Island is a reserve in North Queensland, notorious for its brutality towards my people during their time under the Queensland *Aboriginal Protection Act*. My grandfather was one of six brave men who went on a hunger strike for better conditions for the people. All six were taken away in chains, with their families, and sent to other reserves.

My mother was from Ingham. Her father, Alf Stanley, was a Kalkadoon man from Cloncurry and her mum a South Pacific woman born in Mackay. These were my other wonderful grandparents who helped care for all of the grandchildren, while growing up in Garbutt, Townsville.

From 1955 to 1964 I attended a number of primary schools in Queensland — Garbett, Aitkenvale and West End State School. In 1965 I went on to secondary school at Townsville State High, completing Grade 10. In those days there were no study grants. I scrubbed pots and pans to pay for my education. For one year I was unemployed; few jobs were offered to Aborigines. Then, I decided to go into nursing.

few jobs were offered to Aborigines

I completed my four year nurse's training course, studying from 1969 to 1972 and simultaneously working at Townsville General Hospital. I went on to do post-graduate work for a midwifery degree, later completing the Diploma in mental health. Whilst studying for the diploma, I worked with the Townsville Aboriginal and Islanders' Health Service.

Throughout my nurse's training my shoes had to shine. My dress had to be spotless, exceeding the shine and pristine white of the other nurses on the course. The views some of my superiors held toward Aborigines required it.

The Townsville Aboriginal and Islanders' Health Service was set up in 1975. I was one of the founders and the first registered nurse to work there. It had to be established because of the appalling health of my people, who were reluctant to use European medical services. For a year, I worked in a voluntary capacity for the medical service. During this time, I was also studying for my midwifery certificate. While working at the Aboriginal medical service, I came into contact with indigenous people of other nations. We had a visit from the Papago Indians of North America, who had come to see how our medical service worked. Indians from Arizona, they talked about the cultural similarities and differences between Aboriginal people and themselves. They took the lessons of our health services back to the Indian reserves. Within a year, I was visiting the North American Indian tribes and studying their medical techniques.

In 1976 I received an Aboriginal Overseas Study Award to the United States and New Zealand studying health problems and cross-culture of indigenous people. The grant assisted me to visit my Papago friends and other Indian tribes to look at their 'remote Indian health services'. I learnt a great deal from them. At that time, the Indians were using satellite communication to assist them in delivering expert medical care to their people. Like

Australian Aborigines, many of the Indian tribes are many hundred miles away from modern medical services, and this created particular difficulties for the very young and old, unable to travel easily. The Indians solved the problem by taking the hospital to the patients. Paramedics, often Indians and always with the ability to talk the Indian language, visit tribes on their traditional lands. They use large mobile units equipped with the most needed medical supplies. As well, the paramedics are linked by phone and television monitor to medical practitioners in city hospitals. The doctors are able to obtain advice and information on a patient's symptoms from the paramedic, and even see the patient on the television monitor. Treatment is then prescribed by the doctor and administered by the paramedic.

My trip to the United States also enabled me to visit Indian tribes in New Mexico and Oregon. These North American Indian groups mirrored the problems I encountered in Aboriginal communities. Unemployment was high, housing was inadequate, and (similarly to Australian Aborigines) Indians being accepted within the general community without losing their own cultural identity and beliefs was a problem. Yet generally, the American Indians' health and housing standards, although relatively worse than that of their fellow Americans, were better than those of Aborigines in Australia.

My experience in the United States and here at home led me to conclude that one reason for the marginally higher living standards of the North American Indians over the Australian Aborigines may be that Indians have rights to the mineral wealth on their land. This has given them more independence and a chance to improve their lives for themselves. At the same time, there are strong, noticeable cultural and historical similarities between our races. Both Aborigines and Indians have been overrun by a dominant culture and dispossessed of their land. Both peoples have strong spiritual beliefs and a recognition of the importance of our traditional lifestyles. The tribes conduct similar ceremonies, have their own laws, and retain a strong belief in traditional medicine.

After completing my work with the Indians, I spent six months on an overseas study award in Hawaii studying their medical services. In Hawaii the indigenous people—mostly Polynesians—are underprivileged.

Returning to Australia I resumed my work as a registered nurse, in Katharine, Northern Territory, with the Kalano Aboriginal Health Service, and later with the National Trachoma and Eye Health Program in Queensland. I did a stint with the emergency nursing service, remote nursing in Western Australia, and then set out once more overseas, to continue my research into cross-cultural issues.

I was part of an Aboriginal health delegation to China.

I was part of an Aboriginal health delegation to China. The trip was organised by the Australia–China Council. We went to work on the 'Barefoot Doctor Scheme' in inner Mongolia. Under the scheme, primary and preventative health care is taught to people having no access to doctors. In China, with over a billion people, providing basic health care is a massive physical administrative problem. For me, it was noteworthy that the Chinese rely heavily on herbal medicine. Although they have a choice of three medicines—herbal, acupuncture or western—the most popular and effective are their traditional herbal treatments.

The China visit ran for four weeks, and in addition to working in inner Mongolia, I compared health services in Beijing, Shanghai and Guangzhou (Canton). I then went again to Hawaii where I was offered the position of professional lecturer at the Cultural Learning Institute of the East West Centre. I stayed a year, lecturing on the cultural similarities and differences of Aborigines and other indigenous people. I also studied cross-cultural psychology. I then did a short spell studying medical services in New Zealand and returned to Australia in 1982, working all around Australia with various Aboriginal health services giving any assistance and passing on my experiences. I took up remote nursing once again, this time working in the Nangampa Health Service, with the Pitjatjantjara people in the remote Western Desert of South Australia. Later I moved on, back up north to Alice Springs in the Northern Territory, where for two years I was director of nursing at the Hetti Perkins Home for Aged Aborigines, catering specifically for the needs of elderly, tribal Aborigines. Many of the patients were aged and feeble and had very few resources or facilities for relatives or others to care for them. At the home we cared for their immediate medical needs, with any major treatment being carried out at the Alice Springs Hospital.

My reasons for being at Hetti Perkins were twofold. First, the Hetti Perkins Home is the only Aboriginal hospital of its kind in Australia. It is an example of Aboriginal initiative and self-reliance. I believed it important that the home continue successfully, so that governments and health organisations might support the establishment of other, similar hospitals. Secondly I wished to contribute to helping solve the problems of my people. At the time, I was offered a place at medical school, to become an Aboriginal doctor. I know now, as I knew then, that Aborigines as a people need trained doctors and other professionals to complement our traditional healers. However, I did not want to spend six years training, when already I had so much to offer my people.

> The Hetti Perkins Home is the only Aboriginal hospital of its kind in Australia.

Aborigines suffer one of the highest infant mortality rates in the world. Unemployment is six or seven times higher than in the rest of the community and Aborigines are the most institutionalised people in the world. On average, Aborigines live 25 years less than European Australians and we still have not conquered diseases like trachoma and leprosy, diseases that are no longer problems even in countries classified as 'third world'. When confronted with this, the National Health Strategy impressed me; I sincerely hope both state and federal governments will urgently attend to its recommendations, which came from the people. While matron at Hetti Perkins, my desire was to ensure that simultaneously with providing much-needed services for Aboriginal people, we would prove that Aborigines are competent and successful in looking after our own people's health, if given the opportunity.

My sustaining interest and concern in cross-cultural research and interaction meant that in 1985 I attended the 9th Inter-American conference on cross-cultural and human rights of the indigenous peoples of the world, in Santa Fe, New Mexico. I continued my nursing work part-time at Townsville General Hospital, and in between times took on the role of Commissioner for International Public Health, travelling to Japan and visiting Hiroshima, Nagasaki and Tokyo in conjunction with the International Year of Peace. In that same year I was awarded the honour, in Queensland, of being Aboriginal of the Year.

In 1981 I participated as a keynote speaker at the National Women's Conference, organised by women of Townsville. The conference brought together women from other parts of Australia, and particularly from remote areas of Queensland. I spoke of my work in Aboriginal health, and my role as a nurse, my work 'inside' the system as an 'outsider', and what I hoped to achieve for my people, both by working within the system and directly amongst my people. That same year (as had occurred increasingly in previous years) I was invited to speak at rallies and a diverse range of institutions on Aboriginal health and alcoholic rehabilitation in a cross-cultural context, attending the International Women's Day rally in Sydney; lecturing on Thursday Island to the Torres Strait Island community; returning to the University of Hawaii in Honolulu and lecturing at the School of Nursing, the School of Public Health and the Culture Learning Institute, the East-West Centre, as well as participating as a speaker in a World Health Organisation conference.

By 1988–89 I had become fully involved in work relating to AIDS. There was consultancy work for the World Health Organisation and the Australian government on AIDS. The Australian National Council on AIDS granted me a scholarship for research in the social sciences in relation to AIDS. I began studying for a Masters degree in science at the Tropical Health Surveillance Unit in James Cook University of North Queensland. I wanted to assess the implementation and impact of the health promotion program which was developed in Queensland, and in which I had been involved. Had it raised awareness of AIDS and of factors likely to facilitate the spread of the disease? What was the value of such a program continuing in this and other areas amongst Aboriginal communities?

The AIDS program in Australia began with the Grim Reaper, an advertising campaign starring an emaciated, death-like figure gleefully overseeing the deaths of people from AIDS, depicted as bowling pins being knocked down systematically through the Grim Reaper's expertise with a bowling ball. This campaign raised controversy throughout Australia. Whatever its effectiveness for the Australian European community, it was not appropriate for Aborigines. In 1988 there was a minimum of 10 AIDS deaths nationally, with at least five in Queensland. Aboriginal people would not identify with the Grim Reaper advertisements. Demand had to be stimulated for information about a different set of risk factors: breakdown in community structure as a consequence of unemployment and alcohol abuse, bisexuality rather than homosexuality, and child sexual abuse.

At that time, most states and territories had embarked upon the development of programs to raise awareness of AIDS amongst Aborigines and to promote discussion of the circumstances under which the infection spread. The Aboriginal medical services gave AIDS workshops and seminars, travelled to remote areas, produced AIDS posters and, in the instance of Alice Springs and Redfern, two nationally acclaimed videos. The 'Healthy Aboriginal Life Team' in Alice Springs, a group comprising predominantly traditional Blacks, had used traditional art to get their messages across. This work continues. In 1988 I was aware that only one Aboriginal medical centre, in Broome in the north of Western Australia, had evaluated their program. The evaluation found that the incidence of sexually transmitted diseases fell by 20 percent over the 12-month period following the implementation of Broome's medical centre program.

My research looked at the design, implementation and evaluation of AIDS education for Aborigines in North Queensland, addressing not only AIDS itself but alcohol abuse, child sexual abuse, unemployment, and the breakdown in community structure, all of which influence the spread of AIDS in Aboriginal communities. I headed up a team looking at the health education component. Aida Tillett from the Women's Refuge, Danny de Bosh from the Yuddika Childcare Agency in Cairns, Warren Wilson from the Indigenous Youth Centre in Cairns, Robert Corrie, a health worker from the state Aboriginal health program, and Felicia Morgan, a health worker from the Wu-Chopperin Medical Centre in Cairns worked with me. Together, we visited Aboriginal communities in Palm Island, Lockhardt River, Kowanyuma, Weipa South, Doomadgee, Edward River, Aurukun, Mornington Island, Hopevale, Cohen. The team was invited to the communities by the community councils and introduced to the communities by the Elders. We commenced by giving a talk to the community Elders on Aboriginal way of life prior to alcohol abuse; the medical and social effects of alcohol abuse and how sport and recreation could substitute for boredom which leads to excessive drinking. Case histories of the physical and sexual abuse of women by males within the family following alcohol abuse was a part of the program, as were case histories of children being sexually abused by (mostly) male family members.

Graphs were shown indicating the rising incidence of sexually transmitted diseases in the Aboriginal community, including chlamydia, and drawing attention to the rising numbers of young children being admitted to hospital with sexually transmitted diseases. I then worked together with the audience to ascertain the level of awareness of AIDS and of the factors facilitating its spread; misconception about such factors; the amount of risk-taking behaviour (sexual intercourse between men, non-use of condoms, promiscuity, tattooing and sharing blades and needles) in the community; and factors likely to promote or inhibit behaviour change to reduce the spread of AIDS. We found, overall, that the level of awareness of AIDS was low. There were many misconceptions about the spread of AIDS. For example, homosexuality, but not bisexuality, was thought to be a risk factor. The use of condoms by bisexual men was low, amounting to less than 1 percent. After the lectures and talks, we showed videos and demonstrated the application of condoms by using penile models. The communities were strongly supportive of the team visits, making a room available for the discussions, suspending liquor sales during the team's visit, providing male and female translators, and organising people to attend. We noted the success of the program, as evidenced by the number of people who asked questions, plans to sell condoms in canteens and bars, favourable comments, and being asked by the councils to make follow-up visits.

The communities were strongly supportive of the team visits.

The materials we used in this team effort were developed at a workshop in Townsville, attended by community workers from a wide cross section of Aboriginal communities, and teenagers from Townsville and surrounding communities, with the help of an Aboriginal graphic artist. We produced materials that included story posters to raise awareness of the social effect of alcohol abuse, AIDS and the use of condoms; songs; and a comprehensive plan of action for communities to set up their own health education following the departure of the peripatetic teams. The material was market-tested on 500 Aborigines.

In 1990 I was appointed Special Advisor on Aboriginal Health Issues, to the Queensland Minister for Health, Mr McElligott. My role was to work in co-ordinating a restructuring of community health services. After decades of buck-passing between state and federal authorities, these health services were made a state responsibilty. The Queensland government wished to bring under the umbrella of the Queensland Health Department all hospitals and medical facilities on Aboriginal and Torres Strait settlements. Traditionally, these were administered by a number of state departments, including Aboriginal Affairs and Family Services, or by independent missionary societies. This meant confusion and bureaucratic in-fighting often reigned, where the imperative need was for a co-ordinated approach to basic health problems. Money was not being directed where it could do the most good.

In my role as advisor, one of my first priorities was to open up lines of communication.

There was irony in my appointment. For most of my career I had been a thorn in the side of state authorities. But I was determined that my new position would make me no less outspoken. My work in AIDS, child abuse and Aboriginal health generally brought the realisation that crime and sex-related violence are endemic in many remote Black communities. Child abuse is a growing problem. AIDS has the potential to end the process of genocide begun 200 years ago with colonisation, by introduced diseases such as measles and cholera. It is essential that we get at the cause of the health problems rather than treating the symptoms. This means going after the relationship between poverty and poor nutrition, and the lack of self-esteem that drives people (particularly Aboriginal people) to alcohol abuse. My work as advisor to the Minister of Health coincides with my completion of the Master's degree.

I have now returned to North Queensland full-time. Although I know this area best, and this is where I have frequently concentrated my efforts, my extensive travel throughout Australia and working in remote areas in Northern Territory and Western Australia, as well as South Australia, means that I have a national perspective on the needs of my people. I have sought to combine this national perspective with an international one, in my work with indigenous people from overseas. In this way, I hope to continually increase knowledge and expertise, and (together with others) work towards the creation of programs, policies and practices which hopefully counter the neglect of my people.

For many of us, for many years, to be Black was to be considered inferior. To varying degrees, many of us believed this. I was fortunate that my father, living most of his life 'under the Act' that forced Aboriginal people to live on reserves (and discriminated against us in other ways) did not share these sentiments. Thanks to his guidance I have been strong and able to withstand the pressure of a society which has been, if not at all times openly racist, at least biased towards the anglo-saxon viewpoint. In my career as nurse and activist for my people I have had to be twice as good as a white professional in order to achieve anything at all. Sometimes I have wondered if it is just professional jealousy within nursing circles, or if the resistance is due to old-fashioned restrictions and a narrow perspective so common in nurses trained solely in the medical model.

My mother was and is an important source of strength and support for me. Her life has not been easy, but she has displayed typical coping mechanisms which Aboriginal and Islander women need in their role as backbone of the family. In our families, kinship networks and family structure are very important. Nuclear families are almost unknown amongst my people. A problem affecting one individual automatically becomes everyone's problem. My eldest sister Dorothy has been like another mother, not only to my children, but to my brothers and sisters and their children. For many years I have been a supporting mum. Christopher is now 20 years old, Dorothy (named for my sister) is eight, and Alfred is two. Dorothy and her husband, Sammy, have always cared for my children.

Sharing, a major component in our system, is often misunderstood by western society. Individual aims and objectives are subordinated to the welfare of the family or kinship system in Aboriginal culture.

Since the European colonisation of Australia, 'the Aboriginal health problem' has been the subject of close but misunderstood scrutiny. This has taken the form of government enquiries, colonial, imperial, state and national parliamentary debates, official protection, missionary interventions and private, learned debates. All to no avail. My people, the indigenous Australians, remain the sickest people in Australia today. This precipitated me into the health field. The situation could not be worse. Over the past 20 years, since I have been in full-time health work, there have been no substantial changes in our health, for the simple reason that most programs have been directed from a white middle-class perspective. This became more evident with my study into comparative health, looking at the health status of other indigenous people. I learnt that culturally relevant health programs worked for indigenous people. Those imposed from the outside failed.

For too long, Aborigines have been defined by Europeans. Today, we are reassessing our place in society and adopting our own identities. In doing so, we will become aware of not only who we are, but how we can solve our own problems.

> **We are reassessing our place in society and adopting our own identities.**

Aboriginal women have been deprived alongside Aboriginal men. Yet for Aboriginal women, there is a double oppression—racism and sexism. Aboriginal women today have to take dominant roles in the family. Many are sole supporting mothers; stress from the burden of poor health and education is sometimes too great. The health situation of Aboriginal people as a whole is so critical that the needs of communities have overridden the needs of Aboriginal women. By lifting the standards of Aboriginal health in general, our women's health will benefit immensely.

Historians, geographers, anthropologists and welfare workers have repeatedly said that the conflict which began in Australia 200 years ago remains. Aboriginal and Islander people are still on the frontier. The difference today is that there is not the murder and physical violence, such as reported by Stephen Harris in 1979, in his book *It's Coming Yet: An Aboriginal Treaty Within Australia Between Australians*. He identified the sport made of who could slaughter the most Blacks: 'One hears of the Sunday afternoon manhunts, of sexual mutilation, of burying alive an Aboriginal baby up to its neck in sand and kicking its head off, after tying the severed neck of the husband around the raped spouse.'

Today, a range of emotions and attitudes are expressed in reaction to the Aboriginal presence, ranging from guilt to careless aggression and disregard for any humanitarian redress for the brutal conquest of this land and my people. Images of brotherhood have been superseded at times by the idea that we degraded savages are incapable of participation in a life as full citizens. Both assimilation and segregation have been government policy, at different times, to solve 'the Aboriginal problem'. There is an urgent need for increased Aboriginal participation in the decision-making process concerning health problems. Real progress towards an equal health status will require broad, wide-ranging programs. This is unlikely to occur without greater Aboriginal initiative, leadership and high level commitment with direct support and co-operation from state and federal governments.

Jules Feiffer, quoted in John Pilger's book, *A Secret Country*, expresses well our dilemma:

> I used to think I was poor. Then they told me I wasn't poor, I was needy. Then they told me it was self-defeating to think of myself as being needy, I was deprived. Then they told me deprived was a bad image, I was underprivileged. Then they told me underprivileged was overused, I was disadvantaged. I still don't have a cent. But I have a great vocabulary.

My life and work have told me that the improvement of Aboriginal health programs cannot be addressed until the basic issue of poverty is addressed. Until proper sanitation, clean running water, healthy nutritional food, and good employment opportunities (all of which are enjoyed by the average white Australian) are seen as priorities for a healthy life for all of us, no real gains will be achieved. Millions of dollars on high technology in remote areas is not the answer. Social, political, economic and spiritual elements are each relevant when examining the health status of my people. The uncertainty associated with the western lifestyle, and the loss of the traditional way of life, have to be examined before improvements in Aboriginal health will occur. Our values are different from those of Europeans. We must promote our uniqueness and from that, I believe, a solution will come to our present sad predicament. We must keep what is acceptable from Western society, together with recognising our strengths regarding kinship and the family. In this way, a better lifestyle for all who live in our country will come about, and survival for my own people be possible.

NOT A GUIDED TOUR

Patricia Brennan

Patricia Brennan was the founding president of the Movement for the Ordination of Women (MOW) in the Anglican church in Australia. She was born in New South Wales where, although initially hankering after a career in the theatre, she studied medicine at the University of Sydney. She has practised in Australia and Canada as well as a missionary doctor in West Africa. She worked as a presenter in ABC television and radio for two years, is presently practising as a medical practitioner in preventive health in Sydney, and has widened her reform interests well beyond the Anglican church to women and religion in Australian society.

Poetry is not in my words
It is in the direction I am pointing
If you can't understand that
And if you are appalled by the journey
Stick to the guided tours
They issue return tickets

Chris McCahon

Any attempt to recall major life influences raises questions of memory. Does the selectivity of memory highlight the details of early years or do formative influences fully begin at an early stage, taking all with them? Any attempt to explain how I came to be in my present career evokes an awareness of two areas in me that seem to have been there since time began. The first, a sense of self over and against 'others'. The second, a sense of being 'female' over and against being 'the other', the latter being male (although I never thought of it in those terms).

At four or five, I asked my parents what I would be if I wasn't me. This led to a discovery that others couldn't answer all my questions, and prepared me for a life of trying to tumble to them on my own.

A sense of self remains vital to me, since growing up in a patriarchal society needed a strong sense of autonomy, a fortification against the prescribed role that awaited allotment. Ironically, a religious imagination convinced me that there was meaning and information in the world not accessible by ordinary means. Stereotypes identified girls with sugar and spice and all things nice but I wondered whether there wasn't an alternative. Something unspoken told me it may have augured better for girls if they too had been constituted from snips and snails and puppydog tails.

Attendance at a Catholic school, for my first eighteen months as a student, clothed the search for answers in mysteries that lay halfway between the cosmos and the sacred-heart-of-Jesus pictures hanging on our classroom walls. In the pedestrian gloom of a typical Catholic church of Aussie suburbia, I was gripped by a haunting holiness, a sense of passion on the faces of the saints. I became committed to finding things out despite a world that hid them. Religion opened to me a world of imagination and curiosity rather than fear. I secretly believed the more spooky aspects of Catholic holy hardware didn't work on protestants, so being Anglican rendered me immune: a state I rather enjoyed until my older sister cut it short for both of us by refusing to kiss the visiting cardinal's ring. We were removed from the school. As the Irish priest explained to my mother: 'One bad potato can send the whole sack rotten.'

> Preoccupation with the metaphysical gave me tools to imagine things could be other than they were.

Preoccupation with the metaphysical gave me the tools to imagine things could be other than they were. Things could be changed by mere individuals, a conviction that later attracted me to reform both in society and the church.

That second feature, the predominance of the feminine (not so named), was embodied in my mother, my teachers and my great aunt. They were strong, troubled, buoyant and honestly ambitious that girls should learn. My mother especially. An epitaph I would steal (when the times comes) is Toni Cade Bambara's to her mother in *The Salt Eaters*: 'To my first friend, teacher, map-maker, landscape aide, Mama who, in 1948, having come across me daydreaming in the middle of the kitchen floor, mopped around me.' She gave books as presents, on which she spent hours and pennies meant for other things. Her other favourite gift was pants and singlets. It was as though the exotica of books needed to be balanced by something sensible — sort of keeping the body clothed while exposing the mind.

Unlike other people's mothers, my mother 'worked' and, as if to justify the guilt she felt for being different, used to say she would buy what she liked and do what she liked with her own money. Having a mother who worked was embarrassing since she couldn't serve in the tuckshop or go to Mothers' Union meetings at the local Anglican church. Somehow, she always managed to be at speech days and make the best sponge cakes for the church fête which we took along ourselves as a defiant surrogate for our absent mother. 'Mrs Wilkinson does make a good sponge,' they'd say. I would rather they called her Sister Nugent, her working name at the local hospital. I liked the way she said Mothers' Union was no good anyway because it excluded divorced women.

> Unlike other people's mothers, my mother 'worked'.

Family stories are the stuff of destiny. Mother's story of how she was cut out of her grandmother's will because she left the farm to 'do nursing' in the city against her parents' wishes was oft rehearsed in our house. 'Go on Mum. Tell us about how your father let you wear jodhpurs, and how your grandma said it was fast!'

My aunt made it possible for my mother to do nursing. She was the nearest thing to a radical we had in the family. I've come to think that my strong consciousness of self over and against others and of the feminine were brought together by her. As well as abetting my mother's escape from the farm and the marriage prospects across the river, she took up education of my sister and me in the form of verse speaking. Preparation for the Railway Eisteddfod included instruction that learning to speak properly meant you could go anywhere and meet anyone. Somehow the very first poem taught me the power of words as tools to open the world. I was only seven. I could not perceive the meaning of the phrase 'with a superior air', but my capacity for mimicry convinced the adjudicator, who gave me second prize — much to my disappointment. I had spent the entire Eisteddfod praying earnestly for first. Thus a career in public speaking and a profound suspicion about divine intervention in human affairs began.

I also learned my aunt was right. We were not well off. Elocution was the domain of ambitious society mothers from the North Shore. And here I was with my working mother tired from night duty, the outsider from Hurstville, carrying off the bacon with a superior air that almost had them fooled. So language became the currency of belonging and means of surviving and making sense of the world.

My great Aunt Precious was deprived of her ability to speak properly the day before my tenth birthday. A stroke reduced her fine articulate tones to a sad few vowels and consonants that she shaped despite an excess of saliva and permanent exasperation. Our younger sister would never remember as we did her power with words.

My first career choice was to be a barrister. I liked to argue and Aunt Prec ensured that Doc Evatt was a household name. Somehow Clive Evatt got into the act too by sending a telegram congratulating my sister and me on our Eisteddfod wins (a set-up job by Aunt Prec I'd say). Forever after, he became a career model for me at primary school. Unconsciously but early, it was men's jobs that I was attracted to.

School was my own business. My father liked to help with maths, until I got to trigonometry, when he pulled out. His only claim to academic fame was that he had been dux of Annandale Primary. He was a compositor and I only ever saw him reading the paper. He had been the top apprentice at tech, was hard-working, liked a drink and a good joke, used the words 'rank and file' in arguments with Liberal relatives. He was generally shy with, but pugnaciously proud of, his three girls.

I recall receiving no advice from home about what subjects to choose at school. I let my family think I knew what I was doing, although I was quite at sea. I chose whatever seemed most demanding, with no rhyme or reason until I found myself doing badly.

Maths went out the door after a strong start. History followed, and its absence in my senior year led a grave careers advisor to tell me that law was out of the question. She also told me that girls would find it very difficult if they 'didn't have a relative in the business'. Since my relationship with Clive Evatt had never been consummated, I decided to open up my options.

Throughout high school, my Aunt Prec's spirit followed me into the debating team and whatever play was on. Academically, I liked ideas best of all and so chose physics honours and English honours; physics without the aid of maths, and English without a whiff of history. I brought drama to both, demonstrating off a high stool in the absence of the science mistress that to every action there is an equal and opposite reaction. My chemistry had the same problem, mobilising humour and colour more than formulae. Our science mistress Miss Renshaw was all for girls doing science any way they liked as long as they loved it.

> Going to St George High School in the 1950s was to be taught by a veritable host of latent feminists.

Going to St George Girls High School in the 1950s was to be taught by a veritable host of latent feminists. We despised the notion of needing boys at all, despite the physiological changes racing through our cellular selves. Ideologically there was learning and conquering ahead of us, for which we lacked nothing. What we missed at school was made up for with the less intellectual kind of cowboy model that turned up at boy scout dances.

I indulged in my final thespian fling, applying in all seriousness for one of the first scholarships in drama at the University of New South Wales. Had my minders not managed to instil such a strong evangelical hold on my developing libido, I may have succeeded in giving some semblance of seductive behaviour as a daughter of the Troll King in *Peer Gynt* (my audition). As it was, they turned me down despite a better-than-average sleep-walking scene from *Macbeth*, and yet another Glenda Jackson was lost to the theatre.

I will never quite know what led me to med. school, unless you're prepared to take divine guidance on board as a working hypothesis. Subconsciously it may have been my mother's enthusiastic example. Maybe my Leaving results were simply good enough to get into medicine. It may have been the Judeo-Christian ethic about loving my neighbour as much as myself. Or the prospect of a six-year-long undergraduate course: as I felt very young, I liked the thought of the government paying for my education for the longest possible time. (A legacy of coming from a predominantly working-class background? There certainly was latent hostility to wealthy professionals who put their private-school-educated offspring through medicine or law without the need for academic result to get there.) Was it that I saw a man having an epileptic fit on Central Station and thought I would like to understand why. Such are the vagaries of our life decisions.

What comforts me is that the best resources are often not of the financial kind. Spirit and imagination count. That I got a reasonable education as a girl which led to a male-dominated profession is attributable to my teachers and parents who gave without stint from often meagre resources. The world generously replied out of its institutions of learning. Come try and see what it's like; if you can read and write and are prepared to think, we'll give you a go.

> What comforts me is that the best resources are often not of the financial kind.

Looking back can give a rosy glow to memories that were light on rosiness. My time as a medical student was lost in a haze of too many lectures, working on weekends in nursing homes and never having money for textbooks.

Conscientious students were in a class of their own. I dreaded their knowledge of heart murmurs and obscure drug reactions. The 'in' crowd seemed to be learning by some kind of osmosis. I never felt at home with the male doctor teachers who seemed to tolerate the female medical student like yet another government innovation. There was not the faintest mention of women's rights, but it could be sensed like latent homosexuality in a group of homophobics. One well-known cardiologist commented that women students like me displaced people like his son from medicine. The then Dean of Medicine alluded in lectures to the fact that one-third of women doctors dropped out of medicine altogether.

I remember clearly that women students had no structure of dissent. I endured a desperate kind of silence when among the predominantly male students. Maybe they remember me as vociferous. All the more strange when I recall it that I wanted to shout: 'How can I compete in this competition if you demoralise me by saying I shouldn't be here?'

A late incident awakened me to male chauvinism. I was with my (by now close-knit) tute group. A discussion about marriage broke out amongst my six male colleagues who agreed to a man that they would never marry a female doctor. This shocked me and I asked why. Their answers were along the lines of female med. students were not feminine or were too strong.

That night I cried myself to sleep, feeling the power of a male pact that could exclude me and judge me as somehow less than desirable. I had a foreboding of what might lie ahead.

It emerged in residency years. Working in the male system was much more explicitly sexist compared with studying in it. I was naive and ill-equipped to deal with the subculture of the beer-drinking, macho bravado of residency. My religious background did not provide me with the few choice expressions that may have helped. My love of poetry and language found no outlet in the Philistine world of the operating theatre and the rough social realities of a city Casualty. Gone was the familiar subculture of the feminine, and loneliness accentuated its absence.

Being socialised in the conservative Christian church led to a prudery and defensiveness about sexuality that was thrown up like a macabre shadow theatre on the crude wall of doctor talk about pelvises and penis envy. I felt the butt of unspoken humour about how I wasn't available. I envied the women residents who were married or even, strangely, one nun, who as Hopkins said of the celibate, avoided 'the sharp sided hail' that seemed to cut me daily.

I didn't know how to work the system. I took what was given in hospital appointments, only occasionally risking what I thought was life and limb to talk to the powers that be. I have no doubt that some male residents found the hospital system brutalising at times, but never because they were the wrong sex. I remember with great affection special male mentors who looked out for me in their own ways, both colleagues and teachers. My happiest times were with the nursing and cleaning staff and the occasional wardsman. Patients were equally significant, many of them showing me more compassion than I was capable of showing them with a: 'Come on Doc, you'll be right!'

At the end of basic residency training, I applied for a senior surgery residency, maybe again betraying a passion for the male domain which took me into medicine in the first place. It was an exclusively male domain. Administration accepted me without comment, but placed me in a series of sub-specialties or sent me to branch hospitals. One's only hope was to be invited back as a registrar, and it was obvious I had no hope. The most significant thing about excluded categories of people inside such a system is that nobody tells you that you can't do it. There's no feedback. The year just ends. There is an understanding that you'll have to leave and scramble for the next location.

The next training option was paediatrics. Again I just did the job, changed terms when they blew the whistle, and expected at year's end I would be told if I was wanted as a registrar. I landed a double medical term which was a good sign, but I had no particular mentor and wondered whether 'they' thought I was in the wrong career. I was surprised to be told years later that several honoraries considered me a memorably good resident.

Notable was the absence of solidarity amongst women. It was very much every woman for herself, since we competed for the same few positions and the ever rare favour of the dominant males upon which our careers depended.

Going to Africa as a missionary doctor satisfied a commitment to practice medicine where it was needed, and took me out of the painful process of establishing whether there was a place for me in the system. Africa, and enduring some gruelling times of isolation and professional angst that only inexperienced doctors thrown into lone practices understand, was still more comfortable than being in the Australian system.

When I departed from kids hospital to become a missionary, I decided to get married, and fit my medical career around my husband-to-be's actuarial career. I hardly questioned the understood rule that his career took precedence over mine. Thus began a long story familiar to most women of that era, of moving between pregnancies, intellectual frustration and innovative strategies to stay alive professionally through it all.

Along with many other Australian women, the early 1970s was a turning point in my life. Feminism became a serious subject of study and public dialogue. My sense of self in the world and my identity as a female at last were being articulated by an emerging counterculture that had always been there, but never politically accessible.

Pregnant with my first child in 1973, I now had a rapidly increasing understanding of how I had been socialised to see myself as adjunct to the male. Five years after graduation, I took up the question of post-graduate specialisation. Knowing that pregnancy and motherhood would rule me out of 80-hour weeks (the unbending requirements of the patriarchal colleges of surgeons and physicians), I had the choice of pathology, dermatology or psychiatry. Having worked in Canada in haematology, I decided it was the closest to general clinical medicine, and I got a part-time job as a registrar in my old teaching hospital.

> I now had a rapidly increasing understanding of how I had been socialised to see myself as adjunct to the male.

With a bad back which required me to wear a full brace to stay mobile, the joys of a baby daughter, and a husband who took long-service leave to look after us both, I managed to get through general exams in haematology. All for nought: after 18 months I was told in a fairly casual fashion that there were no part-time jobs available in haematology that year.

Goaded by the familiar return to square one, I set out to take on the problem. Fortunately, a Dr June Raine of the College of General Practitioners had been instrumental in setting up a re-training course for women doctors to enable them to return to medicine. I availed myself of this three-month course. The most critical thing for me was that here, for the first time, I mixed with women doctors whose experiences of sexism in medicine could at last be shared. Each in different ways had struggled within a patriarchal system that allowed them to qualify, but completely ignored the biological reality that 80 percent of women medical graduates marry and have their first child within five years of graduation. We lobbied women graduates and the state government, successfully establishing a retainer scheme for women doctors. This provided funding for 50 women to work in a specialty they were partly trained in, for up to four sessions a week in order to maintain skills through the first four years of childcare.

We had utilised a definitive doctoral thesis by Dr Ione Fett of Monash University's Anthropology Department, in which she demonstrated the entrenched prejudice operating in women's careers in medicine, and blew apart the myth generated by our male mentors that one-third of women dropped out of medicine. Dr Fett documented that despite early and multiple pregnancies, 86 percent of women remained in medicine, and exposed for the first time the surprising information that 5 percent of males dropped out for preferred careers elsewhere. Thus I learned the tools of anthropology could be used to undo the strategies of my own sexist profession. The impotence of being apolitical was to leave me forever.

> The impotence of being apolitical was to leave me forever.

I took this knowledge into the next stage, where my husband's career change saw me out of medicine and into missionary recruitment. I shared the enthusiasm he brought to his job as director of the Sudan Interior Mission for working in the need-ridden areas of the 'third world', where I had already worked as a doctor.

Over the next six years, he and I learned together that with the best motives for care, and involvement with a fine group of missionaries, we could not conform to the conservative requirements of the organisation in Australia. The missionary mandate of the nineteenth century arose at the time of colonial encounter which was insensitive to indigenous culture. The twentieth century could not afford to perpetuate it. There was no longer any excuse for building a kingdom of God that still maintained colonialism, racism and sexism.

A feature of Christian fundamentalism which peculiarly fits it for heroic and often self-sacrificial care is its preoccupation with eternal personal salvation, often at the cost of colluding with injustice in this world. As Bishop Helda Camera said in South America: 'When I fed the poor, they said I was a saint. When I asked why they were poor, they said I was a communist!'

Despite real progress in the mission on issues like cultural sensitivity and indigenous theology, the mounting controversy over feminism within the church-proper heralded our certain demise. The Europeans and some of the Americans were more open to reform, but the Australian board was dominated by the most reactionary elements of puritanism and fundamentalism. During those painful years, I studied anthropology and comparative religion and added to my politicisation new insights into the ideology of religious control. Unbeknown to me, I was preparing for a more basic struggle that awaited me in the church that had both fired my imagination and then socialised it into a secondary form, subject to all that was male including divinity itself.

During my time as the wife of a mission director I look back with amazement at the ignorance and superstition I endured in the oft-cited dictum that my role was to support my husband in the job God had called him to. In my role as a doctor I found it all the more difficult to deal with the women who came to me as patients. The chronic depression they suffered could be traced to the oppressive effects of an authoritarian system which in my role as missionary I was expected to support.

But the feminist 'cavalry' was on the way. In 1973, Dr Barbara Thiering wrote a book on sexism in the Australian church, *Created Second*. I consumed the first half of the book about the sociological features of sexism, but could not in 1973 deal with her criticism of orthodox Christian theology. Any serious study of church history and any serious sociological look at the church as an institution invariably led to some change in perception of its legitimated absolutes which change in the interests of the institutions but are presented as changeless. This is seen in the lengths to which men and women go to maintain the all-male priesthood and the anthropomorphic male divinity.

Theological reflection is pre-eminently a human activity variously informed by experience and a creative imagination. Religious questions are important precisely because we don't have the answer to the reasons for our existence, our consciousness, and our human journey. Women have not significantly participated in the formulation, exegesis or offices of the public church, although modern feminist scholarship has unearthed the most amazing evidence of the counter-culture they have inhabited.

> Religious questions are important precisely because we don't have the answer to the reasons for our existence, our consciousness, and our human journey.

Within the oral tradition, the spiritual authority of women has been kept alive, outside the sway of patriarchal officialdom despite its power to deliver frequent and swift retribution for any female who acted on her own authority. Maybe my background in patriarchal medicine equipped me at least in part to recognise a male construct of reality, once I could take the risk to believe what I saw.

Bearing and sharing the parenting of three children has been crucial to my career and one that I place above most other privileges. Mixing motherhood with a profession allowed me to generalise skills in and out of medicine and gave me extra study options in anthropology and religious studies as well as two years in ABC television and radio. Somehow one's disappointments become appointments.

My career exposed me to people's heartaches as well as their heart attacks and left no doubt that if the church had one problem, it was to perpetuate the worst treason—to do the wrong thing for the right reason. The official resistance to women in both Catholicism and Anglicanism reveals a church in this country that can't even follow the liberating reforms and limited mercies of secular society. To that cause, along with many other women, I have given some of my best effort.

Medicine runs parallel to the church. It is no great haven of enlightenment, even when it comes to healing. Maybe I can offer a critique that will be useful: better to be an ordinary informed doctor than a member of the honorary male club that still defends medical professional interests as paramount. Some of the best critiques of medicine come not from doctors, but from feminist health specialists. Obstetrics, gynaecology and psychiatry are feeling the pressure of consumer insight and demands. The ethical dimensions of medicine need urgent attention, what with IVF technology and organ transplants and the whole complex issue of cost-benefits and health.

A feature of oppression is the assent to it. I reinforced my own exclusion by attributing too much of it to the sexist structures in medicine rather than some of my own idiosyncrasies: for instance, adopting a victim mentality in the face of control rather than challenging it.

After my ten years of effort to see women take up authoritative positions within the church, no longer do I ask what can women do to contribute to the church or to please reform the ministry to let women in. Rather I ask: is the church in its traditional theology reformable? Women are emerging as serious theologians who challenge the church in the face of its own irrelevance.

My chief interests as a child are alive in my decade of reform within the church, not as a devout believer in the system but as an exile within a tradition that asks the best questions and has tolerated some of the worst answers.

Our school song was light on piety except for its mention of the school motto. 'Dieu et Droit'—God and Right. Looking back, it cultivated the only ambition that goes all the way to my gut—an ambition in me for justice that I hope is beyond my own interests, and a spiritual journey that is not a guided tour.

CAREERING THROUGH LIFE

Irina Dunn

Irina Dunn was born on 17 March 1948 in China. After graduating with a Bachelor of arts (honours) degree from Sydney University, she worked as a tutor in the English Department for three years. In 1988 she took her place in the Australian parliament as a Senator, completing her two-year term in 1990. Irina Dunn has also worked as an academic, film-maker, journalist and teacher. She is an activist, committed to contributing to a better world for all. Irina Dunn is interested in politics, feminism, the environment, literature, theatre and music, and aspires to become a source of inspiration and strength to younger women.

My career has been conducted less in the sense of 'making steady progress through life' than galloping through it at full speed.

I have been a teacher, film-maker, politician, restaurateur, all interesting and rewarding occupations. I have always been an activist, and I was born a feminist. The rebellious streak in my character is genetic. I have spent half a lifetime exercising civilising nurture over a recalcitrant and stubborn nature. I concentrated on developing self-discipline, resilience and an optimistic outlook. Money has been much less important to me than living an interesting life and contributing to general welfare.

Until recently, my loyal Russian mother remained my anchor, the still point in my seething world. I caused her no end of trouble, even before my birth. Two weeks overdue, and after 72 hours of labour, I was removed by the brutal caesarean section operation on the 17 March 1948 in a hospital in Shanghai. My Irish-Macanese father was attending the St Patrick's Day ball. Later on, my mother told me parents had but little time to apply a few

Indeed, what was I to do with myself?

formative touches to the rapidly drying clay of the infant personality before it set forever. Her constant efforts belied her wry remarks. She said I had always been an 'interesting' child, and regarded me in awe tinged with trepidation. What was she to 'do' with me?

Indeed, what was I to do with myself?

At school I was particularly good at Latin, mathematics, biology, economics and English. When I saw the vocational guidance counsellor in my final year, the range of choices she offered was most unpalatable— teaching, nursing, librarianship, office work, and, implicit behind it all, the option of 'housewife'. She never suggested that I think of becoming a Senator or a lawyer or diplomat. My hackles rose at the thought of any of her options. Not that they weren't perfectly respectable and interesting professions, but I rejected them because they were seen as 'suitable' careers for girls, and they were inextricably linked in my mind, in a rather sinister way, to marriage. I intended to have none of that.

I knew what I didn't want to do — get stuck in a menial job with sole responsibility for raising a couple of kids. After her divorce my mother, whose nursing qualifications were not recognised in Australia, worked on factory production line or in sandwich bars. For years, she set the alarm at 5.30 am each weekday and took herself off for a 7 am start at jobs that were often grindingly repetitive, dirty and dangerous, to pay the mortgage and to educate her children — my younger brother and me. Meanwhile, my father — not one to be daunted — married for a fifth time and started another family.

This background, and the thought I might, as a parent, have to raise a child like myself, turned me off marriage, families, children.

Perhaps it was because I was a 'foreigner' at a snobbish private Anglican school that I never felt I belonged, even though I was always in the top 10 or so in the top class. Certainly I did not belong to the establishment set with wealth and connections. These were the girls who were going to have the 'brilliant careers'.

My own career at the school was brought to a sudden end midway through the third year of high school by my father's bankruptcy. Despite my outsider status, I was traumatised by my enforced departure from the school I had attended since kindergarten. It was mortifying catching the same school bus in the mornings wearing the uniform of the nearby public school. Usually I saved the money, walking to my new school by the back route. For three months I withdrew into myself and barely spoke.

We moved to western Sydney and a new home and I enrolled at another school; I felt much more comfortable, but I never recovered academic interest in my studies. I skipped classes with my newfound best friend, a girl I much admired not only because of her natural talents but also because she was a voluntary refugee from the private school system. We went to a little bohemian wine bar in Elizabeth Street to discuss existentialism and literature with each other and whoever was there over 2s glasses of sticky alcoholic substances and black coffee, trying to look sophisticated in our school uniforms while choking on strong filterless French cigarettes. Never living up to her early promise, and despairing of a life of prescribed drugs, confusion, pain and failures, my friend decided she'd had enough of life and quit this world not long after her fortieth birthday several years ago. The woman I had admired, loved and emulated, was no longer.

I met the old private school graduates of the class of 1964 at a re-union 25 years later. Very few had had careers at all, opting largely for well-heeled domesticity. And of those who did, none was particularly 'brilliant'. Only one expressed a social conscience. In retrospect, I see that at school there was never any talk of a career, per se. We were being groomed to become well-educated wives for status-conscious husbands.

> We were being groomed to become well-educated wives for status-conscious husbands.

Knowing who I was but not what I was to be or do, I went off to Sydney University after I left school in the mid-1960s to do an arts degree, deciding that studying was a more attractive option than working. The odd jobs I'd had throughout high school and university — as waitress, domestic help, baby sitter, shop assistant, paper girl, artists' and photographic model, interviewer, telephonist, clerk, assistant to the assistant actuarial assistant — fuelled my decision.

'Career Woman' seemed too grand a title for my plans. Later, when my mother used it to describe me to her friends, it surprised me, not only because she used it as a way of explaining my oddity and my single, childless status. She was never able to say: 'My daughter is an engineer' (a profession favoured by Russian immigrants and refugees for both sexes), or 'My daughter is a teacher' (or a lawyer or a dentist). My mother's use of the term 'career woman' was meant to disguise a confusing range of interests and occupations.

My parents had had enough of history to last our family several generations. History — and greed— threw China into turmoil in the first half of the century and attracted scoundrels, missionaries, old and new colonial powers, communists, revolutionaries and idealists, spies, gangsters and opportunists like old Dooley, my Irish grandfather, an engineer. Dooley became manager of the Shanghai Tug and Lighter Company and met Macau-born Sibilina Alvez by whom he had five children. The oldest, my father Timothy Edward, was born in October 1903.

Some fifteen years later, history sent my mother's parents vast distances from the Ukraine to a small village on the border of China and Russia, where my mother was born in January 1922. Not far away, my maternal grandfather, a simple soldier, was later murdered on a railway station for the fur coat he wore.

History stripped my mother of national status and dumped her along with thousands of other Russians in an alien culture although, to be fair, the

Chinese treated the Russian emigrés quite well at that time. History exploded over my mother's head during the Japanese occupation of Shanghai and threatened to annihilate her. History brought my parents together after the war in the American Club in Shanghai: my father was a visitor, my mother a waitress. I was born on the eve of the great Chinese Communist revolution and the beginning of Mao's long reign.

My father's pro-Nationalist sympathies and personal wealth sent us fleeing from Shanghai late in 1948 before the advancing communist brigades. We escaped to Hong Kong with a handful of possessions. Despite the material and political security offered by the 'lucky' country, I have always been haunted by ghosts of times past. I never, in my wildest dreams, imagined I would have the opportunity to be a representative in the federal parliament of my adopted country.

May 1988. My predecessor Senator Robert Wood was referred to the High Court, to determine whether he, as a British subject and not being an Australian citizen, could lawfully take his elected place as a Senator in the Australian parliament. I paced the floor till dawn feeling as if I were poised on the top of the first big dip on a roller-coaster ride.

Robert had been elected for the Nuclear Disarmament Party (NDP) in the double dissolution election of July 1987. With about 50 000 primary votes, the NDP won the last (twelfth) Senate position after Australian Labor Party (ALP) preferences were distributed. This caused some considerable annoyance to the Call to Australia Party candidate Elaine Nile, whose primary vote was about 80 000 but who failed to pick up the necessary preferences to win through.

Distinguished, internationally renowned paediatrician Dr Michael Denborough, NDP founder, had asked me to stand as the NDP's number two candidate. Robert and I were endorsed by members faithful to the party after the traumatic split of 1985, when rock star Peter Garrett and Senator Jo Vallentine walked out of a stormy national meeting in Melbourne.

I agreed to stand on the NDP ticket to help the election campaign. I believed that the single-issue nature of the party, its popularity with young people and the residual support it attracted, would ensure support for the questioning of where Australia was headed. Earlier in the year, when Prime Minister Hawke had invited the United States to test its MX missiles in Pacific waters off the coast of Australia, even his own party was embarrassed by this slavish display and blocked the proposal. If the government was genuinely interested in developing an independent and self-reliant foreign and defence policy, why did it cling to the useless scrap of paper that is the ANZUS Treaty? How could we claim to be opposed to nuclear warfare when our major ally was a leading proponent and manufacturer of nuclear arms? How could we support the South Pacific nuclear free and independent movement when our major ally refused to sign the treaty? The Soviet Union had signed it.

My feminist concerns led me to the NDP. In 1985 I made a documentary, *Fighting For Peace*, about the history of the women's peace movement in Australia. I met a large number of older women activists, and was impressed by their articulate and well-informed grasp of the issues, their longstanding commitment and their energy. They were from the Women's International League for Peace and Freedom (WILP) which was founded in 1916; they were from the Union of Australian Women (UAW), all dedicated workers for women, peace and social justice. I found out about extraordinary Jessie Street through her daughter, lively, warm and gracious Philippa Fingleton, and through remarkable Eve Higson, a friend of Jessie and now close friend of mine. All the participants of *Fighting For Peace* were exhilarated when the film won a prize at the International Film and Video Festival later that year.

The NDP was the only party I ever joined. I once considered joining the ALP, but the local branch was dominated by a right-wing element and would not have been sympathetic to someone with my concerns. I developed close relations with some of the left-wing political parties, working with them on particular issues, and was grateful for their support at times when few others came forward to assist — such as on the Ananda Marga campaign. I resisted joining them, cherishing my independence, with a deep-seated abhorrence of interminable party meetings and procedures from which the NDP was refreshingly free.

When Robert Wood's election was finally known, some two months after election day, I was editor of *Encore*, the trade magazine for the commercial film industry in Australia. It had been enjoyable and challenging work for nearly two years.

Ten months later Robert's capacity to sit as a Senator was challenged after it was revealed that he was not an Australian citizen when he nominated for election in 1987. On 21 July 1988, the High Court decided that, as number two on the Nuclear Disarmament Party ticket, I would receive the votes that the party had gained in the election. After the recount I was declared elected as Senator for New South Wales. Robert pressed me to resign the Senate position in the belief he would automatically be returned after sorting out his citizenship. I was not so sure.

I was declared elected as Senator for New South Wales.

Under the Australian Constitution, a joint sitting of both houses of state parliament is required to nominate a replacement for a casual vacancy created by the death or resignation of a Senator. This provision dated from a period when the Senate was much more of a states' house than it is today. (Only academics could tell you the last time a vote was taken along state lines in the Senate.) With state governments having the power to choose the state's representatives in the Senate, there was no guarantee, if I resigned, that Robert would have been nominated to replace me. I did not think that the Greiner–Murray Liberal–National government was above the obstruction that other conservative governments had been guilty of in the recent past.

In 1975, Bjelke-Petersen's Queensland government refused to endorse the ALP nominee when a casual Senate vacancy was created in Queensland and instead nominated a non-entity, Albert Field, who had no formal party allegiances. It was clear, however, where his sympathies lay. His vote was critical in blocking supply to the Whitlam government in late 1975, which led to the defeat of the government. Ultimately, an amendment to the Constitution was passed in 1977 by referendum requiring that the replacement for a casual Senate vacancy be taken from the same party as the person who created the vacancy.

Even so, in 1987, the Gray government in Tasmania opposed ALP Senate nominee John Devereux on the grounds that he was not a fit person to represent the state. The ALP threatened to expel any member other than Devereux who nominated for the position. A stalemate ensued and, until the election some six months later when Devereux was duly elected, Tasmania was denied one of its Senate positions.

I decided not to jeopardise the NDP's Senate position by resigning. I could do a good job of representing the state, especially on those issues needing a stronger voice in the federal parliament. I did not think my job was merely to be a seat-warmer for a man.

> I did not think my job was merely to be a seat-warmer for a man.

Disappointingly, Robert Wood, who publicly supported feminism and whose 'maiden' speech was about the 'logjam of patriarchy' in our society, would not support his number two candidate. Instead, he attacked me publicly, giving the media the scent of a witch-hunt which they pursued with a vengeance. Robert made it seem as if I had stolen the seat from him, whereas he, in fact, was not entitled to hold it because of his failure to comply with the requirements of the *Electoral Act*. I believed then and believe now that the causes we both supported were more important than his personal loss.

The conflict, which I tried sincerely to resolve, resulted in my decision to enter parliament as an Independent. I intended to represent the antinuclear issues, to which I was strongly committed, and also to represent the cause of women and to raise environmental issues, in which I had some expertise.

To be a woman, an Independent, and more radical politically than just about everybody in the parliament, presented great problems. The only time I did not have two or three of the most rabid opposition Senators frothing at the mouth was during my first ('maiden') speech, when convention dictates that the new Senator be received in respectful silence.

I was horrified at the abuse that regularly flew around the chamber, much of it directed at Jo Vallentine, the Western Australian Independent, and myself. Cross-bench abuse was a ritualised sport indulged in by members of the male club whereas the vilification Jo and I received from both sides of the chamber, but mostly from the opposition benches, was overtly hostile and vindictive. The strong impression was that many of those Senators resented having women in the parliament, and that only those women who played by the male rules were acceptable.

> Only those who played by the male rules were accepted.

I soon developed the greatest admiration for Democrat leader Janine Haines, who was not only able to give as good as she got, but give it with intelligence and wit without descending to the puerile abuse so typical of some of the male Senators. It would be good to have as many women in parliament as men because, whether feminist or not, the women would be less likely to be so combative and aggressive in debates.

I learned Standing Orders on my feet, when points of order were taken against me. On one occasion just before Christmas 1989, during the adjournment, I was getting stuck into the New South Wales government's, and particularly the National Party's, environmentally objectionable proposals; Victorian National Party Senator Julian McGauran, incensed by my attack on his colleagues, broke with parliamentary convention by calling a quorum during the adjournment, when it is generally agreed that Senators should be able to have their say without interruption. I was, in cricketing parlance, bowled out when insufficient Senators turned up in the chamber to form a quorum and the Senate was adjourned for the day.

Next evening, I bobbed up again during the adjournment to complete my speech. When I resumed my seat, Senator McGauran, inarticulate with rage, called me 'the butcher of Robert Wood' and a 'friend of terrorists'. He used such 'unparliamentary language' that the duty Senator for the government, Senator Michael Tate, rose on a point of order, demanding McGauran withdraw his comment unconditionally. He did.

Jo Vallentine, first elected in 1984, was a great inspiration. She demonstrated by her unfailing courage, fortitude and sense of humour how to manage the abuse and insults. Without her support and encouragement as I sat next to her in the chamber I could not have learned the procedures nor borne the insults nearly as quickly as I did, despite the good wishes and support of the like-minded Democrats, who sat on the other side of the aisle.

When I entered the Senate, 17 out of 76 Senators were women. The conservatives did twice as well as Labor, with eight female Senators. Three of the seven Democrats, including the leader, were women, and two of the three Independents were women.

In the House were eight women out of 148 representatives, with only one on the conservative side. That was the remarkable Kathy Sullivan, who has represented Queensland since 1974. The sole woman on her side for a long time, Kathy put up with the unthinking sexist comments of her colleagues and was frequently embarrassed by their disparaging remarks about women.

I quickly learned the difference between having women and having feminists in the parliament. The presence of women breaks down barriers to our visible participation in every aspect of public life. Even conservative women—including Margaret Thatcher—have a useful role in this respect. But conservative women tend to believe they have 'made it' on their own merits, forgetting their debt to women who fought so hard to win political, social and economic rights for Australian women. Conservative women tend to dismiss the idea that women are disadvantaged as a class and believe women can be successful if they try hard enough. The logical extension of this argument must lead to the conclusion that women are either biologically inferior to men or less motivated since they exist in decreasing numbers the higher one climbs up the socio-economic ladder.

I noticed how some conservative female Senators with a sympathy for women's issues have an aversion to the word 'feminist'. To their credit and their intelligence, the women on the government side all called themselves 'feminists', and with some pride.

When the House was debating the possibility of locating a childcare centre in the grounds of the old Parliament House, I was astonished to hear conservative women claim it would be 'out of character' with the heritage values of the old building. Nothing demonstrates so well the macho-mentality of our politicians than the absence of a childcare centre in the new Parliament House. It was not that it was too expensive. In my office there were four imported cedar blinds each worth $1500. With 224 federal pollies, that makes $1 344 000 worth of cedar blinds alone. With less expensive blinds and cost-cutting in other areas, a childcare centre could have been built for all users of Parliament House.

The first legislation I introduced was a Bill to increase provision of childcare services to meet 80 percent of the need by the year 2000. Competent assistance was given me by sociologist and researcher Eva Cox, tireless in her struggle to improve the lot of women, together with conscientious and witty Pam Simons, who joined my staff for several months. The Bill, being introduced by an Independent, had no chance of being passed, but at least it stood as an example of the way forward.

I introduced four other pieces of legislation: Bills to give the government power to protect the national estate, to make the Commonwealth take up its responsibility to protect Australian coastal waters, to reform the electoral system and to remove sexist language from legislation.

I used the adjournment freely. It was the only avenue available to Senators to raise matters of concern in the electorate: I named an alleged wife-basher in parliament, raised allegations of corruption in a mid-north coast council in relation to planning decisions, criticised the New South

Wales government's environmental policies, named police alleged to have bashed Aborigines in a small South Australian town, and many other matters. Wherever possible, I promoted anti-nuclear and disarmament issues. Frequently the government and opposition sat together on one side of the chamber on these matters, with the Democrats, Jo Vallentine and myself on the other.

I had a great deal of sympathy for and considerable rapport with women on the government benches and some in opposition. Some were dismayed by their party's policies on uranium, the visits of the nuclear warships and abortion. In 1989, Liberal MP Alasdair Webster attempted by a Private Member's Bill to eliminate Medicare rebates for abortions. It looked as though it might come to the Senate for debate. The history of anti-abortion in the earlier days of the Catholic-dominated ALP is well-known, and the ALP on that matter allowed a conscience vote as a concession to that element in the party. A government Senator commented that she resented the possibility of a conscience vote on abortion when she was, because of party constraints, unable to vote against nuclear ships visiting Australian ports. I was glad I did not have to face this daily frustration.

Two years to the next elections passed rapidly. I had worked very hard, often 16 hours a day, to make the best use of the position while I held it. I did not expect to be re-elected and I wasn't. An Independent has practically no chance of being elected to any upper house in Australia, except perhaps in Tasmania. In New South Wales, there were 3500 booths to be staffed. This was impossible without a party structure in each electorate. Hundreds of thousands of dollars are needed for a campaign and this I did not have. Although pleased with the result, my vote might have been better without so many competing groups in New South Wales — a total of some 80 running on this occasion — and if the major conservation groups had not given their endorsement to the Democrats. In any case, I felt fatally marked by the bad publicity associated with the NDP.

> I did not expect to be re-elected and I wasn't.

My dear mother, so supportive and concerned for my health and welfare during the often difficult days of my short political career, died in October 1989, leaving a gap that can never be filled. She joins Jessie Street in the ranks of the courageous and dedicated women who have become my heroines and role models. Eve Higson remains a source of living inspiration and friendship to me as do many women who supported, advised, comforted, and nourished me intellectually and spiritually during those frenetic two years.

Many male friends stuck by me loyally, providing inestimable assistance. They include ecologist Dr Harry Recher and environmentalist Peter Prineas who both lent their names to my ticket, and my friend David Shellard who, despite fragile health made worse, I fear, from the strain, provided first-class research and continuous ironic commentary on the nature of political life —

and on my own follies. On one occasion, when walking to visit a member of the lower house, on the other side of the building, I was wearing a brightly coloured dress. It attracted a wolf whistle from a National Party member. He commented loudly this was the way he liked to see women dressed and asked me where he could find me. With raised eyebrow, I replied 'Senator Dunn's Office'. Whom should he ask for? 'Senator Dunn.' He was shocked. I told David about this incident and he replied: 'If you dress like a lollipop you can expect to be called sweety.'

After I completed my Senate term, on 30 June 1990, Dr Harry Recher offered me a six-month appointment as a Senior Lecturer in his Department (Ecosystem Management) at the University of New England, teaching Resource Management Policy. Living in college as a 'den mother' and teaching in the department provided a contrast — quieter but no less rewarding — to the sometimes barely tolerable life of politics.

I do not regret my two years in the Senate. The most interesting job I have yet had, I am satisfied with how I acquitted myself. Eve Higson says that the most important thing in life is to be able to live happily with oneself. With that I have to agree.

GROWING UP IN LAW SCHOOL

Greta Bird

Director of the National Centre for Cross Cultural Studies in Law, a joint centre of Monash University and the University of Melbourne, Greta Bird trained as a lawyer. Graduating from the University of Melbourne as Bachelor of laws, then completing her articles at a Melbourne legal firm, she took up a position as research assistant at the law school at Monash University. In the early 1980s Greta Bird graduated as Master of philosophy from Cambridge University in England.

I've always felt an obligation to work. My parents worked exceptionally hard. Mum left school the day she turned 14 to contribute to her family's upkeep; dad finished Year 9. Both worked much of their lives in manual labour. Mostly dad earned a living cleaning. He worked for a salary during the week and at weekends did contract cleaning. Mum and I often went with him, while the sister closest in age to me stayed home minding the younger children. Throughout my university years, my boyfriend picked me up at university and we went to help with the cleaning. During my articles year (learning to be a lawyer), even after I was married, I kept it up. I did not stop until I took a full-time job as a research assistant at university.

When I was seven years old the priest announced from the pulpit that the Grade 1 teacher had walked out because she was pregnant and there was an outbreak of German measles in the class. He asked for volunteers to take the class of 120 students. This was in the 1950s. Catholic school buildings could not cope with the large Catholic families.

Mum volunteered, spending the next 10 years as an untrained teacher at

101

various schools. She also waitressed some nights, cleaned with dad at the weekends, and raised five children. Mum often said: 'Get a good education so you don't have to earn your living on your hands and knees scrubbing floors.' Consequently I pushed myself at school. I helped mum correct student's work and prepare material for classes. I thought I would like to be a primary school teacher.

The severe overcrowding in Catholic schools meant some children 'jumped' a grade. As my birthday was on 20 April I was still four when I started school and, after 'jumping' Grade 1, ended up 15 at matriculation year. I was at Santa Maria College in Northcote, a Catholic girls' school run by the Good Samaritan nuns. When school finished in Year 12 a teacher shortage at a school in Lalor meant I took over the combined Grade 4 and 5. I took days off to sit my exams, but enjoyed being in charge of a class and earning some money. I had not wanted to complete Year 12. Only Year 11 was needed for teachers' college but, because of my age, I agreed to stay on. However I was determined not to go to university as I saw it as a 'sinful' place full of bohemians and intellectuals. I knew no one who had gone to university. Although the majority of the nuns were enlightened and encouraged us girls to further study, others were anti-intellectual, muttering darkly about 'bad influences' and 'souls in danger'.

I was accepted for teachers' college when a Commonwealth Scholarship Award notice arrived. My parents were keen on my going to university. I said 'throw it in the rubbish bin, I'm not going'.

> My parents were keen on my going to university.

Finally I agreed to defer the scholarship for 12 months and take on a temporary job in the Department of Social Security. There were lots of Catholics in the section, most were male. Two young men were studying law part-time. When they learned I had a Commonwealth Scholarship and could go to university full-time they were encouraging, but also warned: 'Only do law if you love it, don't do it just to get a man.' I was horrified, as I had not thought of meeting boys at university at all. I was 17 and going out with a 16-year-old apprentice fitter and turner. That was my world.

I remember the first day, in the uni. caf', people were reading the *Sun*. Only the *Age* was allowed in our house. Dad said: 'The *Sun* is a pictorial, it is for people who don't read.' Seeing these people with the *Sun* made me feel that they couldn't be the terrifying intellectuals I had feared. I grew more confident. Still, the first term was alienating. In 1965 students at law school were 'well dressed.' Students joked about my jeans and leather jacket and called me a 'Rocker'. I bought some Fletcher Jones skirts. For the first time I learned about 'good schools' and 'old school ties' and 'daddy's firm'.

During first-term break my brother (three years younger) was killed in a car accident. One tactic my parents had used to encourage me to go to university was that it might inspire my brother to go. He was very bright but always 'mucking around' in school. After his death I felt a fraud. Why was I at university now? Somehow I kept going, but felt lost and confused.

The Pop Music Club and the Rhythm and Blues Club helped me survive that first year. Most club members were male. I hung around in a group of 10, nine males and me. The boys in this group were working class, studying either arts or science. Unfortunately all but two of us flunked out. I thought of failure when my number did not appear under the pass section, but to my surprise I had honours in every law subject. A music club friend rang on hearing my results, saying: 'You're a dark horse.'

I had honours in every law subject.

Only a few women were in law. We were generally serious about our studies, achieving good results. I attended the optional honours lectures whenever possible because they were more interesting. I also wanted a chance to get honours.

By fourth year I was heartily sick of university, wanting to be in the 'real world'. To get an honours degree the final honours exams were taken if your grades were good enough. I ignored the notice about the exams. My fiancé (a leading hand in a company that manufactured machine tools) saw it and said: 'You're going to sit aren't you? You've always had good results.' The date to enrol had passed but he pressed me: 'Why don't you see the Dean?' The Dean pointed out: 'Without an Honours Degree I couldn't appoint you as a tutor.' I agreed to do the exams, thinking, this is sheer madness, I would never, ever contemplate being an academic. My younger sister had become pregnant earlier in the year, dropping out of university. She was single, living at home with a beautiful baby daughter. I envied what I saw as her freedom and enjoyment while I was studying for final and honours exams. It was not until I was a mother, years later, that I realised how irrevocably she had lost her freedom. Her pregnancy and single motherhood propelled me into engagement in my final year.

My mother had an aunt who had had dealings with a law firm in Queen Street, Melbourne. The firm's woman partner took on a female articled clerk each year. I bought a woollen suit, went to the hairdressers, and was accepted. I shared an office with a young Catholic man who was studying law at Royal Melbourne Institute of Technology (RMIT). The firm did a lot of hotel licensing and I soon excelled in getting licensees into pubs. As the end of articles approached it was obvious the male articled clerk would stay on while I was to leave. I was now married — unlike the female partner. 'Too soft for practice', I was advised to consider an academic career. Being 'too soft' was a flaw. I lost a lot of confidence about my legal skills.

In retrospect I see that firm worked for a particular class of people: insurance companies, not injured workers; debt collectors, against people like my parents and friends. The hotel licensing work was a 'male' field. My articles year was unhappy as I struggled to reconcile the law as it had seemed at university, and the law in practice. I thought law could be used to empower people from backgrounds like my own. In reality, it appeared oppressive to the poor. The woman partner had insisted I wear hat and gloves to court and deemed my clothes 'unsuitable', suggesting I use her dressmaker. Yet even had I wanted to, it was impossible on my articled clerk 'salary'. I sat dutifully with her at social drinks and sipped lemon squash. We both realised I had no interest in mixing with her social group.

I tried to get a job with a law firm through Eve Mahlab and Associates. At the first interview the solicitor asked if I could type. I got the feeling I would be a glorified secretary. The second interview went well, or so I thought. Later the solicitor rang Eve Mahlab instructing he did not want any women sent for the position. The third wanted to go overseas and leave me in charge of the practice: 'Just put a "Closed" sign on the door if it gets too busy.' The offer was intriguing but too risky professionally. The fourth was a 'factory' with little opportunity for advancement. Without any connections and the wrong 'attitude' I realised it would be difficult getting a job that suited me. This was 1969, before community legal centres. What was I to do?

Monash University advertised for a research assistant. My husband (I married just before my articles finished) and I were living close by and he was working at Monash. The idea of an academic job intimidated me — even if the students weren't intellectuals, the staff very probably were. Where would I be once they realised I wasn't? I applied.

Accepted, I was eager for my first real salary which was to go towards tyres for our old vanguard station wagon. Though full-time research assistant, I shared a room with two other women. There were vacant rooms in the faculty, but the allocation of space was a matter of hierarchy. I assisted senior male academics and the lone senior female academic (a professor). After six months the Dean asked if I wanted to tutor. The Faculty needed to replace a male tutor, off to Oxford to do a BCL (Bachelor of Civil Law). 'How do I learn to teach?' Evidently anybody could teach! I accepted.

I was not consciously aware of the male domination of senior positions in the faculty. It was not until a few years later that I began to see promotions were not just based on merit but also on image. A 'bright young man' who 'got along with people' was likely to be promoted. It was difficult for women to aspire to promotion because of the lack of role models. It was even more difficult for a woman who was a mother. The only woman to be appointed professor or associate professor in Monash law school's first 25 years was a woman with no children, appointed in the 1960s, perhaps partly because of the opportunity for 'radical' appointments at a new university.

This awareness lay in the future. Before I had children I did not perceive gender issues as relevant to me. Until then my non-attendance at a 'good' school, alienation at university, difficulty in coming to terms with the practice of law were connected to my working-class Irish Catholic background. To me all working-class people were oppressed, women and men.

While pregnant with my first child the Dean approved my four weeks maternity leave, and return half-time, in a 'fractional' position. I was grateful as I had thought of resigning. The pregnancy, coming after 18 months of marriage, was unplanned. I assumed this was the 'end' of my career. Another woman on the faculty was pregnant at the same time and had no intention of retiring. Her approach made me rethink the future. I became optimistic about combining a career and motherhood.

I breastfed the baby at 4.30 am and again at 8.30 am to fit in with university work. I came home at lunch-time to feed her, returned to work, and raced home at 5 pm guilty that I was a little late for the baby's feed. After a few months of this I was pregnant again. My second daughter came 13 months after the first. Childcare arrangements broke down. I encouraged my husband to apply for a job in Papua New Guinea, dreading being 'imprisoned' in the suburbs with two babies, no driver's licence, and inadequate public transport. We were soon living in Goroka in the Eastern Highlands. After six months we decided to leave after a man smashed the bathroom louvres while I was showering.

On my return Monash was not making any fractional appointments. I approached the Dean of the new Legal Studies Department at La Trobe University, inquiring about work. He was helpful, giving me tutorial times that fitted with my responsibilities as a mother. I could not bring myself to leave the children all day in a childcare centre. My husband agreed to work part-time, looking after the girls on the days I was at La Trobe. There were opportunities for promotion at La Trobe as it was a new and quickly expanding department. People were being promoted to lectureships at all universities in the early 1970s on the basis of good first degrees without post-graduate qualifications. However, there was a problem. One member of staff treated me in what he regarded as a playful and humorous fashion, but made me anxious and unsure of myself. At that time sexist behaviour and sexual harassment were not formulated concepts. I thought that the failure to take this behaviour in my stride was entirely my own fault. Today I would explain to him why his behaviour was unacceptable. I resigned and enrolled as a Masters student at Monash.

At that time sexist behaviour and sexual harassment were not formulated concepts.

At first I was enrolled as a full-time candidate, to do the degree by major thesis. However, prohibitive costs of childcare and warnings from male colleagues that with two young children 'you would be better doing the degree by course-work and minor thesis' led me to change my enrolment. Only later did I realise that a degree by major thesis was 'more prestigious'.

I obtained exceptionally good results in spite of the demands of two energetic little girls. Rarely did the children go to bed before 11 pm. After they were asleep I worked on 'my hobby', as it was known in the family. My husband had enrolled for a two-year Diploma of education at Hawthorn Teachers' College to enable him to teach in technical schools, making it clear that his studies had to take precedence over mine.

When a supervisor was appointed for my thesis he commenced by saying: 'What do you want a Master's degree for? You're not ambitious.' He was unhelpful and fortunately soon replaced with a supportive woman who told me the finished thesis was 'publishable'. The thesis was on sub-standard housing, involving fieldwork and other socio-legal research. My belief that law could be used to empower people to obtain decent housing was challenged by the data I collected. Yet I still believed that if only the legal system could operate as intended, 'justice' would prevail.

In 1978 the Dean thought I was ready for a lectureship. 'You have served a long enough apprenticeship,' he said. Another senior male member of the Faculty advised me to tell the Dean that I preferred tutoring. I took this advice.

Ambitions for a career lay dormant.

Later that year we took off around Europe for six months. When we returned from Europe I took up a half-time tutorship at Monash. We became involved with a community school, where parent involvement was encouraged. I was soon 'teaching' there in my spare time and attending 'community meetings'. It was like an extended family during the children's primary school years. Ambitions for a career lay dormant. We grew vegetables and baked our own bread, made jam and pickles, and kept hens. Renovating our house gave me practical skills. Holidays were spent camping with the school community. These were good years.

In April 1982 the Dean announced a tutor's scholarship of about $9000 towards going overseas for a post-graduate degree. I applied. Two scholarships were awarded, one to a male, the other to me. I was warned by a male colleague of the need to work hard, as 'Monash University's reputation is riding on your shoulders'. Now I would laugh at the thought of Monash's reputation being so shaky; then, his words made me even more horrified at the enormity of taking two children aged 10 and 11 away and enrolling at Cambridge University for a full-time Master of philosophy degree.

Before leaving I did a fieldwork trip. Elizabeth Eggleston had published *Fear, Favour or Affection*, her work on Aborigines and the criminal justice system. She died and I was to work on a second edition of her book. I decided to do some fieldwork to determine whether I could manage the project. For some months in 1983 my husband and the children and I went through country towns in South Australia and Western Australia where I interviewed Kooris, police officers, clerks of courts and magistrates, judges, barristers and solicitors about Kooris and the criminal justice system. It was exhausting. Then I put away my bulging fieldwork diaries and set off for Cambridge.

What an adventure. The sociology, psychiatry and psychology units were fascinating after straight law, as was sociology of deviance and research methodology. The pace was gruelling. Four unseen examination papers, after seven weeks, then seven research papers plus tutorial papers and a 25 000 word thesis in one academic year. I was tired but exhilarated. My results were excellent and some of the lecturers were encouraging about my work. I formed a strong friendship with Maureen Cain, the British legal sociologist, but also found male lecturers supportive. More confident about my abilities, I applied for a lectureship at Monash University. I was not even shortlisted.

Part of the scholarship included tutoring at Monash for six months. I returned to Melbourne directly after the Cambridge course finished, commencing tutoring within two days. I realised how much I had changed in the 12 months away, no longer interested in a job at the bottom of the academic ladder, confident and capable of great things. At Cambridge a feminist course with Carol Smart, one of the United Kingdom's leading feminist theoreticians, and readings in women's and sociology courses all made more obvious the structures of power and dominance in society. Issues of class, race and gender I now saw as intertwined. Writing up my 1983 fieldwork in Cambridge as *The 'Civilising Mission': Race and the Construction of Crime* I began to see my personal experience as part of a broader canvas. Middle-aged, middle- and upper-class white males had an almost exclusive stranglehold on the elite positions in Western society. I was an 'outsider' on a number of counts. My energy focused on whether it was possible to work to bring about change within the university and the wider society.

I was an 'outsider' on a number of counts.

Within weeks of my return to Monash in 1984 I took on a 15-month project in curriculum development of issues concerning 'Aborigines and migrants' for the law course. The work was full-time and the salary minuscule, some thousands below the tutor's salary I was receiving.

Knowing that curriculum was best developed in a teaching context, I teamed up with Maria Barbayannis. Collaboration worked well. Maria covered the 'orthodox' bits of the course, I introduced new materials. I was introducing an Australian perspective into the law course. Instead of the focus being on the British heritage and British law, I focused on the original indigenous systems of law, their displacement and the development of a culturally plural society. I went further, linking into work being done by the Committee to Review Australian Studies in Tertiary Education (CRASTE). After I had shown drafts of my curriculum materials (using my own money to pay for five trips to Canberra), the committee recommended to the Education Minister, Senator Susan Ryan, that the government finance an expansion of my work into a book. The funding was part of the Bicentennial program. Kay Daniels (of *Uphill all the Way* fame) and Humphrey McQueen (a political scientist) were particularly encouraging, being great supporters through to completion. The CRASTE committee members indicated that as long as I was writing the book it did not matter where it was done. However the Dean at Monash was adamant that the grant be controlled by the university, saying it would protect me as the university would force the Commonwealth to relinquish its copyright in my work to the university. The Dean was concerned that the government might use its copyright power to suppress publication of my work. He wanted control over research to be in the university's hands rather than in the funding body. While I sympathise with this political stand, on a personal level I was later to regret this 'protection', as it left me little leeway for negotiating.

My contract stated that a steering committee would have final control over the content of the book. In an open committee meeting the Dean said this was to prevent my 'damaging the faculty's reputation'. In spite of the 'final control' dictum I was determined not to accept any interference in writing the book and this did not become a problem.

There were difficulties with my being acknowledged as a pivotal point of the enterprise. My success at approaching funding bodies and gaining their support through showing my work and communicating my enthusiasm was downgraded. My role was to be the subsidiary one of 'producing the research' under faculty control. Again I had shown an aptitude for raising research grants, which was seen as a 'male' area of activity.

Because the faculty held copyright in my work it was a party to the contract. The faculty instead of the author received the royalties. Not normal, but it did not particularly bother me. However I was infuriated with the clause that gave the faculty a role in nominating the person who could do the second edition. After getting legal advice this clause was deleted and I was given first option to prepare a second edition. During this stressful period a senior male colleague took me aside and said: 'You are not looking so peaches and cream lately. Are you sure you want to keep working full-time?'

Before finishing the book I approached the Office of Multicultural Affairs tendering as a consultant for the policy options overview paper in law. The tender was accepted. Two male colleagues, close friends of mine, warned against taking on the consultancy: I could damage my reputation through short time-lines, and what of the 'poor pay'? The pay was in fact much higher than the faculty had ever paid me, almost, but not quite, the rate my advisor was earning! I was learning to make my own decisions. While writing the policy paper I also proofread the galleys for my book and prepared for an intensive residential course I had agreed to give at Gippsland Institute on 'Kooris and the Law'.

The policy options paper was widely circulated and favourably received. *The Role of Law as it Operates in a Multicultural Society* argued for structural change in the legal system to include the 'outsiders', those who were not middle-aged, middle-class, male anglo-Australians.

Friends in Canberra informed me of the Department of Employment, Education and Training (DEET)'s plans to establish centres to develop cross-cultural curriculum materials. The Minister expressed a wish that the funding be tied to institutions rather than individuals, but it was understood the grants were for individuals with a proven track record to continue working in the field. Monash University made a submission, without reference to my name. Canberra was well aware I was the person with the 'proven track record' upon whom the submission depended.

Melbourne University also applied for the funding and included my name, stating they would appoint me if successful. Disappointed with the handling of the Monash submission I agreed. Asked by Canberra where I would be prepared to work, I replied: 'I could work with *both* of them.' The grant, $262 000 over three years, came through to both universities.

Monash then advertised a full-time or part-time director's position, a research fellow's position and a research assistant. The director's salary was 'negotiable'. I applied for the full-time director's position. On the night before the interview, friends 'rehearsed' the job interview with me. I was told to walk into the room in a masculine fashion, with my hands thrust deep into my pockets. When asked why I ought to get the job I was to say loudly 'because I'm the best'. I walked confidently into the interview. I was asked would I work as research fellow under a male colleague as director. This angered me. After years of hard work on short-term, poorly paid contracts, steadily building up a reputation in the field, I did not need somebody to provide 'direction'. I had published two books, a government policy paper and established a profile as leading scholar in the field. I refused to consider the research fellow position. Later that day I was offered the director's position, but was told 'the salary is not negotiable, you will be paid the advertised research fellow salary'. The funding was for three years, so I sought a three-year contract, subject to funding. This was refused. I received a 12-month contract.

I was a Director of a Centre. There were few role models within the university. Dr Eve Fesl, Director of the Koori Research Centre at Monash, was particularly supportive, helping me to realise that in the university setting the showing of my 'soft' feminine side, displayed by my willingness to share my feelings of insecurity and vulnerability with male colleagues, was an open invitation to people to make life difficult and justify it by regarding me as not tough enough. As a male colleague said to me on learning I had been appointed director: 'I just hope you survive.'

The bureaucratic battles continued. The grant was for salaries and travel only, with the universities expected to provide infrastructure. There was money for a part-time secretary but no money for a computer or printer. The faculty refused to supply an answering machine. Work was held up for lack of basic office equipment. Finally an application to the Monash Development Fund provided money for office equipment, including filing cabinets and chairs. By the time the equipment arrived the first year was almost up.

In July 1989 the Prime Minister launched the National Agenda for a Multicultural Australia. The Agenda included a reference to the Australian

Law Reform Commission on 'Law and Multiculturalism'. I applied, along with more than one hundred other people, for the position of commissioner to work on the reference. Notification of my appointment arrived in February 1990. The colleague who had said the director's salary was not negotiable approached me: 'How much of your salary will this free up for the centre?' he queried. I decided at that moment that I would stay on full-time and not 'free up' any of my salary.

> I considered I was making a worthwhile contribution to legal education.

I had by now been promoted to Senior Research Fellow. The continual fight for personal survival was, however, becoming wearing. There was delight in the centre's achievement, and in writing progress reports for DEET and the centre's board of management. Reviewing the work, I considered I was making a worthwhile contribution to legal education. I had visited every state in Australia stimulating interest in cross-cultural curriculum design and had had a deal of success. In 1990 the centre reached its third year of funding so I applied for further DEET funding. The colleague whose name was put forward for the directorship put in a competing submission on behalf of the faculty. My submission was successful.

Looking back on this 21-year period in academia, it is difficult to determine whether men or women have been more supportive. Very few of the women have been in senior positions, though this is now changing. While I was content with a tutor's position I had a great deal of warmth and active encouragement from people of both sexes at all levels in the hierarchy. Once I had undertaken the degree at Cambridge I became more self-confident and interested in a 'real career', rather than in playing a supportive role to other people's careers. The attitudes and behaviour of some of my colleagues changed. I wanted to be treated as an equal by people higher in the hierarchy, because I felt I was their equal in intellectual capacity, hard work and dedication. My lower position in the salary scale was connected to time spent mothering, rather than any inferiority. However some people were obstructive when I wanted plain recognition. With ego stroking I could possibly have achieved it with much less pain.

Not only was my work a challenge to 'the way things had always been done', my way of operating was 'unorthodox'. Brought up without the 'benefits' of middle-class thought and speech patterns and without any inside knowledge of workplace politics I made decisions and acted without forming alliances in the faculty. I spoke my mind plainly. I chose to teach and research in fields that attracted me because I believed that through the work I would, in some small way, alter the balance of power in society by empowering 'outsiders'.

I do not want to paint too pessimistic a picture. As the years went by I found a network of like-minded people in universities and colleges throughout Australia and in the public service. Unfortunately their numbers in any institution are small and they do not form a critical mass sufficient to alter the culture of the institution. We are good friends, especially in times of adversity, and are making an impact on Australian society. Hopefully as more women are appointed at senior levels, the position for women in universities will improve dramatically.

I am aware that had I confronted the difficulties of my past years with the wisdom and strength I now have, my behaviour and my perceptions would be different. To a great extent my lack of confidence and a desire to lead a 'quiet life' contributed to the way colleagues related to me. I am optimistic about the future and feel a great deal of affection for Monash, the university where I 'grew up'.

Over all these years my husband has been supportive; my two daughters, now 18 and 19, are great mates. 'Keep it up mum' they say: 'You're doing this for all women.'

PART III

Breaking the Barriers

NOT FOR THE MONEY

Melba Marginson

Melba Marginson is a Filipina married to an Australian national. As Melba de Guzman, Melba was a familiar name in the popular movement for change in the Philippines. In Australia, Melba Marginson continues her activist work, devoting her energies to organising Filipina victims of domestic violence, organising support groups and lobbying for the empowerment of Filipinas in the Australian community. She is spokesperson of the Collective of Filipinas for Empowerment and Development (CFED) and national co-ordinator of the Centre for Philippine Concerns – Australia.

My development as a woman activist was to be expected. The life I chose to pursue eventually led to it.

Both my parents came from Central Luzon, the hotbed of the HUK rebellion, a peasant resistance which was perhaps the most important and certainly the largest social uprising in modern Philippine history. Its roots go back to smaller uprisings and scattered incidents of peasant anger early in the twentieth century. By the 1930s, discontent had grown to a rage that united a few hundred peasants in the rice and sugar producing plains of Central Luzon. This widespread unrest developed into a rebellion between 1946 and the 1950s.

Like other peasant families in Central Luzon, my parents' families led a life of fear and uncertainty before, during and after the Second World War. They were targets in the massive witch-hunting of suspected peasant subversives, widely branded as Communists by, at different times, the Americans, the Japanese and the Philippine military.

My father's father was witch-hunted for joining the Sakdalistas, a peasant uprising before the war. My mother's brothers were targets too. It was during the war that one of them was executed by the Japanese soldiers who killed Filipinos by the dozens on mere suspicion that they were HUKs.

Even after the war the Philippine government, in close collaboration with the United States of America government, continued to pursue the HUKs because they knew that this peasant-based rebel group had expanded its membership widely during its fight against the Japanese. Philippine historians are at one in the analysis that had it not been for the HUKs, the Americans would not have won the war against the Japanese in the Philippines.

This was the political environment that compounded the misery of the already marginalised families of my parents, and of all peasant families in Central Luzon. This was the main reason for my father's family deciding to transfer to Mindoro after the war, a province separated by water from the southern tip of Luzon.

Both my parents learned to become independent from their families as soon as they reached adolescence. They saw that life in the country was poor and slow, so they decided to try their luck in Manila. To many Filipinos after the Second World War, Manila was the land of opportunities.

My mother was an enterprising woman. She had a small dry goods store in Manila from which she earned sufficient money to send her youngest brother to school. Filipino families, like other patriarchal families, invest more in the male siblings than in the females.

My mother was an enterprising woman.

My father left his family during his teens to study fine arts in Manila. He took odd jobs while studying but finally quit studying when he got a regular job as an advertising painter.

When my parents decided to marry in 1950, the Philippines was beginning to feel the pangs of its economic ties with the United States. The country was swamped with duty-free, non-essential American commodities, and war damage payments went mainly to rehabilitate American companies and import–export interests. A balance of payments crisis produced inflation and increased unemployment. Prices of goods went up to almost eight times the pre-war level, vastly eroding the workers' purchasing power. Fifteen percent of the available workforce was unemployed.

My life as a child in the 1950s was nothing extraordinary. I learned to help my mother look after the two boys who were born after me, Ramon and Danilo. The first, Ramon, was two years younger than I. Later, my sister Sally and then two more boys followed. This may be large compared to an average Australian family but, in the Philippines, this size is average.

My family's financial situation became fairly auspicious. With a bit of trading skill and a lot of industriousness, my parents established a dry goods store and a tailoring shop which prospered, giving them enough money to start other small-scale businesses. Subsequently, life was better. We were sent to private Catholic schools. I went to an exclusive school for girls. There, I fared well. I was an honours student from primary school and through to graduation at second from the top in fourth year high school (equivalent to Year 12 in Australia).

I matured early. This made it easier to acquire a deeper understanding of the issues of our time. I had developed self-confidence easily. I felt on par with the opposite gender. Being the eldest in a family of four boys and spending 14 years in a girls' school might have contributed. Another factor indirectly affecting me was my mother's dominance in the economic activities of the family.

After completing secondary school in 1970, I passed the admission tests of the premier university in the country, the University of the Philippines. This university played a significant role in my political development.

> **I felt on par with the opposite gender.**

The major international issue during the late 1960s and early 1970s was the American intervention in Viet Nam. Throughout the world, the 1960s also saw a resurgence of student activism, particularly in the United States, South Korea, China, Mexico and France.

Faced with a crushed peasant resistance and a government that proved itself to be another instrument of United States imperialism, the anti-imperialist struggle in the Philippines shifted to the middle class sectors — the teachers, students, businessmen and other professionals — with the sympathetic support of the mass organisations of peasants and workers.

Starting in the 1960s, the University of the Philippines (UP) became the hotbed of student activism. Inspired by the revolutions in Central America, Asia and Africa, the radical literature of Marx and Lenin, and the nationalist writings of Filipino leaders like Senators Claro M. Recto and Lorenzo Tanada, UP students were to become key figures in the continuing struggle for nationalism and democracy in the Philippines. From the campuses of the 1960s, this activism would find itself in the factories, fields, churches, communities, and later on in the mountains, waging a protracted people's war.

When I came to UP in 1970, the atmosphere was dynamic. Many organisations represented a wide spectrum of differing radical left-wing Kabataang Makabayan (Nationalist Youths). As well, women's groups existed across the political spectrum.

Faced with unabated economic crises, unsolvable because of subservience to United States foreign policy, and driven by his own unquenchable greed for wealth, President Marcos was unable to run the country without resorting to violence. Mass demonstrations almost daily in Manila and outlying provinces were met with teargas and beatings by club-wielding riot police. The more the state used violence to stop the protests, the bigger the demonstrations became. Later, students were not only beaten and bashed; they were also fired at indiscriminately.

I came to UP after the violent demonstrations of January 1970. Consciousness of the 'red menace' was widespread among Catholic schools during that time and I was naturally fearful of the radicals. However, other Catholic school-bred students were recognising the futility of peaceful demonstrations. These were the moderates who joined the January 1970 demonstrations and experienced state violence.

As could be expected, I chose to join the UP Student Catholic Action. It was becoming militant and more left wing as the dominant nationalist student movement on campus succeeded in influencing a growing number of moderate students. I began joining mass demonstrations. My interest in theatre also led to my involvement in 'street theatre', the most effective form of protest theatre during that time.

My participation in street politics was short-lived. In September 1971, President Marcos declared martial law in the country. Hundreds, including government officials critical of Marcos, were arrested. In two years, more than 50 000 would be detained.

The Congress was padlocked, and so were all major newspapers and broadcast stations. On campuses known to be centres of activism, military checkpoints were set up and military agents were deployed to monitor activities. All student organisations were banned. Left-wing activists went underground.

All student organisations were banned.

There was a lull in student activities for more than a year. I went back to serious studies. In my drama classes, my drama professor continued to vent his nationalist aspirations and criticisms of the government. My classmates and I began a theatre company as venue for student protest in the campus under the restrictions of martial law. The theatre company brought me closer to the exploited masses through our travelling performances. We staged Filipino plays tackling poverty and state violence. At first, the university officials and military agents were unmindful of our stage plays. However, the growing numbers of our regular audience caused suspicion. Our drama professor was arrested and detained for three months. In his absence, we continued our theatre activities. By that time, other student organisations had been established so the surveillance by military agents was diverted from us.

I completed my tertiary degree in October 1975. By that time, I was deeply involved in theatre so my natural affiliation was with a community-based theatre organisation. We performed in depressed communities while organising community theatre groups. These experiences played a strong role in raising my political consciousness.

In 1976, I was accepted as an instructor in a government secondary school. There I established a drama group for students which became the target of surveillance by the military intelligence officer in the campus. I was sent for interrogation to the NISA, the country's intelligence unit. I was accused of being a MAKIBAKA member during my university days. MAKIBAKA was the leading organisation of women activists that went underground after martial law. I had not been a member, so I denied the accusation. I was also accused of being treasurer of the theatre company during university days, and told that the money we earned from our performances was sent to the New People's Army, the armed group of the Communist Party of the Philippines. Again, this was not true, so I denied it. These sorts of interrogations were aimed at intimidating public servants, especially public teachers like me. Though I did not lose my job, the directress of our school and other right-wing teachers at school took turns harassing me. I had around me supportive students and co-teachers, so I ignored the pressures.

Simultaneously, my community involvement was deepening my aspirations to serve the people. I resigned from teaching. It had been fulfilling for me but, as well as guiding students toward a nationalist view of their country, I thought I would be more useful to society if I integrated with the exploited classes.

Through community contacts, I began assisting workers in their education courses for genuine unionism. It was an enriching experience. I learned to live a simple life, sleeping on mats or wooden or hard cement floors. Food was always a combination of rice, fish and vegetables. Meat was only for special occasions. Men shared household work with women. Comradeship was strong among us because of the collective life we led. In other words, we had shed the lifestyle of the bourgeoisie.

Even in these communities, monitoring of workers union activities was conducted by the military in collaboration with the owners of the industrial companies. Close association with the workers made me an easy target for surveillance. After eight months my collective and I had to leave our rented house because we were informed that our house would be raided the next day by military agents.

My family sent me to a relative's home to cool the 'heat'. After four months in hiding, I surfaced by returning to teaching. Mass work, to my mind, could also be done in organising teachers and students.

In 1982 I taught in a college for dental and medical students. The following year, Cory Aquino's late husband Benigno Aquino was assassinated. Protest demonstrations were held almost every day. I encouraged my students to attend the rallies. In the meantime, I became a member of the Alliance of Concerned Teachers — Philippines, a militant teachers' union in the country. I was elected secretary-general of the union in 1985 and resigned from teaching to devote myself to full-time work in the union.

It was in the teachers' union that I was able to maximise my talents and skills while at the same time expanding my horizons. My awareness of gender issues became more pronounced. Of the 15 to 17 board members of the union, 40 percent were women. The union's membership then was around 50 000 — 85 percent of whom were women. The chairperson was a man. As secretary-general, I undertook various responsibilities which widened my influence and power. Further, I became popular with the media. Little did I suspect that some men in the union were uncomfortable with this. The chairperson would support me only if I were subordinate to him. The height of his sexist treatment occurred during an international conference of teachers in Melbourne when he and another male officer ganged up against me on the issue of who among us should run for a position in the Asia—Pacific Committee of the international federation. He ran and, as I expected, lost the position.

Although I survived four years as secretary-general, the fifth year proved disastrous. My male detractors used a past personal relationship to destroy me in the eyes of some of the members. They even pressured me to resign from my position five months before the next elections. Given I was democratically elected by the assembly, I refused to resign. Some male and all female members of the secretariat were behind me. The regional leaderships, amongst which I had strong support, were generally confused. My detractors used every means to wage war against me by sowing intrigues in the regions. I continued to function but with extreme difficulty because of the sabotaging efforts of my male detractors. At that time, I was already engaged to be married to Australian Simon Marginson, so the prospect of leaving the organisation and settling in Australia was the most viable option for me. A week before the elections, I submitted to the union board a letter expressing lack of interest in running for any position because of my plan to settle in Australia.

On 31 July 1990 I arrived in Australia to join Simon. The first community issue that welcomed me was the death of Gene Bongcodin at the hands of her Maltese Australian husband. I went to the burial, attended largely by the Filipino community. I took interest in the case, joining the community organisation that was collecting donations for Gene's family in the Philippines. Invited to attend the organisation's tribute to Gene Bongcodin, I volunteered to read an excerpt from a play about the sad plight of mail-order brides in Australia.

To understand more deeply the phenomenon of mail-order brides and its related issue of domestic violence became an obsession. I obtained several Australian studies that had been done on the issue. Having developed the skill in handling campaigns on specific issues while a teacher unionist, I directed the 'Justice for Gene Bongcodin' campaign which the Filipino community had initiated. My new position as media officer of the Philippine Resource Centre proved to be strategic for the campaign.

In January of 1990, I was granted a scholarship to the Deakin Women's

Studies Summer School through the kindness of Robyn Rowland, senior lecturer and social psychologist, who has been instrumental in bringing political issues surrounding new reproductive technologies and genetic engineering before public, academic and scientific forums. The summer school broadened my understanding of feminism and its relationship to racism, ethnicity, class and gender. My association with different types of feminists in the course contributed much to my increasing respect for women as a gender. Several women teachers and students have continued to support me in my work, even after the course. They include Jenny Coate, lawyer, Jan Pettman of the Australian National University (ANU) peace studies centre and several women from my class.

Following the summer school, I gave a talk about the Filipino Women's Movement proposing that a women's group should be at the helm of any campaign on women's issues such as that of Gene Bongcodin. The audience agreed, and a group formed, now organised under the title of Collective of Filipinas for Empowerment and Development (CFED).

CFED and SAMPA (the Filipino group which spearheaded the Bongcodin case) together followed up the case until its resolution on the 9 July 1990, exactly a year after the murder of Gene. On that day, Charles Schembri, the late Gene's ex-husband, was sentenced to eight years imprisonment, with a non-parole period of five and a half years. It was a plea bargain, him pleading guilty to manslaughter, not murder. We protested on the steps of the Supreme Court against this injustice. For the first time, the Australian public saw the Filipino community led by women who questioned the Australian legal system's sense of fairness to women and especially to Filipinas. I was particularly touched by the support from the women journalists and broadcasters.

As a 'career woman' who has found her work in political movements for freedom of the working people, and particularly the Women's Movement, and succeeded in paidwork of my own choice, I have never been paid sufficiently for my work. I do it for love of country, not for the money. Money has been and is a means to be mobile without being hampered by lack of transport and food. I realised my political work was 'career' only when I started becoming sufficiently well known in the Philippines that my credentials as a teacher/leader were enough for me to get teaching jobs in some universities. (This meant I was paid while I kept my political work as my primary involvement.) Other people played a significant part in the development of my work, my perspective, and my career. I had role models in the past, but I never consciously modelled myself on them. Some observers have said that Etta Rosales, the first chairperson of the teachers' union which I served as secretary-general for almost five years, and I share similar styles of work and public speaking. At times I was fondly called 'Etta Junior' by some comrades in the popular movement.

Women have been consistently supportive to my ideas. I am rich with women friends in the Philippines and Australia. During periods of depression, I have only to call any one of them and they're available to cheer me up, keep me company, or guide me towards better understanding of myself. In the same way, I am available to them. I also work very well with and find support from men who accept gender equality and who value women's contributions, but never with patriarchal men or men who are obsessed with power. Because my personality and style of work exhibit assertiveness, such men find me threatening.

The greatest pleasure in my political life comes from watching a person change her or his view of the world from the metaphysical to the dialectical. Part of this process is that person's increasing empowerment, through linking her/his actions to a larger community. In Australia, our success in reversing the Filipina image through our Bongcodin campaign has given me a strong sense of achievement. Prior to the protests that culminated on 9 July 1990 in front of the Supreme Court, the Victorian public's image of the Filipina was of either a manipulative mail-order bride, docile domestic helper or a wandering prostitute. These negative images were largely created by the media, by Australian companies which send their workers to the Philippines for holidays as a form of incentive, and by Australian males who go on sex tours. After the protests, a different type of Filipina emerged —courageous, strong, militant, articulate.

> Our success in reversing the Filipina image has given me a strong sense of achievement.

I don't see myself as ambitious because I do not aspire for success in my political work for myself. I am happiest when I see other Filipinas developing as leaders too. I am most sad if I am left doing the work alone: it not only burns a person out but it is bad organising. I am ambitious for the institutionalisation of our gains in the women's sector. I want to establish a Filipina collective in every Australian suburb (and the world over) where there is a concentration of Filipinas. I want to set up a community centre for Filipino facilities which Filipinas can use for their education, assistance and work for disadvantaged women. I want to publish a magazine or newsletter for women which will not only become an instrument for educating them but will also harness their talents. I want to form a cultural group that will hone Filipinas' talents for the propagation of a Filipino-Australian culture.

If I have children, I hope to pass on to them my aspirations as a Filipina in an Australian setting. To the minimum, I wish our child to be a girl or, if the child happens to be the opposite, I wish him to be a staunch supporter of women like his father.

Even in my old age, I intend to continue my political work. It is my greatest dream to help in the reconstruction of my country. I'll probably settle in the Philippines when the political conditions there permit. Specifically, I'll work for the continued emancipation of women. My feminism is central to my political work. Now I am convinced that Filipino women have to simultaneously free themselves as they pursue national liberation. Genuine national liberation can occur only when women are liberated from gender and patriarchal oppression.

BUT YOU COULDN'T POSSIBLY ...!

Jackie Huggins

On 19 August 1956 Jackie Huggins was born in Ayr, North Queensland. She completed a Bachelor of arts at the University of Queensland, and has worked in the federal public service. In 1989 she completed an Honours Degree in history/women's studies and a Diploma of education at Flinders University in South Australia. In 1990 she made a conscious decision to spend some years writing, and in particular writing a biography of her mother, as well as working on Aboriginal history and Aboriginal women's activism.

In November 1958 Jack Huggins died of a massive heart attack in Ayr, North Queensland. Jack had been a prisoner of war in Burma/Thailand, one of the many Aboriginal men who had fought and died for their country while back home their children were being denied access to a full education, atrocities were occurring daily against Aboriginal people, and Aboriginal people were not even citizens of their own country. At age 38 Jack died and was not afforded the status of an australian citizen.

In the 1940s Jack was possibly the first Aboriginal person to hold a position in the post office, a rare sight to see a Black man in any public office in those days. Rita and Jack's union produced three children. Jackie is the middle one. Rita also had two daughters by a previous relationship.

I came from a single-parent household which possessed a very strong Mother. She instilled into us the importance of pride in Aboriginality, to fight to overcome racism and other injustices, to be proud of who we were and never duck into a corner and hide it, to deal with white people as if we were equal to them, involving children in Aboriginal activities from a young age.

My early childhood was 'ordinarily' Aboriginal but 'differently' anglo-wise. Different, because we were not 'anglo-australian'. Ordinary because many Aboriginal families are single-parent families and we are all one big family.

Rita returned to Brisbane in 1959, after Jack's death, to the comfort of her extended family network. The extended family provided solace for her grief and an anchor for her children. Without this Jack's loss would have been more devastating to her. Rita thus became a 'war widow' and has received a pension all her life.

My father's death influenced my life more than I ever realised. He died from war injuries inflicted in a needless war, and before he could witness some of the more positive steps taken to address the injustices to Aboriginal people. There was the 1967 federal Referendum, recognising (for the first time in anglo-australian history) Aboriginal people as citizens; the Northern Territory Land Rights cases and many other historical events.

Throughout my life my driving force has always been my Aboriginality in whatever I do. I am nurtured and guided by it. My foremost identity is as an Aboriginal. My family gave me a strong and proud upbringing and reinforcement that to be Aboriginal was the greatest honour in the world. We just had to educate other people into believing this was true.

I've wanted to 'be' many things. Perhaps it has been too many things to too many people which has impeded some of my progress: when offers come up I see them as equally important and find it hard to say no.

Whilst all my immediate family have a keen sense of pride in their Aboriginality, I am the most public and outspoken member. I've sought out, and followed through, opportunities coming my way. My political activism has been my identity; commitment to my people and community, my entire existence.

I knew I'd be working in some field/s of Aboriginal affairs as I could not be a whole person if I didn't. (As a child, I had fantasies of being an air-hostess, a paper boy and a ballerina— of all things! and I thank God those ideas never came to fruition.)

Two strong Black women have been my role models: my Mother, instilling me with the fight and determination to succeed, and my cousin Lillian Holt. Lillian, eleven years older than I, was a fighter in Aboriginal affairs long before it was fashionable. As a young girl I admired her immensely, her wisdom, strength, tenacity, good humour and unconditional willingness to share all her hopes, fears and aspirations about the plight of our people. With much pride I say I didn't need to look outside my family to find role models.

From the time I was born I have been political. Aboriginal people are born political. Political awareness and action is a way of life. I could not hide, nor did I ever want to hide the fact that I was Aboriginal and always knew who and what I am. Perhaps the greatest influence in my life has come from many bigoted people who have low expectations of my race. It's the rising above that I find the greatest liberating force.

In Year 10 at high school I saw the senior mistress to discuss future schooling and other vocational options. I told her I'd like to complete Year 12. She laughed: 'Oh but you couldn't possibly do that!' My grades were good and I was taken aback. Bewildered I asked why not. 'Because you're Aboriginal and Aboriginals have got no brains.' I felt dehumanised and powerless. At 15 years old I had neither the words nor guts to challenge her. What a different story it would be today. I crawled out of the office, my dreams shattered. She erected a stumbling block in my psyche which remained for 11 years: I thought I was too dumb to achieve any scholastic accomplishments.

At 26 years I enrolled at the University of Queensland. I began to receive high distinctions. I realised I was not dumb or biologically mentally inferior to non-Aboriginals, and grew to love my studies and the challenge of university. I graduated BA (Hons) in history and women's studies, going on to complete a Diploma of education. So many young Aboriginal people have been discouraged because others don't see their goals as achievable and equal to others. My story is not an isolated case, it's happened and continues to happen through people's notions of vast superiority over Blacks. It is this concern that largely motivates my work. To prove that we are just as good and even better than most.

> So many young Aboriginal people have been discouraged because others don't see their goals as achievable and equal to others.

Brisbane became home. The extended family left the Cherbourg Aboriginal Reserve (which was in the heart, or should I say thorn, of the old Bjelke-Petersen electorate of Barambah) for the greater freedoms of city life and employment. Rita's motivation was to return from Ayr to the strong institution of assistance, love and stability of her family after her husband's death.

Aboriginals in Brisbane faced difficulties being 'newcomers' and were primarily rural or small town and reserve people moving into an urban area. In addition, Aboriginals also faced racial prejudice and discrimination. My family moved house 14 times in three years, due largely to discrimination by landlords and their intolerance to the sharing of homes with transient relatives and friends. The house where we now live has been a family home for 18 years. My brother owns it but works in Cairns. It has provided much stability and comfort for two generations of families. It is the longest time in a place that the family has ever lived; our home is cherished.

Every few years I like to go 'walkabout' to recharge my batteries, to a place where I am not well known within the Aboriginal community and where I can find some space to do what I deem personally fulfilling like studying, writing and working. This is necessary because, amongst other stresses, many community expectations are placed upon Aboriginal people who are successful and educated in the western sense. Demands to render assistance, such as writing submissions, organising conferences, lecturing to recruits, sitting on committees, talking to groups, are pressed upon Aboriginal people more so in their local communities than elsewhere.

I survive by breaking away to another city. When I enter another state the pressure is immediately lifted. There's more autonomy and less ties to my mob. Nonetheless Brisbane is my home and the centre to which I gravitate. My family is also here and I miss my community and other Queensland Murries (Aboriginals) if I am away too long.

In 1978 and 1979 I worked for the National Aboriginal Council (NAC) secretariat in Canberra. In 1984 it was Canberra again, in the Department of Aboriginal Affairs (DAA), and in 1988 and 1989 I studied at Flinders University in Adelaide. The moves have been well timed. In 1988 I had to escape from Queensland during the Bicentennial because I couldn't stand the hype and hypocrisy associated with the celebrations. Being somewhere else I could become a recluse. I tried hard to ignore it and concentrate on the 50 000 plus years of Dreaming rather than the 200 years of nightmares following colonisation.

> **I survive by breaking away to another city.**

A magical highlight of my life was participating in the Aboriginal march in Sydney, January 1988. An overwhelming sense of pride engulfed me that day. I woke up with bursting emotions, as if I were standing on the shore the day Phillip and the 'First Fleet' arrived, or even when Captain Cook set foot. I said to one of the four Aboriginal sisters who had travelled down with me from Brisbane: 'Do you feel how I do?' With tears in her eyes she said: 'Exactly.' We needed no more words to know we felt the same emotion. Our non-verbals magically described the whole scene.

We marched that day for our ancestors and for the generations to come. When we turned the corner into Belmore Park, a huge sea of non-Aboriginal, white, Asian and South American faces were ready to take the baton and march with us. We marched proudly in solidarity in the colours of black, yellow and red, never before realising the number of our supporters. The media reports stated only 20 000 marched. It was more like 60 000. Aboriginal people came in droves, the best way they could manage, from thousands of miles around australia. The solidarity that Invasion Day turned my mourning into joy for once and has given me great hope for the future and our children.

Establishing the new office of Indigenous Women in the old Department of Aboriginal Affairs — now ATSIC (the Aboriginal and Torres Strait Islanders Commission) has been my greatest achievement. I headed a national unit comprising 50 Commonwealth Employment Program (CEP) Aboriginal and Islander women to assess the needs of women, youth and children throughout australia. A 100 page report specified the needs and concerns of Aboriginal and Islander women in australia. Permanent positions were then created in DAA regional, area and head offices.

At DAA my duties were to direct and control the Aboriginal Women's Unit; formulate and develop aims, objectives and policies in respect of the social development of Aboriginal women and children; assist in ensuring that the department's functional programs reflect the needs and concerns of Aboriginal women and children; co-ordinate the development and implementation of appropriate programs and strategies; undertake appropriate investigations and analyses of policy issues. During 1984 I travelled extensively throughout australia to attend and advise Aboriginal women's groups in setting up their own organisations. Highly visible and growing numbers of Aboriginal and Islander women's organisations now exist within community and bureaucratic structures. They cater to the aspirations of our women and children. Women's units are now established in government departments such as the Department of Social Security (DSS) and the Department of Employment, Education and Training (DEET).

The white men in DAA put obstacles in the way. It was a fight every day to educate the whites in the place that Aboriginal women had vital statements to make about health, housing, education, employment and areas which required attention. Of the 50 women employed, about five had tertiary experience, ten had been employed before, and the rest were previously on pensions or benefits, involved in home-duties and had limited education. With a crew like this the white staff thought it was doomed to fail. It didn't. It's still there — thriving.

Simultaneously with our project, the Office of the Status of Women employed other Aboriginal women to perform a similar task. I suspected this duplication was designed to create havoc, fighting and non-productivity between the two bodies. However the competition served only to extract the best possible information from women in the field. The thoroughness of this information was published in *Women's Business*. Overseeing the Aboriginal Women's Task Force was an all-Aboriginal Women's Steering Committee of which I was a member. The hard slog and the solidarity of all women who worked with me in the AWU will always be remembered. The innovative nature of our job meant we had to be the pioneers. We began with nothing. It was a milestone for Black women.

> The innovative nature of our job meant we had to be the pioneers.

Many people have told me that they see me as 'an expert on Aboriginal affairs'. I feel humble, but I guess they say this because I have a broad-based knowledge of what is happening in Aboriginal affairs and keep up with contemporary events. I see myself as a multi-faceted and multi-talented person and an advocate for Aboriginal people. Other people see me as a role model for Aboriginals, particularly young Black women who have aspirations of working in community affairs. They see that I have done much along the way: establishing community-based organisations, organising the First

International Indigenous Women's Conference, completing tertiary studies, achieving a high position in the public service, writing articles in journals and chapters in history books, membership of national and state Aboriginal advisory boards.

Out of all this, the most important aspect of my life is other Aboriginal people and their existence in this country. My greatest achievement came at a time when I knew we could accomplish great things. I was relatively young — 27 years of age, and full of energy — when I worked in Canberra as the National Co-ordinator, Aboriginal Women's Unit (AWU). A precedent was established where a government department was prepared to look at the specific needs of Aboriginal and Islander women, then turn them into policy.

Today I am writing my mother's biography. My plan is to write for five years about Aboriginal history/affairs/women's issues. My political activism is unpaid, but unstoppable. I cannot write in isolation as I need to be in touch with Aboriginal issues. I'm on several committees both state and federal — health, employment, prisoners, women. The most exciting is my appointment to the Legislation Review Committee which will provide recommendations for legislative alterations to enable Aboriginal and Torres Strait Islander Communities to manage and control their own destinies. Study has been postponed. Offers to speak to conferences, classes and gatherings, and to participate in cross-cultural workshops and give lectures are ever increasing. I have been declining more and more. I am not the only articulate Black around; nor do I speak for all Blacks which is sometimes the expectation that burdens Aboriginal speakers.

> My political activism is unpaid, but unstoppable.

My life now is a natural progression of my experiences in childhood and growing up. It's a new direction that we, Aboriginal women, are taking and directing: challenging white feminists about what the Women's Movement's exclusion of us has meant, issues of race, propriety of knowledge, and information. It also means looking at ways in which we can form alliances with each other.

At school I felt different because other kids never saw or liaised with their relations very often; they didn't stay in crowded houses; they didn't know what it was like to wear one dress to school every day and what it was like to go without food. The older I got the more 'different' I felt from other people. It was a growing political awareness to feel I was different. It was also a strength and a comfort to know I wasn't the same as everyone else. Some differences are creative and should be respected for what they are. The colour of my skin and my Aboriginal features are integral components of my identity. There are beautiful aspects of my culture like sharing, non-competitiveness, non-materialism, respect for others as human beings which I never saw reciprocated in anglo society. I never wanted to be white because my dignity and spirit would be dead.

In my political activism I have not felt different from other Aboriginal people. But when engaging in debates about feminism I feel very different from Aboriginal people. The isolation of being the only Aboriginal woman at feminist and women's studies conferences is unbearable at times because I prefer the solidarity and group nature of Aboriginal society and sisterhood. I wish there were 'more troops in the hills' and reinforcements lining up but the signs are not encouraging.

I would like to see the Aboriginal history of our country taken seriously, significantly placing Aboriginal people and restoring their past to a respectful place. I would like to rid the world of racism and capitalism to make it a better place for us all. This means 'changing the world'. Yet it is hard to think globally. 'Changing australia' would be a good starting point.

I am a single mother with a six-year-old son. My Mother also lives with us. She and I have a wonderful relationship (when we're not fighting). Relatives and friends pass through staying with us. It's refreshing to receive news from other places about people. Working from home means I have flexibility. With my Mother's and sister's support I attend conferences, meetings and other important events. Their unconditional love and support nurtures me.

My activism is not restricted. On the contrary, it is becoming far broader. While many activities and actions I have undertaken have not been deliberate, I sense components are being channelled in particular directions. One concerns Aboriginal women's representations within the Women's Movement (that is, the exploration of race within the Movement), another my writing of Aboriginal women's history.

Given the opportunity, I would have studied at tertiary level much earlier in life, say five years. Then I would be five years advanced and ready for my next step. But I am laying the foundations for greater things to come. As for my community activities, I'll stay in them until I die, because they are my bloodline.

Life is a game of chance and I have been in the right place at the right time, and have given it 100 percent. Being thorough is what's important, and following through no matter how small something may appear because it could be a matter of life and death for others. We must fight against all oppressions, but we are usually stereotyped in those we know and feel the most: mine is racism against Aboriginals.

GENESIS — TENNANT CREEK

Sue Schmolke

Victorian-born, Sue Schmolke has spent the past 22 years in Australia's Northern Territory. In the 1980s she was appointed by the Chief Minister as convenor of the Territory's Women's Advisory Council. Sue Schmolke is known in the Northern Territory for her commitment to the life of the community and to raising awareness of women's issues in what is recognised as 'redneck' country.

My life began in Tennant Creek in the Northern Territory. Born in Melbourne, raised in Victoria, my life has been a series of circumstances — some that connected, others that did not — leading me to where I am now.

I have not had a 'career' — rather a succession of jobs, much the same, I suspect, as huge numbers of other women: from shop assistant, waitress, clerical office worker, receptionist in my early working life to the more dynamic and self-motivated roles that have come with added years. Now nearly 44 years old, I feel as if I am just starting to get my act together. Long ago I realised I would always be learning, growing and changing — nothing is predictable and certain. Especially if life is to be interesting!

I have always felt a nagging sense of personal failure in all aspects of my life — particularly with employment, professional skills and income. It is only in the past few years that I have realised that 'the system' has been stacked against me as a woman, and to have succeeded in the way I yearned for would have been a small miracle.

The oldest child in a family of three brothers and two struggling parents, I grew up with an understanding that somehow I would receive an education, get a good job and live a nice, secure life. I see this now as a hope by my parents

131

for something better for their child. At the time it was my reality. I worked hard at school (in the professional stream), did very well in matriculation and received scholarships for university study. At the time I could choose between attending the established Melbourne University or travelling by circuitous means to the closer, but fledgling, Monash University.

I embarked on my first momentous life-affecting major wrong decision — I say with the benefit of hindsight. I enrolled in a commerce degree at Melbourne University. Based on my lack of life experience and any knowledgeable advice and guidance, I chose the security of the established place of learning and the acceptability of the staid and safe discipline. After all, what do those arts students get up to and how useful will their degree be to them in getting a job? My decision to study commerce was based on school and social influences. At that time there was great optimism for the future. Opportunities existed for those who wanted to take them up — and there was an expectation that everyone would be gainfully employed, either in the workforce, or at home as a housewife. I only ever saw myself working in the workplace, for the whole of my life. If family was to come, I imagined that I would somehow juggle all aspects to fit together but I would keep working. So the practical world of commerce seemed to be the means to do something really interesting, make some money and do something different.

> I only ever saw myself working in the workplace, for the whole of my life.

I headed off to Melbourne University—unprepared for the reality and quite alone. One year on campus, and an attempt to do two failed subjects part-time, effectively ended my formal academic phase. I had been living away from my parents' home for some time. However, I was now on my own in a serious way — I had to earn a living.

In the 1960s jobs could be found relatively easily. But I was without the usual useful skills and interests of women. Most difficult of all was that I could not type. So I took myself to an evening course and acquired rudimentary office knowledge and the most basic typing skills. Typing has continued to strike terror in my heart, at least until the recent advent of word processors, with the option to correct and change before the final printout.

However, faced with what I saw as failure, I ran away. I entered a relationship and shortly after left to travel Australia. I had the usual range of jobs — housemaid, receptionist; I had the chance to see and experience some of this country's remote and rugged realities.

I discovered that the wandering life was not what I wanted. I was losing my connectedness with people and events. When man walked on the moon, I was living in isolation in outback Western Australia without the most basic form of radio communication and nearly 300 miles to the nearest town. I missed out on sharing that momentous occasion!

I found I hungered for the basics of city life — people, information, communication, libraries, electricity that was available at the flick of a switch, effective refrigeration and, my biggest craving, ice-cream. The total alone-ness of living on a remote property where I could see the horizon in three directions and a low range of hills in the other, and without the means to communicate with the outside world, was not for me. Yet this period of my life gave me valuable insights and experiences that I would call on in later years. If I hadn't done it then, I would always have had a hankering to 'see the rest of Australia'.

Next stop was Darwin and, 22 years later, I continue to live in the Northern Territory. Darwin felt good then, as it does now.

Yes, I started broke and at the bottom as always. We pitched our tent in a caravan park and looked for work. The wet season came and necessity forced us to hire a caravan. Eventually buying our own caravan marked a massive step forward in life and a huge financial commitment.

Darwin felt good then, as it does now.

Clerical and typing jobs followed. A move to Alice Springs brought total readjustment to new conditions, weather and setting out on making my life real to me. My son was born in Alice Springs and spent the first few months of his life in a Bureau of Mineral Resources bush camp 100 miles north of Alice Springs.

A move further north to Tennant Creek brought new challenges, trials — and comforts. The bliss of running water and connected electricity! Tennant Creek marked what I now recognise as the beginning of my life. It offered me opportunities and openings that I don't believe I would have had otherwise. It gave me employment, skills, confidence and a network of people that would stand me in good stead for many years to come.

I had been 'alone' all my life and I continued to be alone and thrown on my own resources and survival instinct. Being a housebound mother nearly drove me out of my mind. When my brain had stopped functioning, to the point that I could not add up or think straight, I decided I needed a job to widen my horizons and challenge my thinking processes. It was boom time in the mining town of Tennant Creek and peak population meant that there was enormous demand for few jobs. I got the only job available for which I was remotely suited — I joined the Commonwealth Public Service as a typist. The agonies of coping with that job were indescribable.

Yet I soon began to understand the workings of the office. Christmas Day 1974 brought massive changes not only to Darwin with Cyclone Tracy but to my life as a functioning real person. With the acting district officer in Alice Springs for his Christmas holidays, and no other senior office person available, I was called on to participate decisively in the town's role in caring for evacuees from cyclone-devastated Darwin.

I did things I had never done before, I took responsibilities I had never had to consider before and, like the rest of the town's population, I gave all my time and energy to assisting the evacuees and speeding them on their way. For the first time I was part of a team effort: service organisations, police, business people and individuals banded together to operate from the Country Women's Association (CWA) hall. Initial estimates had suggested that 300 to 500 evacuees would pass through Tennant Creek. The reality was thousands of distraught people every day. It became apparent that a proper, organised system of registration of names and destinations was needed as well as providing help with food, clothing, fuel and so on. So the main operation moved to the District Office. I had the keys — I let them in.

Limited phone connections out of the town and a desire to keep travelling meant the evacuees relied heavily on us to get messages to their families. With the help of a somewhat startled telex operator somewhere in Australia I learnt to use the departmental telex machine. (I had been avoiding this for months!) Registrations, vouchers, fuel, information and advice were dispensed. Rostered shifts were worked out. For over a week the office was staffed for 24 hours-a-day, every day. We all worked on the run.

It has been said that a small town is a microcosm of the world. In it you discover the good, the bad and the ugly — right alongside the inspirational, the funny and the lovable. At its peak times Tennant Creek's population is a mix of many races with all the richness and frictions that this brings. The Aboriginal population and culture is an underlying and interwoven mat of constancy and growth. Views and horizons reflect the environment; opinions and emotions are intensified.

The doors to opportunity opened. The District Office was one of the last vestiges of 'colonial rule' from Canberra. Effectively, it was the hub of local government decision-making and the contact point for government departments and agencies. I was thrown into an environment of people and was totally involved with the workings of a town. Local government issues gave me a peg to hang my interests in humanity on. I worked long and hard, and was promoted. Eventually I had the opportunity to act as the district officer.

I worked long and hard, and was promoted.

Tennant Creek has always been a man's town. The fascinating yet austere landscape breathes miners, prospectors, an assortment of bushies, fighters, drinkers and law enforcers. For a time, it was my responsibility to keep the town running. I was responsible for the Municipal Gang of thirteen men, I was Mining Warden, a marriage celebrant, I officially opened local sporting events, I inspected rubbish dumps, I met visiting dignitaries — I was stressed and worn out. But what a learning curve.

After a short stint as Tennant Creek's clerk of courts (another previously undreamt of opportunity), I moved to Darwin. I returned to familiar buildings and streets — but a totally new world of opportunities and challenges greeted me. Using my life's skills of survival and coping, my ability to analyse and express myself clearly, the 'female' skills of being a good organiser, and based on the absolute need to make a go of it, I launched myself into the world of the public service bureaucracy in Darwin.

It was 1978 — the time when the Northern Territory was given self-government status. It was a time when Territorians were first able to make decisions about government, infrastructure and more mundane matters, previously made in Canberra. Politicians rode high. It seemed that anything was possible.

By a series of circumstances I found myself in the Ceremonial and Hospitality Unit of the Chief Minister's Department. It was a brand new unit in the Territory's own public service. As part of a small team, I set out to establish office and official procedures; to meet, greet and host visiting dignitaries; to research protocol procedures in other states; to find my way through the bureaucracy, get to know people, familiarise myself with the projects and developments of the Territory, and to stay afloat.

It seemed that anything was possible.

I had the pleasure and the terror of being in at the beginning of something new. I often had to make major decisions quickly, decisions I could live with — and justify at the highest levels if called on. I had to be pleasant, organised, articulate, informed and thinking a few steps ahead of everyone else. One media identity took enormous pleasure from attending the Chief Minister's functions wearing work singlet and shorts! A European ambassador felt so uncomfortable with a woman that he refused to look at or speak directly to me. However I met many interesting people and had a fascinating view into the Territory and what makes it tick.

A few years later the need for change and growth saw me return to the field of local government. A new city was being developed from the ground up just south of Darwin. I joined the Palmerston Development Authority as Municipal Services Manager when there were roads and basic services but, as yet, not one resident. The authority focused on planning, engineering and the associated services to meet these ends. I went in as the first member responsible for the introduction of local government and, eventually, an appropriate style of town council.

This phase was another trail-blazing effort. Starting from scratch, and with the benefit of the vast resources and expertise of the Northern Territory public service, the 'normal' services of suburban living were established in a town carved from the bush. I chased wandering buffalo from the smorgasbord of succulent young trees newly planted along the roads. I inspected subdivisions with an eye to the effect of future habitation on drainage and run-off from tropical wet season downpours. I established the first official waste disposal area, liaised with postal authorities for mail deliveries, was responsible for the bus service to Darwin before population numbers tempted the big operators, worked on the first by-laws and welcomed the first residents.

My office, staff and responsibilities grew. Effective communication was the essence of our operation. Residents were consulted on open space and park areas, a town management advisory committee was established as the forerunner to a full local government council. I published regular community newsletters and I staffed and set up an office.

My skills were honed and refined. My confidence in public speaking and meeting procedure grew even further with the combination of my working life and membership of a public speaking group. I developed links with the media and became deeply involved in the public relations and promotional aspects of my job. My life was exciting, challenging — and exhausting.

Leaving the public service after ten years on the payroll was not difficult. I was unwell, tired and could not see where I would go if I continued in the public service. I was not a career public servant and needed a change of environment. Outside the public service, Darwin and the Northern Territory do not offer lots of openings for a woman at middle management level who is a generalist rather than a specialist. There were no firm thoughts for the future — other than the chances were that I would survive. My first priority was to recuperate and look after me. I then discovered I had always defined myself and found my identity in terms of my job, or the job I aspired to. Suddenly, in my eyes, I was a non-person. I didn't have a job and it didn't look as if I ever would again. Well, not a real job anyway, with status, good income and doing something meaningful in the world. I indulged in another side to life that, in all my years, had not touched me because I was so busy working. I discovered that during working hours Monday to Friday plenty of people are not working: they shop, visit, go to the beach or just sleep in. It took me over 12 months to adjust.

Having lost my reference points in a lifetime of working, conditioning and the need for security, I had to work on finding myself. It has been painful, difficult and an illuminating process. I embarked on the road to becoming a different me.

I found help and support for this process. It took me into the areas of alternative healing and self-awareness. I met different people with different reference points and ways of looking at the world.

At this time my husband and I established our own public relations business. We worked from home, minimal overheads with an emphasis on client service and contact. I enjoyed this experience enormously — and found myself once again in the traditional female support role.

I was limited as much by myself as by anybody or anything. I felt trapped. How could I get out of my self-imposed comfortable little life? I had no professional qualifications, my skills were general, my interests broad, I was not a hot-shot secretary, and I was past the stage of being at a boss's beck and call. It seemed that my aspirations exceeded my expectations. How could I hope to get something reasonable and fulfilling to do with the next few years of my life?

SUE SCHMOLKE

Then a new opportunity arose. The Chief Minister of the Northern Territory invited me to be convenor of the Women's Advisory Council. This body of women, drawn from throughout the Territory, reports to and advises the Chief Minister on a wide range of issues affecting women.

My year with the council saw a heightened public awareness of its functions and role. We visited and talked with women throughout the Territory, from Yulara to Borroloola, hearing their concerns and achievements and their need for support. We reported directly to the Chief Minister and linked into government departments with recommendations and reports on such issues as the implementation of changes to laws on domestic violence; 'de facto spouse' legislation; regulating for the safety of people travelling in the back of uncovered vehicles; counselling services; childcare centres; and accommodation of needs of women from remote centres seeking medical treatment in the major towns. I wrote a weekly article for the Sunday paper, talking about the activities of women throughout the Territory. It was much sought-after by women, even when the paper arrived by the weekly mail plane on the following Thursday.

As had happened in the past, this opportunity came to me courtesy of a man. And it tied in with a book that came my way during a period of external studies in Tennant Creek — *Damned Whores and God's Police* by Anne Summers. This book gave me the first inkling that there was another view of life and history. It was a revelation. Reading it in the 1970s in Tennant Creek was like an illicit act.

A realisation of the influence of any strong women in my life has come about only in recent years. I often felt out of kilter with the world and the expectations of those around me — but I didn't know why. I simply believed that I was slightly weird. Now I know that I am not and that there are plenty of other women with similar views and concerns.

I had spent my life working hard, trying to do the 'right thing' and feeling alone. I now accept and understand that this was part of a major learning process for me. Where in the past I knew very few women as friends and all my attention was on the male-orientated work sphere, I now have a growing network of women friends and contacts. My lifelong interest in people has a real focus — women.

> **My lifelong interest in people has a real focus — women.**

Life has taken me to a job as executive director of a community foundation with the aim of enriching the quality of life in the community. I am in contact with a wide range of issues and people and I have responsibility for taking on the projects decided by the board, of which I am also a member. We target often untouched areas, such as initiating a club for new arrivals, awarding a prize for outstanding voluntary community service, establishing a research grant open to the general public for ideas that will benefit the community, and playing a leading role in a research project into the situations of youth in the greater Darwin area.

I have a small staff and a busy office. We are daily kept in touch with the community as our meeting rooms are hired out and people contact us with information and enquiries. We distribute a much sought-after monthly listing of community events and liaise and work with all levels of government, community and business. I use the skills and experience that I have acquired over the years — and I thoroughly enjoy my job. At last, I no longer face the pressures and stresses of trying to succeed in an area that is new to me. I have time to reflect and to be creative. I can nurture, consolidate and expand my network of contacts and information. What luxury.

Where to from here? I have embarked on part-time study for a law degree, at Darwin University. There will be more growth and more changes. I will always be working — whether paid or not. My focus and interest is women. My income-producing activities of the future may not have women as their central concern. But I know the interests, needs and friendships of women will be at the heart of my personal activities for the rest of my life.

To some extent I envy people who can map out their lives and careers and follow through gaining qualifications and achievements as planned. My life has been and will continue to be unpredictable, varied and interesting.

BEWARE, OH TAKE CARE

Dawn Rowan

Dawn Rowan grew up in Adelaide, South Australia. She initially trained and worked as a secondary school music teacher. As a mature-age student she returned to university, completing a degree in social work. A veteran of many media interviews and programs on domestic violence including the first ABC national special 'Pressure Point' and 'Open File on Domestic Violence' in 1985, Dawn Rowan has worked and campaigned extensively with the problem of violence against women, and women's health, in Australia and the United Kingdom and pioneered the development of training programs for workers in the field of domestic violence in the early 1980s.

In 1991 after 20 years in the public sector, Dawn Rowan took up private practice specialising in personal counselling, running groups and training workers in the field of domestic violence and sexual assault. She is the proud mother of three-year-old twin Labradors.

Born 1946 (15 February, 4.10 am, in Adelaide, South Australia, for the astrologically inclined), I am the consummate Baby Boomer. Childhood was an unquestioning journey through the post-war fever of sex-role stereotyping when 'girls were girls' and 'boys *would* be boys'. It somehow didn't work on me. I couldn't accept the 'don't bother your little head with thinking 'cos you'll only be getting married and ...' line. I was never one for the dolls and pram or the tea set, but mudpies did have appeal.

BEWARE, OH TAKE CARE

I was branded a 'tomboy'.

It was difficult for my parents to present with any confidence to ageing relatives, and I was not conspicuously or willingly active in the kitchen. In short, like so many girls with strength, enthusiasm and independence of spirit, I was branded a 'tomboy'. This was accompanied with a re-assuring: 'But she'll grow out of it.'

If childhood was restrictive, teenage life in the 1950s and 1960s left us with an excitement deficit of gargantuan proportions. All the 'real' work was done by males, the females expected to be nurses, teachers, shop assistants or secretaries. I fell into teaching by accident.

Always good at music, I lived only for music lessons. I have vivid memories of hopping, skipping or galloping in time to the music of the Australian Broadcasting Commission (ABC)'s school broadcasts and was totally elated when my parents bought me a piano and I began lessons.

I had no expectation of going to university. My secondary school achievements were generally in the 'could do better if she applied herself' category. It was with considerable amazement that, by the age of 21 years, I found myself endowed with a Bachelor of music and a Diploma of teaching.

These academic conquests channelled me irretrievably (or so I thought at the time) into a life of secondary music teaching. This, in 1967, meant filling up empty pubescent vessels with culture, 38 at a time, and then, like yoghurt, leaving it to multiply in the fullness of time in a warm place (usually on the beach).

Not very satisfying stuff for them or me!

I have a consuming passion for justice and humanitarian pursuits. Since early childhood I have 'defended the underdog', often to my great personal peril (as events will reveal). Almost always out of step with the prevailing view, I have been willing to take risks for my beliefs — to be at the barricades of social change.

Leaving high school at the age of 17 signalled the introduction to exciting and indeed awesome new ideas. It was 1964 and Baby Boomers were faced with a dreadful and, to us, unbelievable injustice. The Australian government committed us to fight in Viet Nam — an unjust war, since confirmed as the brutal absurdity we declared it to be at the time. The ultimate wickedness was that, without referendum, the government ordered one in seven 18-year-old men to be 'called up' into the armed forces for two years and to be sent to Viet Nam after six months training, to fight and, very likely, die. The one in seven were chosen by a 'marbles in a barrel' lottery. Conscription by lottery was happening to *our* boyfriends, *our* brothers, *our* friends.

For the first time in my life I was outraged by an inhuman abuse of government power and took to the streets to demonstrate against the Viet Nam war and the use of conscripts to fight it. My life as an activist had begun. We were filled with optimism and an unshakeable belief that we could change the world to a peaceful, loving, free and equal place. The Hippy generation—flower-power at its zenith—we wanted a *new* society. Naively we believed we could create it. Around the western world in the late 1960s and early 1970s, we challenged the established order—politics, religion, sex, marriage, class, culture and (eventually) sex roles.

Women challenged their second-class citizen status and the media was instantly on the job, instinctively subverting the message. 'Bra-burners', 'Castrating Butch Bitches' roared the media. 'Need a good lay,' said the men with whom we demonstrated against the Viet Nam war. 'Biology is destiny' proclaimed the scientific fraternity.

And many women simply developed an acute case of LAM (Looking After Men) — including me.

I was taken to my first Women's Liberation meeting in 1970 and took home a few published articles to read. (By this time I'd been married for three years and was teaching music at high school.) I sat in bed that night reading roneoed articles, 'Why I Want A Wife', 'Christian Oppression in the Family', 'The Myth of the Vaginal Orgasm' and 'The Politics of Housework'. I needed no more convincing. From that night, I've been committed to development of equality and social justice for women throughout the world. My passion and focus have been the empowerment of women, for us to take control of our lives, loves and well-being. **My life as a feminist activist had begun.**

My first Women's Movement work was in the Adelaide Women's Liberation Centre. In 1970 we set up the first crisis counselling service for women. I worked voluntarily (there were no paid jobs in this area then) two nights a week or on weekends, on roster, and was horrified at women's stories. We were overwhelmed by domestic violence, rape, legal injustices, homelessness, difficulties with the health system, and the poverty of women and children. Almost none of these problems had been acknowledged previously, at least not in such a public way. Injustices against women and children were hidden behind the closed doors of the family.

In 1970, we did not fully realise the profound impact of the power of men over women and children. It remains incompletely understood. We still do not recognise the sacred inner sanctum of male power is man's historic and current right to violate his wife and children privately using a combination of physical, sexual, emotional/psychological, social and financial abuse. From this inner sanctum emanates the patriarchal power to abuse outside the family, in government, law, business and the media.

Increasingly I became aware of the enormity of the social, personal and political problems facing women. As a generation of feminists in the 1970s we thought we had *discovered* women's oppression and were the first women in herstory to experience a Women's Movement with its component beliefs, ideology and action. We were wrong. We thought it was *new* to discover brutality and injustice based on gender alone. We were wrong. Surely, we thought, it must be happening only because it's hidden and private, and if everyone is informed and educated about the truth, society will stop it. We were wrong. Without knowing it, we were facing great dangers. And we are still.

Perhaps the greatest danger is lack of knowledge of women's lives in the past. Without this, we keep reinventing history. Without this we will not be able to confront the real problem, the real agenda. We need established, effective practices to stop private and public abuses of women.

The latest wave of feminism precipitated the beginnings of women's services. In Adelaide, the first women's health centre opened in Hindmarsh. I was privileged to work as a volunteer, hearing the stories women told of their ill health and of how doctors treated women as ignorant, neurotic problems. I learnt about the trivialising by doctors of serious and even life-threatening illnesses of women.

In 1973, whilst in the United Kingdom on a trip with my (now) ex-husband, I bought a copy of Erin Pizzey's book *Scream Quietly or the Neighbours Will Hear* — the first book on domestic violence. Not having personally experienced violence, my father and ex-husband being gentle men, I was profoundly shocked. The book outraged me. My desire to do something about it lead me into voluntary and, ultimately, paidwork in the women's shelter movement.

In 1980 I became administrator of the Christie's Beach Women's Shelter in Adelaide. The media continued the image of women's shelters as doss houses where rampant lesbian separatists trained innocent homeloving housewives in basic feminist terrorism. Male-dominated and -defined society at large had a strong investment in believing this. The image is no accident, but the result of active and studied ignorance on the part of the media. The end result is that one of the most effective and powerful sources of aid to battered women and children is denied to them because of fear and mistrust generated by the media image and swallowed by the community.

> The image is no accident, but the result of active and studied ignorance on the part of the media.

I was determined that Christie's Beach Women's Shelter would fight this image, thus enabling women to escape from abusive homes to a place which was peaceful, safe, clean, tidy and dignified. I established an attractive shelter environment with purpose-built childcare, administration and counselling areas. A team of committed and highly competent workers was devoted to provision of high quality services properly and powerfully supporting abused women and children.

This shelter was the first of its kind. Frequently state and federal politicians and other workers in the health, welfare, education, legal and housing arenas visited us. My policy was to have an open place where women did not feel hidden away and further victimised. The shelter's operation and diversity of resources and support networks was used as a model for the development of new shelters. We had great success working with the battered women and children in our care because of the conscious and active processes used in raising self-esteem and sense of personal power in a nurturing and powerful way.

We, the workers, were role models for women, concrete evidence women could make changes to the housing system, to welfare policy and to the legal process. It was a source of great joy to us to see defeated and terrified women blossom into confident and assertive individuals who began taking control over their lives, whether they returned to marriage or left permanently.

The South Australian women's shelters waged a long, united and effective campaign to establish a proper level of funding which acknowledged that we didn't just provide a 'safe bed' but a range of services necessary for abused families to re-establish themselves successfully in the community. Christie's Beach Women's Shelter was a leader in this campaign.

The image of women's shelters being so poor, I decided that, to be taken seriously by the community, the bureaucracy and government, I needed a qualification. At 36 I returned to university and completed a second degree — in social work.

This I did whilst working at the shelter full-time and was alarmed at the lack of relevance and reality of the academic process to the human condition. There was, in 1982, no reference to family violence in the course, which was lofty and theoretical. The most valuable skill I learnt was how to write a good academic essay — a remarkably useless talent for anyone working with people with serious personal problems.

The work and public image of the Christie's Beach shelter went from strength to strength. The media image of battered women moved away from 'nagging trouble-makers' who 'deserved what they got'. The horror suffered by approximately one in three families was being exposed and, in that exposure, acknowledged. Women had begun to trust and use the women's shelter networks. The unique first hand knowledge of the workers was gaining recognition and respect.

There is a sinister aspect to that success though. Client confidentiality precludes workers in women's shelters from revealing information received from the women and children in their care, but their knowledge of the behaviour of some of our leading public figures inside and outside the family leaves individual workers dangerously vulnerable. So it was with us at Christie's Beach Women's Shelter.

I could not in my worst nightmare have predicted events that followed. Without realising it, as leaders of this successful program of social and personal justice for women, workers at the Christie's Beach shelter were vulnerable. Dale Spender

> **I could not in my worst nightmare have predicted events.**

records in *Women of Ideas — And What Men Have Done To Them* how powerful, outspoken and effective women throughout history have been brutalised, humiliated, disgraced, silenced and even executed. Burning 'difficult' or competent women at the stake is an historic tactic of the patriarchy effectively terrifying other women into silence and complicity. The modern method of 'burning at the stake' is character assassination. Wicked lies are widely publicised about innocent and usually altruistic people whose political or philosophic beliefs differ from those of the current regime.

According equality and justice to women is inherently threatening to the men who wield power and control today. Feminism is challenging male power at its personal and political roots. The inner sanctum of patriarchal power is under threat if we succeed in empowering women. When we succeed in empowering abused women, particularly the wives of powerful men, there is considerable personal danger to those working with these women.

> Feminism is challenging male power at its personal and political roots.

Christie's Beach Women's Shelter had become too powerful in its ability to defend and support victims of criminal assault in the home.

In August 1987, under parliamentary privilege, the (then) Minister for Health and Welfare in the South Australian Bannon Labor Government, Dr John Cornwall, released what was described as an 'independent' review of the South Australian women's shelters, *Shelters in The Storm*. No consultation regarding complaints or allegations about our shelter was undertaken by the review committee with the shelter. Department for Community Welfare files formed the basis of the review. Unsubstantiated allegations were made. The review committee completed the report without shelter workers being informed that we were *accused* let alone *of what* we were accused. This denial of natural justice was condoned through the parliamentary process. We learned of details in the review from the television news. Without forewarning, life's work, and personal and professional reputations were destroyed in 90-second news 'grabs'. Not only unsubstantiated, the allegations were untrue. Yet they were carried in the front-page headlines of the *Adelaide Advertiser* the following day. News stories on television and radio for days after repeated these lies.

Before we could document our innocence, John Cornwall announced at a press conference that funding to the shelter had been withdrawn. On 12 August 1987 the *Advertiser*, South Australia's major daily newspaper, reported upon the projected closure of the shelter 'after allegations of maladministration and unacceptable professional and personal behaviour'. The article appeared under the heading 'Negligence row shuts shelter for women', and reported accusations made under the protection of parliamentary privilege. The article continued, saying *Shelters in the Storm* 'alleges there has been misappropriation of funds, sexual and physical harassment and intimidation, professional negligence, persistent overspending and inadequate financial recording at the Christie's Beach shelter'. A ministerial statement by Cornwall was quoted:

> Concerns about deficiencies in financial management, unacceptable management practices and a number of unsubstantiated allegations of professional and personal misbehaviour were forwarded to me. These allegations and other information have been referred to the Commissioner of Police and the Commissioner of Corporate Affairs, both of whom have instigated investigations.

On Wednesday, 7 October 1987, the *Southern Times Messenger* reported that three of us had been charged by the Corporate Affairs Commission with breaches of the *Associations Incorporation Act* governing the shelter, by failing to keep proper accounting records of a shelter bank account; and not ensuring that the financial statement for 1985–86 was audited by an authorised person: 'Charges relating to the bank account are alleged to involve about $1,500, mostly donations for Christmas and Easter presents for children at the shelter.' (The accounts had been audited by an experienced accountant qualified to diploma rather than degree level.)

My colleagues and I were obliged to go on trial before the Christie's Beach Magistrates' Court on the charges. On 2 June 1988, following the trial, the *Adelaide Advertiser* reported (on page 3) that money spent prosecuting us 'would have been better spent on the women and children for whom the shelter was set up'. These were the words of Mr W J Ackland, SM, who heard the case. The article pointed out that the Magistrate was 'reluctant to find the women guilty' but was 'obliged to do so from the evidence before him':

> 'I say reluctantly because, in my opinion, if the allegations before me are the only substantial allegations of wrongdoing made against the defendants the not inconsiderable amount spent on this prosecution would have been better spent on the women and children for whom the shelter was set up ... These were technical breaches of an Act and in my opinion you can't get much more technical than this.' Mr Ackland said there was no allegation that any money in the [bank] account had been used for any 'improper or unworthy' purpose or that the women had tried to conceal the existence of the account. 'The defendants were preoccupied with other tasks which they reasonably considered more important and pressing than contemplation of the *Associations Incorporation Act*,' he said.

Mr S J Kenny, appearing for us, opposed an application made for $700 prosecution costs, asking Mr Ackland to record no conviction against any of us. He said: 'These are honorable women who have worked diligently for the community. These offences are of the most trifling nature and it is inexpedient to inflict punishment on them.' The *Advertiser* reported his statement that our crime was 'less "in the eyes of the law" than keeping a dog without

a licence' and went on:
> Mr Ackland, after taking a short adjournment to consider the matter of costs, said 'although the taxpayer has been put to considerable expense' by the three-day trial the breaches of law were of a very technical nature and did not disadvantage anyone.
>
> He said that, under the circumstances, granting costs would 'be unfair' to the women. He ordered the costs incurred by the prosecution be borne by the prosecution.
>
> He found the women guilty of the charge but did not record a conviction or apply a penalty.

That was not the end of the matter. A parliamentary select committee was established to look into how we had been treated. On 12 April 1989, more than 18 months later, the *Southern Times Messenger* ran a banner headline on its front page: 'Shelter staff cleared of charges'. The *Adelaide Advertiser* ran an editorial on 17 April 1989, stating:

> The double-edged sword of parliamentary privilege is a vital weapon which must be wielded with care. It can allow politicians to expose criminal and corrupt practices without fear; but if mishandled, it can cause serious harm to the persons and reputations of innocent people — as in the case of the Christie's Beach Women's Shelter.
>
> A 1987 report tabled in Parliament labelled seven women workers at the shelter as dishonest, incompetent and sexually and physically violent. On this basis, the Government withdrew the shelter's funding.
>
> Many of the workers have since been unable to find employment because of this blackening of their names.
>
> Last week a unanimous all-party Select Committee found the allegations to be completely baseless and condemned the flaunting of them 'in the strongest possible terms'. When questioned about the unsubstantiated allegations in the 1987 report, the chairwoman of the committee that prepared it, Ms Judith Roberts, said that women had made allegations to the committee which 'it was not our duty to substantiate'.
>
> This is worse than gossip.
>
> Following the allegations, three of the women involved with the shelter, including the former director Ms Dawn Rowan, faced financial charges which a magistrate described as technical and trivial. He found them proved but did not apply a penalty. No other charges were laid.
>
> The women have called for compensation and reinstatement — only to meet a stone wall in the government that caused their suffering. It is hiding behind one line in the 11-page report which says funding for the shelter

could have been withdrawn for persistent over-running of budgets — also true of some other shelters - 'if that course was considered appropriate'. This is spurious coming from the Government that has itself been revealed as responsible for serious financial mismanagement with the Justice Information System and the South Australian Timber Corporation.

For the Government to have accepted the first report with no proof of the allegations, and with little thought of the consequences, is reprehensible. For it to continue now to turn its back on these women, and refuse to consider restitution, is cowardice.

The time has now come for the Government to admit a mistake, to face the blame for an appalling abuse of parliamentary privilege, and to prove that the sobriquet of Cowards' Castle is unfairly earned.

The *Southern Times Messenger* followed up on 26 April 1989, publishing letters to the editor supporting us and our work. B. Davies of Morphett Vale wrote:

> ... As an ex-resident of the women's shelter I am pleased to hear that the staff have been exonerated of physical abuse or mismanagement. These ladies have my sympathy for what they have been through in this past two years.
>
> It has been a harrowing experience for them, and I think now their names have been cleared of any impropriety that they should be reinstated.
>
> They have done marvels for the Christie's Beach Women's Shelter in the past, even beyond their call of duty, to be of help in any situation that arises. I commend them for the help they have given me and many others.

Today, I still do not know exactly what allegations were made. The government and the Department for Community Welfare have been unable to produce details. The unsubstantiated allegations have remained vague and unspecified.

The impact of private and public abuse is to frighten, control and disempower us. The stronger and more outspoken we are, the greater threat we are, the stronger the attacks.

We were subjected to four inquiries after the initial report— Criminal Investigation Bureau, Department of Corporate Affairs, the South Australian Ombudsman and a South Australian Legislative Council All-Party Select Committee — all of which debunked the lies and strongly criticised those who used them. Furthermore, over 100 letters of defence and support were sent to the *Adelaide Advertiser*. NOT ONE was printed.

I was unable to work for several years because of the catastrophic effects of this experience. The Minister of Health subsequently resigned. The government continues to refuse to re-fund the shelter or compensate the workers for our great personal suffering and that of our families.

I invite you, readers, to read between the lines. I do not have parliamentary privilege and cannot legally tell the whole story. Those who abuse and violate others are protected by the power of their own legal and political system. Our civil liberties and fragile democracy are ultimately dependent on the honourableness or otherwise of our members of parliament.

Political strategies used against women activists serve several ends. Strong groups of women are divided. We are terrorised into silence and inaction. The positive image of women's shelters is gravely damaged and credibility that was established disintegrates. The most effective service to empower women to escape or challenge family violence is gravely undermined. What was done to Christie's Beach Women's Shelter and, by implication, to all women's services is tragic evidence of the degree to which we are a threat to patriarchal power. We are fooling ourselves if we believe that those who maintain power will willingly give it up simply because others suffer injustices as a consequence of their holding, exercising or abusing it.

I have learned from this experience. First, we survive! Profoundly changed, my world view shattered and no longer naive, but, against all odds, surviving and able to continue working towards goals set by women over centuries. If you are willing to work at the barricades of social change, be wise, be prepared for the battle, be certain of your supports. Don't believe that *all* women are your friends because some are on the other side. Don't believe that all men are enemies, because some are on our side!

Power is not the problem. The abuse of power is.

My greatest hope is that others can grasp the baton and keep pushing forward. My greatest fear is that we will return to the starting post and begin yet again. And as for advice to women considering work in the women's services: remember the words of an American folksong (written by a man) —

> Beware young ladies, they're fooling you
> > Trust them not, they're fooling you
> Beware young ladies, they're fooling you
> > Beware, oh take care.

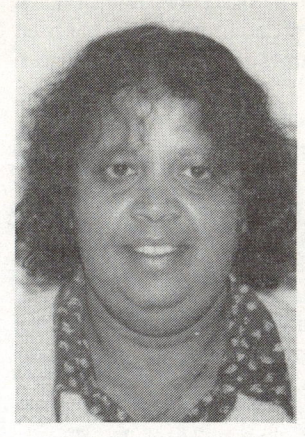

HUSTLING POOL

Lariane Fonseca

Lariane Fonseca is a health worker at the Women's Health Service Barwon/South Western Region in Geelong, Victoria. Her family immigrated to Australia in 1967 from India. After completing her final year of schooling at Geelong in Victoria she studied nursing going on to complete a degree in computer science and a post-graduate degree in medical science at the University of London. She later completed a Master's degree in medical sociology and a graduate diploma in education. Lariane Fonseca has worked in both community and academic institutions, whilst maintaining a commitment to grassroots action. An activist for some 20 years, her work has spanned a diverse range of issues, including women's health, violence against women, the cross-cultural needs of women, women and work. From 1984 to 1988 she was national co-ordinator of FINRRAGE, the Feminist International Network of Resistance to Reproductive and Genetic Engineering.

Retrospective explorations of self give way to curious exercises. There is a distinct choice — either the simple 'safe' method or opening the proverbial 'can of worms', a somewhat dangerous but more honest catharsis. I choose the latter.

One of the central tenets of feminism 'that the personal is political' often manifests as part of our lives as women long before we conceptualise formal notions of 'feminism'. Confronted by the question when did my oppression as a woman, a Black woman, and a migrant woman, became a part of my conscious knowledge, and what experiences led to my acknowledgement of it, I realised the answers lie not in the obvious, but in a set of complex and intricately woven series of life experiences which in an evolutionary manner gave way to political and personal commitments.

I have often wondered why the position farthest from the centre feels so appropriate — why extremes, although difficult and sometimes painful to maintain, are more comfortable than the unchallenged line straight down the middle. I have always had a particular kind of determination. It has been stubborn, painful, and infuriating — but most times it has, in the end, proven worthwhile and self-satisfying.

Born in India, in the newly post-colonial era, into a racist, male-preferring and alienated culture, I grew up desperately trying to understand my parents' own denial of their Indian identity. This struggle has continued to haunt me, invariably winding its way through my life, surfacing at different points in time, with varying intensity and fury.

The oppression of sex, race, and class inevitably underpinned the construction of my 'unreality' as a woman in Australia. The prevailing social order provided a racist and misogynist hall of mirrors rendering my existence invisible and annihilating my own reality, my parents', my own experience. At 16 years I was exhausted by the struggle. Temporarily, at least, I was willing to give in to a system that seemed too big to handle. My parents' generation had tried to teach me my powerlessness. By their own words and actions: their lives of subservience to colonisation, the edification of the culture of their oppressors — the deification of so much that was alien to my reality. Ultimately, the position adopted by my parents was racist in itself. This may be viewed as a strategy of survival in an alien culture. However it gave them a false consciousness about their own class and racial location in the culture they chose. My parents invested in this image of themselves, taking pains to hide us from their own powerlessness.

> **My parents' generation had tried to teach me my powerlessness.**

My family migrated to Australia in 1967. I was 15 years of age, and the eldest of five children — three sisters and a brother. While keen on the idea of life in a new country, I was apprehensive about separation from my friends and peer group. Like so many others, my migrant experience in this country has been harsh. Nevertheless it has had a significant contribution in bending and shaping the metal that has served me well.

The humiliation of 'difference' in an alien culture is not random. It is calculating and ruthless, and reared its ugly head through my only year at school in Australia — Matthew Flinders Girls High in the provincial city of Geelong, Victoria where my family chose to settle. The learned answer to this humiliation was — if you cannot change the reality (and this seemed to be the case), then change your perceptions of it. We were the ones who were supposed to be grateful for the lucky country, our gratitude expressed by the surrender of self. I legitimised my partial acceptance of the demanded position by recalling the trepidation that had filled me at the thought of being married off to some Indian man. Surely this is better I thought, measuring my luck by comparative atrocity.

I was given to believe that I could have the whole world in my hands, at least for most of the time, and with a few provisos: I had to act correctly, be subservient, have a sound work ethic, be obedient, unquestioning and god-fearing. (My parents resorted to their religion of Catholicism as the antidote to their own oppression.) What a lie. Any doubts about the reality of my experience were rapidly and summarily put down as small but intolerable rebellions against divine authority.

I had to escape. The next years reflected my desperation. In school, I lived for sport; hockey was my essential love. I escaped my oppression temporarily. The wall I so carefully erected helped me avoid the issues as I immersed myself in the excellence I aspired to in the field. Cultural reproduction (read education) came easily, merely existing like eating to keep functioning. Friendship attachments were superficial. The wall was my path to self-preservation. For the most part I lived a contradictory existence. I was the 'clown', the 'troublemaker', the 'rebel'. In the meantime, my other self rejected god and patriarchy (I had conceptualised this by now), rejected capitalism, colonialism, nuclear families. Yet this did not make life any easier, and under the surface I simmered and stewed over the possible directions of my life. I was not quite 17-years-old.

I cannot consciously remember bothering myself with notions of a 'career'. The idea of paidwork and economic survival did not feature as immediate concerns. No one had really asked me or seemed to be concerned with what I might do after school. In India, the expectation was that one must perform well at school and go on to achieve an academic career. My parents appeared to almost expect that my sense of responsibility as the eldest of their five children should prevail, carrying me down a perfectly paved path, but they were busy coping with their own traumas of survival and adjustment to the new life.

The idea of paidwork and economic survival did not feature as immediate concerns.

Something remaining as a source of anguish to me was my parents' focus on the negative. I cannot recall too often receiving praise for achievement, yet the chastisement for not performing as expected remains well ingrained. This had a major influence in my working life for, as I grew, I invariably found myself attempting to seek the approval of my parents by 'proving' myself to them.

My mother, a trained teacher, on coming to Australia returned to paidwork for the first time since her marriage. My father, a talented man in his field of marketing, was rejected by the world of business because of his race and colour. After a trying time, at which he practised every one of his highly held principles, he re-trained as a teacher, remaining in that career until his retirement.

My immediate means of escape from the frustration of living an unreality was to flee the 'nuclear' family and the small-town environment — fast becoming claustrophobic. I had chosen a science stream at school, and was accepted into nursing at St Vincent's Hospital in Melbourne. The idea of a Catholic hospital and the caring profession allowed me to slip off the shackles, for I was sure my parents would not have settled for any less reason to let me go. I enjoyed nursing. Academically and practically, I succeeded.

I began, at a general level, to grasp the notion of my oppression — a kind of shorthand of my consciousness as a woman/Black. However, it was one thing to encounter the concept, and completely different to understand a general idea such as male hegemony. I now perceive in a whole series of moments how this affected me. The past 20 years has been about the communication of these moments, recognition of self through a process of reconstruction of my own reflections. The journey of self-discovery and identity traversed a number of painful years and became architects of momentous changes to my life.

Soon after completing nursing training, I injured my back. The course of life I had begun to accept as 'my lot' was completely changed. The years spent nursing had not completely released me from family ties. Anxious and reckless in my quest for freedom I married a white Australian male, and had a male child. This marital experience served merely as transfer of father/property to husband/property, this time with the added ingredient of violence and emotional abuse. Up to now, this was what happened to other people, for there had been no evidence of it through my childhood. Nothing had prepared me for it.

My back injury kept me bed-ridden for almost 18 months. My life was quickly transformed from one of action to imprisonment. I had succeeded in nursing. For the first time, realising the wage inequities for women's work, I had been active in the wage campaigns for nurses, and the rights of women to work. I had had a fair share of success in hockey, and had charged through the past four or five years with hardly a thought to my direction or purpose. The months in bed provided space to think. Where had I been? Where was I heading? Would I walk again? What was my life worth? How could I — did I — value it? Did other people? Why did I feel so alienated from my son? What would I do if I ever got out of there? Questions, more questions. Angst, introspection, analysis. The turning point began to emerge. I knew that if I did get out, on my own two legs, there was a life I could not go back to, and getting out just had to be done. I kept wanting to go back to the beginning, to find out how things happened and why.

I did walk again. Hell bent on change, and with a steel determination, I shed the old skin and slipped out into a sunny world. Left behind were the marriage, child, shackles of dependence, the immobility of disability. But issues I had not really considered before had to be confronted. Of immediate importance was the question of career, how and who would support this new-found independence. For the first time, I started to value the pragmatism of a career and appreciate that the key to independence lay in access to paidwork.

I turned to assessing my options, and calculating how to achieve the most worry-free and financially lucrative path open to me. University and further study appealed. I gained entrance to the new computer science course at the University of Melbourne and grabbed at it with a thirst for knowledge and skill.

Yet my university years were fraught with new-found frustrations. Women were a minority group in the course, the discrimination often unbearable. It quickly became evident that intense visionary moments would not help me to survive! But commitment to pre-occupations with self-discovery pulled me through. I was here to prove I could do it, and that I could be self-sufficient. There was the excitement of discovery, the exhilaration of the freedom of expression. I was exposed to the praxis of Marxism, to socialism, Viet Nam, peace, and the re-discovery of feminism and its meaning for my life.

On the more practical level, I survived thanks to a small scholarship and hustling pool at Johnny's Green Room in Carlton. I proceeded into an honours program with the assistance of a scholarship from one of the larger banking organisations, where I spent the next few years as senior programmer/analyst. The position as senior programmer realised success, and saw me travel to assist in setting up a data centre for the bank in London. However, the challenge of work in an essentially male arena took its toll. Men sought to trivialise my existence and disregard my presence, often totally. The administrative and operational responsibilities were fast becoming impossibly oppressive.

> Men sought to trivialise my existence and disregard my presence.

Sexual harassment, verbal abuse, and racist and sexist jokes were part of everyday life. I attempted to maintain a non-hierarchical mode of operation, with a devolution of power in leadership. My aim was to share knowledge and responsibility with my co-workers. However, this was abused and ridiculed; as far as most were concerned, what I needed was a 'good man'. Unfortunately, women were drawn into the ridicule by the men and were easily co-opted into their perceptions of me as 'enemy'. Devastated, frustrated by the failure of my efforts, I sought refuge in another survival strategy — I became 'one of the boys'. I drank with them, defeated them at snooker, laughed at their jokes. Surprisingly, it worked. They paid attention, met their responsibilities — yet all the while I squirmed inside. How could I prostitute all I had come to believe in as worth fighting for. I knew then I had to get out: if male power was needed to survive, I certainly did not need it.

During the next four years I travelled extensively in Europe, Africa and Asia. I had developed and adopted a strong sense of existentialism. Now, is what counted. Life was too short to procrastinate. I followed the sun, took risks, learned from different cultures and worked in a variety of jobs that had me programming in Reykjavik, Iceland, and harvesting chestnuts in France. I spent three months with a Kurdish tribe travelling across Iran and Afghanistan and proceeded to India to re-discover my earliest beginnings. Once again I was confronted by confusion about my identity. Although obviously not foreign, I was rejected due to my non-stereotypical behaviour. Women in India are expected to be quiet, passive, non-political, and to dress in a prescribed manner. I fled, disillusioned, and swore to come back only as a tourist.

Returning to London, determined to find a reason to stay, I enrolled in the only available course useful to me at post-graduate level — a Masters degree in computer/medical science. I learned about the Women's Movement, becoming increasingly conscious of how we gain knowledge as women: the negativity of men's definitions of us — how we were always wrong, we were 'other', we were less than the 'norm'. In my spare time, I worked with a group of women to set up a house for the collective, 'Women Behind Bars'. In a more theoretical way, I began to appreciate that while women are seen as a deficient category, the deficiency was not with women but in the ways of knowing. 'Research methodology' was made by men, and worshipped. So, if you wanted to ask questions or do research that was not comfortable to men, the research became instantly inadmissible.

Completing my degree, I returned to Australia empowered by my achievements and experiences, and with a new zeal as a feminist and socialist activist. However, something still bothered me. I was not happy with my role in the sciences, and had begun to critique science as a patriarchal construction to control knowledge, analysis and understandings of the world.

I had had enough of the long cold winter in England. I travelled to Queensland in search of sunshine and a possible new direction. While working in a pathology laboratory as a medical technician for the Queensland Department of Health, I enrolled in a Bachelor of arts-sociology. Sociology provided the analytical framework for my previous concerns with male science. Yet it soon became painfully obvious that sociological research was part of the male epistemological production. I thought of ways in which to construct life-enhancing knowledge about women: how could we make the personal political and make it recognised?

Thanks to my growing awareness and political conscience, the increasingly oppressive regime in government in Queensland led me into a series of involvements both personal and political that required my immediate attention. A sense of urgency developed. I studied full-time to complete my degree, simultaneously working full-time as women's rights organiser for the student union. Administration of the fourth Women and Labour Conference in Brisbane was a painful experience for it became evident to me that while feminism provided a framework for analysis and its potential was exciting, its underlying impetus remained divisive.

My involvement in the union movement became part of everyday life, which was increasingly oppressive. Through the Trade Union Training Authority (TUTA), I helped develop and conduct courses in Women and Unions. I worked on programs relating to workers' health. Inevitably I was caught up in the historic Electrical Trades Union (ETU) dispute in Queensland. Industrial agitation occurred as a response to the imposition of working conditions and deregulation of the industry by the Bjelke-Petersen National Party government. Lasting some six to nine months, the dispute symbolised life under the oppressive regime, eventually drawing in several unions and almost resulting in a general strike. Many activists, including myself, joined a resistance movement. For our efforts we experienced police harassment, including being locked up for street marches. (Legislation had been passed by the government some years before to prevent protest and street marches and demonstrations.) The dispute ended in legislation sacking the striking workers and appointing workers on contracts with restrictive conditions. The resistance continued, finally resulting in the demise of National Party rule in Queensland.

Completing my degree, I took a teaching position at the Queensland Institute of Technology. I also taught sociology and medical sociology in a number of courses at Brisbane, at the Department of Social and Preventive Medicine in the University of Queensland, the Princess Alexandra Hospital, and disability training programs at Basil Stafford Training Centre.

I began to use the classroom as an arena for the politicisation of teaching others. I utilised my power positively and enjoyed my work. In teaching I had finally found my niche. Tired out by the political fight, I moved to South Australia as guest lecturer to the University of Adelaide, Department of Community Medicine. I was increasingly involved in the movement against the rise of the new reproductive technologies and genetic engineering after having my consciousness raised by leading activist Robyn Rowland of Deakin University. She became a friend and contributor to a new set of analyses in my life.

In teaching I had finally found my niche.

Over the next three years I worked as national co-ordinator of FINRRAGE (the Feminist International Network of Resistance to Reproductive and Genetic Engineering). We ran a national conference, and worked hard at community development on the issues. It was through FINRRAGE that I have been fortunate to meet one of the most identifiable personal and political role models to influence my life: the example, the challenge, the encouragement and support of Renate Klein (who with Rita Arditti and Shelley Minden edited *Test Tube Women*, the first international anthology challenging new reproductive technologies) continues to provide direction.

Determined to pursue my developing commitment to the bridging of theory and practice, I continued working at a grassroots level to 'keep me honest'. In South Australia, while completing a Masters in sociology at Flinders University, I worked to set up the Migrant Women's Domestic Violence Service. Then followed a two-year teaching contract with South Australian TAFE and the Aboriginal Health Organisation in co-ordinating and teaching the health worker program in the state. The health worker program took me to remote areas of South Australia, into isolated Nunga communities. The insights I gained are crystallised in my analysis of social justice and the inadequacies of a system that continues to ignore the atrocities against the Australian indigenous people.

The need to return to Victoria, closer to my family, began to emerge. I had grown older and had essentially missed most of the significant family 'happenings' over the prior 20 years. My parents had retired. I was an aunt three times over.

The opportunity to co-ordinate the project of setting up Victoria's first Women's Health Centre arrived. It was too good to pass up — I took on the task, completing it in 1988. This was an exciting time at a practical level, but once again was tarnished by the divisiveness of women unable to understand power. The group's management ultimately identified with men instead of women, and in doing so took on the notion of their powerlessness and victimisation. I was devastated, disillusioned, and vulnerable. No longer believing in my own skills, I was rendered invisible. I refused to allow this pain to continue, and moved back into the mainstream, determined to salvage my self-esteem in the quiet anonymity of the classroom in a large bureaucracy.

For the next two and a half years I worked at the Gordon College of TAFE in Geelong, as a teacher in social and community studies in the area of disability programs. Here my only other significant role model entered my life. Colleen Lindner, friend, confidant, provider of support, encouragement and the space to reconstruct the self that I had put aside. She has continued to tear away the threads, making me believe in myself again. With this, I have let go of the pace which was starting to take its toll. I have discovered a love of photography, gardening, and of fiction. Our friendship has had an holistic effect on my life, for it has permeated my philosophical framework and perspective. Together, eighteen months ago, we started Colari, a women's bookshop and gallery that operates in Geelong today as space for women to stop a while, talk to each other and discuss their lives.

One more accomplishment remained — to return to the arena of women's health and regain the confidence and self-esteem I had lost during my work at the Women's Health Service in The West, Melbourne. Since 1990, I have been working as community development worker with the Women's Health Service Barwon/South Western Region. My work continues to do the job I hoped it would; the healing process is slow, but well on the way to completion.

I have never valued ambition. I do not see myself as ambitious. However, I have highly valued the sense of personal power, that is: knowing who you are, being proud of it and fighting to retain it against all odds. I've had a romantic notion about being 40, and if all goes well it will be attained soon. I cannot recall the significance of the age, suffice to say it has provided a focus for a temporal framework to get things done. I cannot say what the future holds for me. There is so much more to do, but some days I feel enough is enough. Having achieved much more than I had envisioned, it will be interesting to see if I do set another age marker for the same purpose.

> **I have highly valued the sense of personal power.**

There is no easily identifiable source of the directions I have taken. This reflects my central philosophy that, despite the extraneous influences and players entering my life, the real changes have been born from within. There is the need to be committed to the struggle for one's beliefs and the strength to stand up and be counted. My career has changed to adapt to the personal and political changes in self. I do not believe that the knowledge, experiences and skills I have gained along the way are ever wasted.

My parents have played a significant role in my search for identity and the struggle it has presented. In their own way they have also led by example and good intention. Many others have entered and exited my life with varying degrees of influence. Ultimately, part of the struggle is belief in self. This is not to disregard that the historical, cultural social and economic times each contribute to one's life chances. Many factors may dictate that we withdraw — take the conflict with us, and let others get on with it. This is a better option than energy spent on resentment and recrimination. I hope this is now what I am about. I look forward to the years ahead from day to day, maintaining the level of existentialism I did fifteen years ago. However, the fire is now tempered by a healthy level of cynicism and a disillusionment with humankind.

No doubt I will not calculate, and change my path any more or less than necessary. Nor will I permit the influence of time, person or place to intersect my life more or less than it has in the past.

PART IV

In Practice

SLIPPING THROUGH THE NET

Jennifer Coate

For seven years, through the 1980s, Jennifer Coate ran her own legal practice in Melbourne, Victoria, first together with a partner, then as a sole practitioner. Jennifer Coate was born on 8 February 1953 in East Melbourne, Victoria. Spending her first decade post-secondary school working as a teacher and educating herself, she commenced the 1980s holding a teaching diploma, a degree in arts and a degree in law. In 1991 she sold her legal practice, and began working with the Legal Aid Commission on an interim basis, until determining upon her future plans. A member of Feminist Lawyers and the Women's Legal Resources Group, in 1991 she was appointed by the Premier to the Victorian Women's Consultative Council.

My earliest memory of life in North Dandenong is being held suspended by each hand with my parents jumping me along as children love to do. I wore hard leather shoes and we were inspecting the home where I was to grow and mature over the next 21 years. It was a Housing Commission Estate newly built to feed workers into the General Motors Holden (GMH) and Heinz factories. I stamped along with all my might to be heard, to enjoy the noise I was making and to express some power over my environment. I was three. I'm still stamping 35 years later. I'm still making noise that I enjoy and I'm still striving to gain some sense of my world. Only now, not with my hands held by my parents.

I was allowed to feel my strength and wanted to explore my potential. I had no strong sense of on-going desire in any one direction, but always ahead.

In 1956, we moved from St Kilda to Dandenong enabling my father to continue with his roof tiling business. It was a short-lived success. Before beginning school I rode around on the little carts that carried the tiles inside the factory. My father seemed a bit awkward having me around without my mother there. Perhaps he didn't quite know what to do with a little girl, especially one wanting to ride in the conveyer boxes and stack roofing tiles at four years old. Things went downhill. The business was sold. My mother returned to paidwork. My father bought a truck and worked as a truck driver. That truck created havoc in our household. My father adored it. My brother adored it too. My mother hated the truck. It cost more and more money, breaking down constantly. My father got ulcers and was often irritable with worry and beer in the evenings. Eventually, the truck was sold. I was glad.

I grew up with the notion that girls who wanted careers, who were often smart at the expense of being attractive to men, could find security in nursing or teaching. My teachers, my peers, my mother and myself each knew I was smart enough to be a teacher. The holidays were good, pay was all right. You could always leave, have children and return. It was safe, secure and ensured one's ability to support oneself if times got tough. Careers weren't something anyone thought about as fulfilling. It was rather that a girl needed an education in case she had to work if she didn't marry successfully.

> A girl needed an education in case she had to work if she didn't marry successfully.

I had a few fantasies about being a writer or a lawyer but was loathe to share them for fear of being mocked. Fear — class and gender based. I finally told a trusted teacher about my idea of being a lawyer. She arranged a visit to a local solicitor in Dandenong. He is still in practice in Dandenong and I long for the time when we are opposed to each other. I'll remind him of his words to the guileless awkward 15-year-old who sat in his office: 'Do you know anyone in the law?' 'Does your family have any money?' 'Have you got any relatives who are lawyers?' 'Why do you want to be a lawyer?' 'Where did you get the idea from?' Overwhelmed, I responded: 'I just want to ...' He summarised: 'Look dear, you don't know anybody, you haven't got any money and you're a woman. This is a tough world. That combination will make it impossible. Haven't you considered teaching? You seem like a bright girl ...'

I can still feel the sense of combined depression and embarrassment. I went to vocational guidance trying to broaden my horizons. After the IQ test, the tester gives out the results and talks about career options. Teaching was the answer. What would it have been were I a boy from Brighton?

At a young age, to my eternal frustration, I understood about the differences in freedom between boys and girls. At the swimming pool, I didn't want to wear my bathers' top. I wanted to run around the streets dressed only in my shorts. To feel, see and enjoy one's strength and developing body. Conscious of the restrictions of traditional female clothing on myself and hating it, I protested vigorously at wearing dresses other than the compulsory school attire. I could not achieve the same physical prowess in a frock. I didn't like the feeling sitting, standing and trying to run, hampered by girls' clothing. At school, girls were largely forced to become passive onlookers whilst the boys played vigorously.

My feminism and principles, though always there, have often been undisclosed. My mother was probably the first to put feminism into my psyche. Mother was strong on the notion of getting an education: 'You always need independence. Being able to support yourself.' Once I decided to go into law, she was encouraging, spurring me on. Her horizons grew too as I pushed them further.

But I paid a price. It's a syndrome I call 'soon I'll be discovered and asked to leave'. It came with a sense of having pushed the boundaries of class and gender. Gone above my station as it were. Even after graduating in law and commencing in practice the flashback returns: 'You couldn't really have become a lawyer. That little shiny eyed, black haired creature running half naked around the streets with constantly grazed knees.' Leaving teaching was a symbolic act challenging a position I'd been trained to accept.

A long process of gradual education both through institutions and people moved me on. I think sometimes of the women in my street. All of them, with few exceptions, were tolerating, mothering and caring for falling-down men. Mrs Lean would ever be making excuses for the insensibly drunk and belligerent Mr Lean. Mrs O'Shannessy never even came out into the street to pick up Mr O'Shannessy when he arrived home in a taxi every night from the pub, falling down, drunk. Those were the old 6 o'clock closing days and kids used to fight over who picked him up and took him inside. The one who did got two bob. I was scared of him and wouldn't ever touch him.

As a child and early adolescent I was heavily involved in swimming, training for competitions. Memories of the swimming club, the people who taught me, the smell of the chlorine, the sound of the starting pistol, and the cheers are filled with overwhelming nostalgia for me. I seemed much younger and much smaller than everyone else. Seeing photographs of those years bears that out. I learnt to swim at six and by eight was competing at state level. At eight years old I was swimming the mile marathon with the 16-year-olds and over. I loved the sense of power and endurance and fed off my will to continue on and on in the pool.

I now see the enormous significance of what I never understood then: developing strength and control of one's body, and the psychology of being primed into competition. A great heroine of my life, Dawn Fraser (later to become an independent in the New South Wales state parliament), was my first outside inspiration. At various times we trained at the same places. To this day Dawn remains oblivious, but it was important to me. At 5 am my mother roused my brother and me, taking us to Burwood,

Dawn Fraser was my first outside inspiration.

the closest indoor pool from Dandenong, where we swam for an hour. Training was an hour in the mornings, an hour at night. My mother took us to stroke correction classes on a Friday night at the city baths. News got out that Dawn Fraser was in the big pool training. I was far too awe struck to approach her. This was in the early 1960s at the height of her career. Dawn was strong, tough, independent, anarchistic, fearless and a winner. She defied the rules of imposed femininity. A working-class girl, she took on the world and won. I watched as she powered up and down the swimming pool under my unknown but adoring gaze.

One night my brother and I stood at the chocolate machines putting in our two bob to get out a bar, trying to pull the next drawer out before the other went in and get one free. She approached. I could hardly look up as I handed her a thrown away entry ticket I picked up from the floor and asked for an autograph. She smiled, writing: 'Kind regards, Dawn Fraser.' She was a larrikin, a rebel, a fighter, a winner and a symbol of the physical, mental and emotional strength of women. I was proud to identify with her, and I've still got that ticket.

I grew up with a sense of refusing to accept that my body or spirit was any less powerful than my brother's or the boys in the neighbourhood. I was out on the street playing cricket or football, pushing the billy-cart or having stone-throwing competitions, doing anything that the boys were doing and making sure I was at least as good as any one of them. I recall standing on the volley ball court at age 13, so confident of my strength. I had just seen a boy push my girlfriend and next door neighbour off the court, saying he got there first. He hadn't, we all knew that. But he was a boy and therefore more powerful, unarguable it seemed. I walked straight up to him and punched him right on the nose out of sheer frustration and indignation that he could be so unjust, unfair and dishonest. I did not contemplate the possibility of being defeated. Schoolyard justice still has its attractions.

His nose bled, my hand hurt but I made my point. The girls around me were horrified. Clearly this was forbidden. The feminine socialisation process struck a blow that day. I had to learn that you hide your strength, stop running and fighting, care for your appearance and agree to be beaten.

Ms McDonald was my Grade 1 and 2 teacher. My introduction to school was positive and encouraging in her class. I was conscious of being bright and strove for excellence. I felt driven to be top. Ms McDonald liked me and let me be the best. Ms Brown, my English teacher in high school, was a shy, quirky, awkward woman, sensitive, bright and astute. She pushed me out of the 'near enough is good enough' syndrome. But the thrill of the win waned. Girls who are too clever don't get boyfriends or husbands. She didn't have one. I gave up swimming. I started to menstruate. I stopped trying to beat the boys. Tried to tone down my act. I was taunted for looking and behaving like a boy because I wanted to be strong and independent. Girls were openly criticised, taunted and mocked for such behaviour. Ms Brown persevered with me and I made her teach me how to do better. She was frustrated by my pragmatism and lack of vision. I only wanted a recipe to get better marks, a means to an end. I didn't want to think differently.

At our high school farewell dinner, Ms Brown sat beside me and asked me about the future. I knew I had a studentship to go to teachers' college. I told her that's what I would do as if it was a choice. She responded: 'You weren't meant for cutting out pieces of paper and playing with glue'. I was hurt and disturbed by her words. I felt flicked on the raw and there was nothing I could do about the course.

I matriculated in 1970 at Lyndale High School in North Dandenong in the first Form 6 the school had ever had, despite its 10-year history. Only nine or 10 students out of the group of 36 passed. Then, tertiary education was a question of money, not just entry results. I had been accepted to university but had no money. My father was not well. His working future looked dim. My mother's health was not good either. I didn't want to upset her by being too unhappy about ending up at teachers' college. She had to cope with my father dying of cancer. Sadly, university had to wait.

In the meantime the college at Frankston was a way of getting a tertiary education. My years at teachers' college from age 18 to 20 held great personal turmoil. I dreaded reaching the end and teaching. Yet I did not find the course challenging or demanding. Consequently I spent many hours in thought, discussion, reading, and walking along the Frankston beach.

However, I discovered the discipline of philosophy, taught by an unconventional and inspirational European woman. I developed a taste for the challenge and appreciated the intellectual stimulation of something beyond Cuisenaire rods and Piaget's theory on child development. It helped maintain my resolve not to be held in primary teaching.

1971 saw the emergence of Germaine Greer. I bought my copy of *The Female Eunuch*, reading it non-stop and attended a function in Camberwell where she spoke. I idolised her as I had once Dawn Fraser. My adulation wasn't set in any clear feminist perspective, but I wanted to understand what she was saying.

In my final year I saw a notice at the college about extended studentships, whereby I could go to university. Forms were available. I completed one, telling nobody in case I failed. Awarded a studentship, I was overjoyed. It was the break I needed.

In March 1974, my father died and I began my BA at Monash University. I was still on a studentship, assisting my mother with the loss of my father and working part-time at the local swimming pool. I studied philosophy, literature and linguistics. These were often lonely and alienated years for me. I had missed my peer group and no one from my neighbourhood or school or even from miles around was there. I wrote in March 1975: 'In this melancholy menagerie, I am all mimes and mumbles.' I lasted two years full time but the overriding spectre of those three years of 'bonded' time I had to teach hung over me. At the end of 1976, I made a fairly spontaneous decision to start teaching off the bond and get the whole thing over and done with.

I could finish my arts degree part-time. A number of friends thought I'd made a big mistake; I would never finish. But that kept me going through those three years of teaching. I attended university lectures two nights a week during term and wrote essays and studied for exams in the school holidays and after school. I taught Grade 2 at Hampton Park outside Dandenong for a year. Bored, empty and frustrated, I transferred to Collingwood for the next two years. Then I was free. I had also finished my arts degree. It was 1979.

Leaving teaching in 1981, deciding to study law full-time, was symbolic. It was the act of breaking out of my station in life, challenging the position I had been trained to accept. A long process of gradual enlightenment, inspiration and encouragement moved me on. Ultimately, however, I see myself as a driven woman. My longtime friend and neighbourhood comrade Norin Malone, who died tragically at 31-years-old, was an inspiration. She had come from my street, my life, had grown up seeing what I saw and had gone to university too. We talked long and often about how we both suffered from the recurrent fear that one day we would be discovered and told to get back to North Dandenong.

I got my first paid job when I was 13-years-old working on the shop floor at what was then E C Hattams. I wanted the independence of money. Earlier, I had taken over the chicken house in our backyard and after an initial contribution of six hens to my stock, my business began. I sold my eggs in the neighbourhood and bought feed from the proceeds. The business venture never really prospered. Disease hit my chickens and my interest waned. I had a beer bottle collection too in the days when the bottleo came around, paying a shilling a dozen for empties. On weekend mornings, I took my mother's shopping jeep to the park. The 'take' was often over two dozen bottles. It was particularly ungirl-like to indulge in such enterprises. I tried to go early, so I wouldn't be seen by the neighbourhood.

I worked as an emergency teacher throughout my law degree, counting the weeks and days until the last time I would go into a classroom. I had worked as a swimming teacher throughout my teachers' college years and first degree, and went back to it again during my law degree. I worked as a school teacher to earn enough money to travel the world for a year. Paidwork was always a means to an end. Now, as a lawyer, it feels like a luxury to finally reach my mid-thirties and be able to say I have a fulfilling and satisfying job that I do as a means in itself.

What motivated me to do law? An inexplicable fascination with the courtroom from an early age, and a magnetic love of language and mastery over words; power, the sense of power of language, people, systems that an understanding of the law offers. I was keen to be in the debating team, studying and discussing philosophy, making speeches, anything to play with words, the weapon of the law. Perhaps it gave me back the power I lost at age 13, after realising one could no longer openly match physical strength by fighting.

Our household was openly engaged in politics. There was the scandal of my mother's friend Bernice Morris living under some horrible cloud in the communist purges of the 1950s. I visited at Bernice's poultry farm in Dandenong frequently, collecting eggs and sliding on the lounge-room floor, listening to the adults discussing things in low-pitched tones. I instinctively knew we weren't allowed to talk about this outside the family. Eventually Bernice, her husband and two sons left Australia for China.

The massive power of a system that sent Bernice and her family into exile left a lasting impression. I spent some years grappling with adolescence, and in my middle teenage years was introspective and not particularly motivated by political matters. However, during the late 1960s, an awareness of the system's tentacles developed, during the Viet Nam days when I supported the Draft Resisters' Union. I was reminded of 'something out there' controlling our lives. My idea was to discover what it was, dissect it, analyse it, understand how it operates. I accepted that knowledge is not only one's individual strength, but a key to change.

In 1979, with bonded teaching and arts degree behind me, I sold my car, cashed in my superannuation, withdrew all my savings and took off to see the world.

Twelve months out of Australia, 12 months out of my environment, having no identity other than that you self-create on a daily basis, put the finishing touches on my resolve to change paths. I spent three months in Mexico and Central America after three months in the United States of America. I knew I could not return to Australia to where I had left off. I had to take a dramatic plunge, extend my horizons and push myself. Upon my return, my mother was joyful at having me back again. She was positive and encouraging when I announced my decision to resign from the education department and attempt law full-time. Even when I panicked in first year, feeling overwhelmed and out of my depth in that alien environment, her encouragement and continuing confidence was a substantial and important factor for me worth more than any wealth. It's only now I realise the importance of that faith.

I was not conscious of modelling myself on anyone. If anything, I was aware of trying to break the mould I felt born into. Always struggling against what looked like my destiny, I knew I didn't want it, but got lost in my own search for self before I could emerge in my twenties and start making a decision for me.

In my first few months at law school it seemed everyone was speaking in tongues. I was in shock. I could identify with no one. On several occasions

I had to run out to the parking area, desperate to reach my car before tears poured over me, overwhelmed, alien and isolated. On one such occasion, I drove to my mother's house in Dandenong, confiding in her that I wanted to admit defeat, accept I'd tried to go too far and could not make it. To calm me down, she suggested it was not too late to return to teaching. That was the sobering thought I needed. What I was never able to explain to my mother, but what I know now, is that I instinctively knew I was on the brink of something big. I was about to be allowed a special view of the inner workings of the machine that controls us.

> The breakthrough came after my first test in contract law.

The breakthrough came after my first test in contract law. I had been anxious about my capacity to understand, think or write like a lawyer. I had been around the law school for just two months and still felt totally intimidated. I had the impression that all those privileged young men and women had a different intellectual make-up, putting me out of the running.

I was relieved when my first test was over, because I hadn't dropped dead in the exam room. With some trepidation I entered the lecture room the day our papers were returned. The lecturer was grim and full of doom. My heart sank; I was hardly listening. When she said she was only going to mention one person who had achieved the top mark, I vaguely came back into focus, thinking how unfair it was because of course it would be some judge's son or daughter who had achieved such greatness.

I heard my name. Everyone was looking to see who it was. She said it again. I went to collect my paper. The lecturer had no idea what a turning point that was for me.

In my early years at school, I was good at all academic subjects as well as good at sport. I got the sports award in high school as well as honour subjects and the others tolerated it, I think, because I wasn't good looking. I was humble and modest as my mother had taught me to be. When you're good, let other people do the talking, you don't have to tell, she always said. However, into my middle adolescence I dropped behind in maths especially. In Form 4, I failed and was shocked to the core. I didn't ever really understand what happened except that I remember maths and science being something that boys did and girls did English, art theory and languages. I loved literature, language and philosophy, and got no joy from maths and science. As an adolescent one learns nothing of the world from $E=mc^2$ but John Keats, Andrew Marvell, John Donne and Shakespeare and Emily Dickinson all created a world I adored. My mother read to us, listened to us read and bought books for us.

Over the years I have been in practice, my feminism has grown and developed and taken shape in a far more articulate way. What the law can and should do for women but fails to do is a constant source of work, discussions and action. It is central to my daily life in practice. But just as important is what knowledge of the current legal system can do for women too. A feminist approach to the practice of law means one is open to issues much larger than a piece of legislation. Even if one can do no more than explain the law in a clear and sympathetic way to a woman who seeks advice, it is a feminist act. To be a committed lawyer is to be a fighter and an advocate. To be a leftist feminist lawyer is to engage in a constant struggle, inciting fear and anger in hearts.

I have not felt much difficulty in being a woman when it comes to clients but that is because of the law I practice. Were I working in corporate law, I am sure there would be an entirely different attitude. One favourite story springs to mind. I exited from a harrowing day at the Family Court. My client was calm, sensible and rational but her de facto husband was the opposite. He had come to be her support. He understood nothing of what had happened that day. Outside the court as we were leaving he made a snide remark to me: 'You've gotta have balls to do this job.' I comforted myself with the line in my head: 'Yes, sonny, but who wants them between their ears.' Generally I have enjoyed good relations with my co-workers. However, on a number of occasions I have gained a definite sense of being patronised. Middle-aged male solicitors form the largest single such group: 'Look dear, I think you'd better let your boss handle this one—' My steely reply: 'I am the boss, now give me your best shot.'

Working in family law provides an insight into how much or how little we have advanced in equality of the sexes.

Working in family law provides an insight into how much or how little we have advanced in equality of the sexes. Affidavits prepared by male colleagues contain gems like the Husband who thought he should have custody of his two small children because over the last six months the Wife had got depressed and 'sometimes failed to properly prepare the evening meal and this task fell to me'!

Other difficulties can arise with male members of the police force. Once I arrived at a police station at 7 pm to attend upon a client. Cold, hungry and tired, I intended to take instructions as quickly as possible and leave. I had earlier confirmed my visit by telephone and struck no problem. Upon arrival I was told to wait, which I did for five minutes, then a further 10 minutes until I again approached the counter, explaining I had arranged a professional visit and could I please see my client. There appeared to be no barrier: he was in the cells waiting, I was nearby. Upon my becoming insistent the sergeant was summonsed. I was led to the cells. My approach was heralded by the yelling of the sergeant: 'Hey, Brown, there's some sheila here to see ya.'

Out there in the community, sexism is thriving. Drinking one night at an hotel in Carlton with some female colleagues, a couple of well-heeled boys standing at the bar questioned us: 'You in the teaching game girls?' 'No,' we replied. 'Law.' Not to be outdone they replied 'Oh secretaries, we were close.' 'No, lawyers, you're miles off, boys.' We left, but smiling.

There is genuine camaraderie amongst female members of the profession. A sympathetic ear is available for the sexist difficulties one confronts. Nonetheless, some women in practice haven't yet lifted the veil. In 1990, a female practitioner at the Family Court was heard to say, while speaking of a group of women who ran an outer suburban women's refuge, that they were 'sensible, good women, they're not feminists or anything'.

I went into law knowing that it was part personal journey and part public struggle. I cannot yet see the end of the road. The struggle brings its own motivation, energy and inspiration that comes from the victories, however small. For as long as I still have the energy to offer my skills to combat the oppression and degradation of women I cannot see myself sitting easy and still.

The greatest reward in the practice of law has been 'cracking the code': the mysteries of the system gradually undraped. It is difficult to describe the process of learning that the system is nothing more than a set of unspoken codes and networks. This revelation provides strength and insight, the knowledge that action brings change, and the capacity to show other women that there is light at the end of the tunnel. The excitement is knowing you've been let into a secret — and now you're telling everybody.

Optimism instilled in me as a child has served me well. It carried me through the blacker periods when the way seemed steep and hard. However, I have experienced great frustration from time to time in periods of failing in confidence, my reversion to the scared girl from Dandenong. I do not accept the proposition that if I can do it so can all other women. Growing up in the 1950s and 1960s, the boom time in Australia, the popular myth of the lucky country was the rags-to-riches syndrome. But it was a male dream. I dreamed of greatness, but I do not remember sharing my dream with anyone except my mother whom I trusted implicitly to be enthusiastic and encouraging. Many young women from Dandenong in the 1950s and 1960s would not have had their horizons lifted in the way I did. As well with women continuing to be repressed and oppressed on account of race, ethnicity and religion, we have a long way to go before we all have equal opportunities, even amongst women. I feel as if I slipped through the net rather than achieved what my peers could also have achieved. My mother told me I was born under a lucky star and I think it helped.

WHY AM I DOING THIS?

Diane Fingleton

Diane Fingleton commenced studying for a Bachelor of laws at the University of Queensland in 1980. Earlier, she worked as a secretary in Australia, England and the United States of America. Diane Fingleton was instrumental in establishing the Women's Legal Service in Brisbane, Queensland, and, with the election of the Labor government in Queensland in 1989, was appointed advisor to the attorney-general. She is currently working as a solicitor in a Brisbane suburban law firm.

My 'struggle' to achieve a career is exemplified for me be my memory of a conversation with my late, dear mother in 1981, the second year of my studies towards a law degree. It was a conversation over breakfast— just before I was leaving for an examination in torts, a second year subject. Mum had been to stay with me at my flat overnight. I hadn't seen her for a while, as I was ensconced in my 'swot vac'; however, I had given in to her desire to come and stay and help me by cooking me meals while I studied.

On that morning, heading out the door I said to Mum: 'Well, I'm off to become a lawyer!' She said something like: 'Well, good luck, love' —but not too enthusiastically, I thought. So I shot back: 'You haven't got a clue why I'm doing this, have you?' (I should add she and my father had been supportive of my change of career and helped me financially when I was a full-time student.)

Mum replied: 'No, not really— I really wish you were married with kids.' What I was attempting to do was something so alien to my mother, who did the traditional thing of marriage and children — first and foremost.

I was struck by the honesty of my mother's comment, but it didn't deter my ambition to become a lawyer. I was then 33 years old and finally was

171

WHY AM I DOING THIS ?

admitted as a solicitor in 1984 at the age of 37. I am not married nor have I children of my own. This is not to say that I think the combination of home duties and a career is impossible — I'm sure it's even more hectic.

My mother, until her death in 1988, grew more than used to my being a lawyer. My 'career' became something of a hobby to her, including, as it did, media appearances and a degree of notoriety and public profile. She never gave up her wish for me to be (happily) married and become a mother. I have been lucky enough to enjoy many special relationships, including those with my nieces, nephews and children of close friends — my 'borrowed kids'.

I encouraged my mum to accept my career by including her in activities which showed what I did and why I did it. She came to my admission as a solicitor. She attended functions at which I spoke or where others referred to my achievements. I alerted her to when I would be appearing on the media. She loved those occasions and all her neighbours listened. She was less than impressed when, during my student years, a neighbour would remark she had seen me on the TV news at a 'Right to March' demonstration. I know, after a while, that the penny had dropped for her...that she knew what I was on about, that what I was doing was socially useful and intellectually stimulating for me.

My mother may also have realised that it had all been at something of a cost; that life, especially for a woman, has its trade-offs and the single-mindedness, one way or the other, can leave her in a one-way tunnel. However, the search for balance and total fulfilment goes on. Recently, a bright, attractive woman who had married young and had three children alerted me to this. At about my age, she is beginning part-time studies and enjoying it. What I most noticed was her lack of self-confidence and later I thought to myself: 'I'm glad I've got my self-image worked out.' When I suggested I may have missed out by *not* having children, she said: 'I don't think so — work is *very* important to us all, don't you think?'

I first realised the importance of work while working as a secretary in London and then in New York in my early 20s. When I left school I had become confused, turning my back on my life-long ambition to become a school teacher. I knew I wanted to travel and, at the age of 21, set off on a working holiday to England and Europe with three good friends.

While working at a bank in London, I was influenced by an English woman who took her job as secretary to the manager of the bank very seriously and appeared to enjoy her work very much. Until then, my work as a shorthand typist was what I did for part of five days a week. The real point of life then was travel, having fun, dating. I imagined eventually I would marry, have children, and that if I worked after marriage, I wouldn't need any further qualifications or experience. My friend in the bank taught me everything I was to know about being a secretary, about organising time, prioritising, protecting the boss, and being pleasant about it all. When I went to New York (with the same bank), Australian and English secretaries were the 'flavour of the month' and my London training was useful.

Between 1969 to 1972, the Women's Movement went from its early to strong days in the United States. Ms magazine was required reading. In an 'equal opportunity' bank, I worked with Black women and men for the first time in my life. I met strong, confident women, like my American sister-in-law and her family. She came from a family of strong, New England women, not themselves in positions of power, but influential nonetheless, who expected a lot more from their men than did their Australian counterparts. I remember acutely when I realised I may have to support myself for quite a while — if not always. Living in New York, my budget failed me in one pay period. Sending for money from home was out of the question, as I needed money to live on. I did not, out of pride, want to ask my brother who was always most generous to me. I was, after all, attempting to be independent.

> I remember acutely when I realised I may have to support myself for quite a while — if not always.

Finally I borrowed money to survive, but vowed to take control of my life and consider the possibility of having to be serious about jobs which would provide me with security.

My American sister-in-law was the first woman I had known to combine career with motherhood by using childcare. After the births of both my nieces, Pam was back at work within weeks, my brother and she employing a series of childcarers who came to their home daily. My 'New York' brother was most supportive and they are a good example of a 'teamwork' approach to marriage. My nieces are now most splendid — and I have been a supporter of 'childcare babies' and parents ever since.

Upon my return to Australia in 1974, I landed a job on the staff of Bill Hayden, then Minister for Social Security and, later, Treasurer. I was one of the secretaries in the office and, as we often travelled back and forth to Canberra together, Bill Hayden and I became good friends. I learnt from Bill the value of hard work and how to make use of all available time. He often dictated letters to me on planes, reading from notes he'd made to himself on the edge of plane tickets.

As I became more politically aware and my involvement in the Australian Labor Party (ALP) grew, our discussions on planes became more political. I became one of the people he bounced ideas off. I had begun a degree in arts at the University of Queensland. He encouraged me to undertake further study, suggesting I should think about law. I was mixing with a lot of lawyers working for the federal Labor government but, at that time, I saw law as the private profession dominated by conservative males. However, Attorney-General Lionel Murphy (later High Court judge) was establishing the Australian Legal Aid Office. The concept of combining the practice of the law with working towards social justice appealed to my political consciousness.

The use of the law as an agency for social change continues to be my reason for being a lawyer. For some of my friends and acquaintances their aim has been practice in the courts to push the limits of the law; for others the aim is to become judges, to influence the direction of law; for still others, to use their status as lawyers to lead organisations pushing for social justice, such as civil liberties and Labor Lawyer groups and, for some, becoming parliamentarians. I became a full-time student in the law school at the University of Queensland in 1979 with a set goal: I wanted to work, as a legal aid lawyer, either in a community legal centre or at the Legal Aid Commission.

This carried with it some problems, but I am glad I took to the study of the law a critical, political perspective. Although it meant I felt alienated at times from the knowledge itself and the structure of the discipline, I was glad I had an ability to fit the concepts into the broader social spectrum. This was somewhat an unpopular stance to be taking at a conservative law school, so it was with great delight that, in my second year, I met some other feminists and we established a Women Law Students' Association. The friends made through that group (together with a few young male friends) made the difference, for me, between loneliness and fulfilment at law school and we remain close friends.

Women Law Students' Association activities included guest-speaker functions, public speaking workshops and a regular newsletter. We had a reputation for being much more radical than we were, but it was, after all, in the conservative climate of Queensland in the early 1980s.

Out of this group also was formed, eventually, the Women's Legal Service, in late 1983. What began as two rooms in Women's House in West End has developed into a vibrant, busy centre today in its own premises, still in West End.

When contemplating becoming a law student, I was terrified of being poor. I met Roisin (Hirschfeld) Goss (a social worker before she studied law) a couple of years before I decided to give up work to try to live on 'tertiary assistance' — TEAS (as Austudy was then called). I thought how brave she was, to cut herself off from regular income to study for some years. Roisin made it through, setting a great example to the women beginning to undertake law at the University of Queensland in growing numbers, assisting as she was to establish the Aboriginal Legal Service in Brisbane. She also was generous about sharing her excellent law lecture notes.

I began to understand real poverty only during my two years as an articled clerk.

Surviving four years at university, in my spare time I was a political activist, research worker, waitress, house-cleaner, shorthand teacher, babysitter, clerk. I began to understand real poverty only during my two years as an articled clerk. The rate of pay was low, and as I was completing the law degree part-time and studying post-graduate subjects towards admission to practice law, part-time work was not possible. I experienced an acute feeling of panic when I received a telephone or electricity bill. However, both at university and during that time, my friends and I could always make up a good party—with everybody bringing something along.

After 18 months' post-admission experience in private practice, I achieved my goal and got the job I had always wanted, as legal co-ordinator of the Caxton Street Legal Service, whilst remaining closely involved with the Women's Legal Service. Working for the Caxton Street Legal Service for almost five years, I took it to stage two of its development, past the struggle for survival in the early days, to a consolidation. It is now seen as a model for other community legal centres in Queensland (itself having been modelled on Fitzroy and Redfern Legal Centres in the south).

For me, Caxton represented a chance to combine skills accumulated to date — organisational, legal, political. The beauty of work in a community legal centre is its lack of structure. The workers, in tandem with their management committee, decide, largely, what they will do and when. Whilst studying at university, my main concentration was on such subjects as criminal law, torts and family law. I believed these would be my areas of involvement as a legal aid lawyer. Ironically, commercial law and company law should have dominated my attention at law school, as at Caxton, I became more involved with consumer credit issues. It was through this involvement that I felt close to challenging capitalist interests: frequently hitting at the sensitive issues of overcommitment of debtors and harassment by creditors.

In 1990 I reverted, in one sense, to a more political position: policy advisor to the attorney-general in the Queensland state government. The chance to be part of a government which was to institute reforms of what had been shown to be a corrupt system, was too much to resist. The opportunity to see the workings of the government, the bureaucracy and the legal system at a high level also propelled me toward the job.

Looking back at the last 20 years (dating from the time the idea of a 'career' started to occur to me), the obvious question arises — would I do it again? Friends and acquaintances often consult me about studying law and are surprised when I exercise caution. I don't believe many people are suited to it; I have seen the study and the practice of law change people, until they begin to take themselves, and the law, much too seriously.

Mixing with a large number of lawyers spoils one in one way; lawyers are usually clear and organised thinkers, and are good at isolating the key issues in a debate. The most negative aspect in lawyers is their self-absorption and narrowness of thought, and the belief that there is a legal solution to everything. Some, indeed 'fall in love with' the law — to their detriment.

Being very sure of what I wanted, older than average and having been a

WHY AM I DOING THIS ?

little well known may have prevented difficulties associated with being a woman I may otherwise have experienced. This is not to imply that I do not believe impediments to women in the legal profession remain. I was impressed by a comment I heard recently at a meeting of women. The convenor, a high-ranking bureaucrat, pointed out that people often tell her that she had 'made it', because she's special. She went on to say that all women are special and any woman can achieve her goal. Whilst the thought is a good one, problems still exist such as the structure of the legal profession, lack of part-time work and lack of maternity leave and childcare. Reluctance in offering partnerships to women, as well as inequality in levels of salary paid to women solicitors, demonstrate that there continue to be real barriers to women in the profession.

Retirement exercises my mind often. I anticipate an active one, with the chance to do at my leisure those things I don't have time to do now — like travel. However, that necessitates a comfortable financial situation. Hence my determination to have a healthy superannuation scheme in place.

In the meantime I face, along with other women engaging in careers to a greater extent than their mothers, extra stress. The search goes on for a balanced lifestyle.

I am grateful to all those women and men who lead from 'the top' like Justice Elizabeth Evatt, formerly Chief Judge of the Family Court and now President of the Australian Law Reform Commission, and Justice Mary Gaudron of the High Court of Australia. I also admire women working at community level like Zoe Rathus of the Women's Legal Service in Brisbane and Narelle Sutherland of the Caxton Legal Centre.

I thank also my friend, Monica Cowell, who proofread this piece for me — she knows the whole story, and was always a part of it, and Carol White, who has done the whole thing differently from me and is just beginning the story of her career.

SURVIVING AS A PEOPLE

Irene Watson

Irene Watson is 36 years old, a descendant of the Tangankeld people. The Tangankeld, prior to the invasion of Australia, occupied lands surrounding Kingston SE in South Australia. Today few of the Tangankeld people live in the local area. In 1985 Irene Watson graduated from Adelaide law school and was admitted to the roll of barristers and solicitors that same year. At present she lives outside Adelaide with her partner and three daughters.

I did not consciously decide I wanted to become a career woman. I did know what I didn't want to be: a victim of racism and dispossession. My modus operandi has been to arm myself against both.

Have I been successful? No. There is no escape from racism, as yet; dispossession for the majority of Aboriginal people remains and, on current trends, will continue. My mother, her mother and her mother before her suffered the same experiences of racism and dispossession. I inherited that suffering. My greatest desire is to change that social disorder. I have never sought to become a part of the hierarchy of a society that has so brutally dispossessed my family and continues to deny this ever occurred.

I was never ambitious in any of the areas traditionally the domain of men. Yet on another level I am ambitious: to be a well-placed Aboriginal person living in harmony with both the ecological and the human environment. That is the most ambitious thought I could have.

The most difficult aspiration for Aboriginal people in Australia is simply to assert Aboriginality. It is a struggle for us to live with the appropriate social standards, because Australia is a racist society. An individual who opts for assimilation (by absorption into the dominant surrounding culture) has limited opportunities for survival. Only if a person fits in, and doesn't rock the boat, is she allowed to stay there and even grow rich and prosper. Society prohibits the growth and development of the Aboriginal people as a people. Aboriginal communities all over Australia are in crisis; whether the community is an urban or a bush community the suffering is the same. Dispossessed of the basis of our lives, our laws, religion, land and the loss of our people we struggle to remain intact.

The poverty I have experienced was not self-inflicted; poverty never is. My family's poverty was caused by a history of racism and dispossession. As a child it was difficult to understand why my family life was different from most other families. When I attended school, to be an Aboriginal was to be intimidated, by what seemed like the entire school, for the spearing of Sturt. Social studies classes became something to endure with the images of my culture constantly referred to negatively. The education system reinforced the racism, alienation and isolation. Remember we are just 1 percent of the population. A people who 200 years ago were a majority, and in possession of Australia, are now dispossessed. Most who have survived struggle to hang on to a lesser, dehumanised existence.

> My family's poverty was caused by a history of racism and dispossession.

As a child I despised the ugliness of the city and urbanised environment. We lived in a suburb of Adelaide in government housing. Every house in the street, and in the entire three surrounding suburbs, was exactly the same, except for an occasional change of colour. Trees did not exist, gardens were a rarity, open green lawns were the thing. For most of my childhood we rarely left the area. I often felt one could die from the total boredom, and sadly that continues for many young people stuck in that environment.

I don't understand a society that expects sensitivity from a youth experiencing only harshness. I know, from my own life in poor urban centres, that if a person has no regular breaks and visits to the bush, the energy of the cities seems to take over.

I made a decision, as a child, that I would struggle to change the ugliness surrounding me, try to find a better world for the people who needed it. Studying law was a means of achieving that aim, yet my decision to study law was made much later, at 27-years-old.

Initially (I was about 18-years-old) I attempted to create change and awareness through film. As a film-maker, I wanted to use this effective medium to communicate to the world what was happening to Aboriginal people and our natural environment. It was the 1970s and I lived in Sydney, greatly influenced by the Redfern Aboriginal community initiatives. I completed a number of documentary videos with Aboriginal people talking about their lives. One story was of young children in juvenile institutions, *Political Prisoners No. 1* (it was the first of an intended series). I quickly discovered that the resources to make films are scarce in Australia and even scarcer for films critical of Australian society.

I never visualised myself as a lawyer; it was not a burning desire. Soon after I was admitted to practice, one of the women who graduated with me suggested how I might look wearing a wig and gown and asked was I 'excited about the prospect?' I wasn't. For me, becoming a lawyer was about using whatever means were available to negotiate change. 'Doing law' was more about ensuring I would continue to wage a struggle to empower myself in the world. Over the years in a number of situations I was intimidated by the law, its traditions and language. To become a lawyer was a means of self-defence; finding a way of not letting the system take control; and to help make the world a better place. I'm not sure I still believe in the simplicity of that idea.

> For me, becoming a lawyer was about using whatever means were available to negotiate change.

Paidwork was never a priority. In Aboriginal society the concept of wealth is not relevant. My family life has been a balance of taking only what is necessary. I've tried hard not to get carried away with western materialism. The Americanisation of our lives through exposure to television poses problems for all Australians. Subliminally viewers' identity becomes overwhelmed by another world, which is remote; conflict of identity arises when fulfilment of the television vision is unattainable.

Those who are poor tend to watch a lot of television. I did. A part of the struggle has been to de-program myself from a television non-reality. I understand how difficult it is for people who spend so much of their time sitting passively before a television set. Our lives would be richer without the uncontrolled influence of television. It is not that there should be no television, but a greater awareness of how it affects our lives is necessary. I try to keep external influences in check and analyse how those influences affect both myself and family. My adrenalin pumping to buy–buy–buy is about being a poor person looking at so many luxuries on television.

For us to survive in peace the affluent must stop extracting and start sharing. As an Aboriginal person I am not advocating equality of lifestyle with the western world but campaigning to Aboriginalise the western world. Our global survival suggests there is no other course; anything else will result in the death and destruction of the environment and its people. We cannot all be hunters and gatherers, but the few people who monopolise most of the world's resources can learn to live more simply.

The attitude one has to money is important. If money is merely a means of acquiring necessities, then it is not something to attach a great deal of importance to; for me it is about basic survival. If money had motivated me in a career sense I would have been working full-time and possibly in a highly paid position. Also I cannot cope with a humdrum position: work has to be valid, a position I can see will achieve results and changes, challenging the basis upon which Australian society is built. I have never applied for a position because the $ looks good. The work I do is related to what I know must be done and in the best way I am able. My present involvement with the Aboriginal Legal Rights Movement as chairperson is not a paid position, but it is important.

Even the work done by the Aboriginal Legal Service is mostly crisis management work, dealing with the total stress under which the Aboriginal community lives. Such work is demanding, with marginal rewards. After you have said 'goodbye' to the same person three times around, on their entry to gaol, you begin to ask why am I doing this? If you know the people, and feel a part of them and the community, you can't do that work all the time. Your spirit grows tired. I have been criticised for stopping work to be at home with my family. I've even been criticised for having a family. I reached such a level of stress that there was little choice but to just stop, reflecting upon what I was doing.

I didn't want to become the greatest gunslinger in the court room. (It certainly does wonders for the ego but I wanted more.) In those situations I felt spiritually vacant. That was intolerable. For my own survival as an Aboriginal woman I have had to go slow, stopping to look at the world spinning out around me so as to gain the ability to focus again on where I am going. Now, I'm strong and ready again. The work that needs to be done is endless; and I hope to see us making positive inroads and changes.

Early in life I learnt that where money was involved, one had to make a sacrifice. I never minded working hard, my mother worked hard most of her life, providing me with a model. I have also worked hard as a waitress, cleaner, clerical officer and fruit picker: sacrificing my time and labour. The sacrifices that most concern me are those where a person is required to denounce principles and loyalties to family and community. Working in the public service was stressful, particularly in Aboriginal Affairs, because the policies and outcomes were never of any lasting benefit to the Aboriginal community. More often the initiatives of government were about undermining Aboriginal self-determination, rather than implementing the policy.

I grieve for all the good values and traditions rapidly passing from our lives. There was a time when our people were happy to be together in each other's company. But there is so much sadness in our lives, so much that has been stripped from us; when you are a people dispossessed of land, culture and language it is an eternal battle to keep the spirit strong. I become very tired but fortunately many other battle-worn allies keep the fires burning. Australian society does not understand how we feel.

The only way I feel right about myself is when I'm fighting for what Aboriginal people have fought for in this country for 200 years: the right to be recognised as Aboriginal people, and to be self-determining of our lives in a real sense. That will fully occur only when the Australian government and governments throughout the world recognise Aborigines are a sovereign people. Until then it is vital for our survival as a people to assert the right to self-determination on all aspects of our lives — our legal rights, health, housing, education, all functions of our existence must be determined by ourselves, from the perspective of positive Aboriginal development and not of welfare dependency.

The federal government from the 1970s onwards has boasted of a policy of self-determination for Aboriginal people. It's not true. An enormous struggle is waged by the Aboriginal organisations to provide basic services to the communities. Sometimes there appears to be a conspiracy by government to demean the Aboriginal people directing and determining community initiatives. The common experience of most Aboriginal organisations is the critically short supply of resources and the constant review and scrutiny by what was once the Department of Aboriginal Affairs, now ATSIC (the Aboriginal and Torres Strait Islander Commission). Our organisations have never been adequately equipped to do the necessary community work. Achievements say much for the determination of Aboriginal people who have made things work even under duress. Paternalistic over-administration of our affairs has been largely responsible for the absorption of the budget allocated for Aboriginal affairs, and the control of grassroots initiatives. The racist assumption that we are a people in need of managers, administrators, and spokespersons, undermines traditional Aboriginal structures — for example, the Aboriginal elders, and community-based decision-making. Traditionally decisions were arrived at following lengthy community discussion, and based upon consensus. Aboriginal communities throughout Australia, dispossessed, relocated, fragmented, in crisis, attempt to revive Aboriginality in the decision-making process.

This seems the most difficult process to regenerate. So much of the decision-making for allocation of resources is decided by governmental structures remote from the people. Even ATSIC remains remote. Although it boasts of broad community-elected representation, self-determination and recognition of Aboriginal people, ATSIC, like previous administrative structures imposed upon Aboriginal people, is merely a window-dressing exercise designed to dupe the Australian public into believing something positive is being done. ATSIC will become the mechanism used by the federal government to mainstream existing Aboriginal programs. The recession creates increased political pressure to do this.

The ATSIC regional councils will have the unenviable role of making hard decisions on funding of Aboriginal programs. Ironically the Aboriginal people are being given some degree of autonomy when decisions have to be made on how thin to slice the cake, or who should go without. Continued imposition upon Aboriginal people of structures that do not recognise our status as a people, our rights to be self-determining, and the right to be compensated for dispossession, will not correct the injustices of our history.

SURVIVING AS A PEOPLE

Life is a journey. To view anything as simply a career feels too narrow and simple. It's like referring to your life in fragments: this part is my career, this is my creative side, this is my family side; I have a perception of myself as one whole. I'm an Aboriginal woman, who is a daughter, a mother, a sister, a partner and, yes, I am also a lawyer. I am annoyed when people say 'hello nice to meet you oh, you're a lawyer'.

My role models are people who were close to me in my growing up, particularly the elders. The main influence was my mother; I didn't consciously model on mum; I think that just happens. Many of our people have been denied that relationship through policies directed towards the total disintegration of our society, those of separating Aboriginal children from their homes and family. This was an attempt to speed up the process of assimilation. I was spared that, and am grateful for the relationship I was able to nurture with my mother. Learning from my Aboriginal mother who has hung on to the remnants of the teachings of her mother, and mother's mother, and on down the line gives me much to be grateful for. My mother is a strong person, maintaining a sense of humanity when many others I know caved in under pressure. My mother's strength rubbed off onto her children, all five of us. That is my strength and will be the strength for my children.

Our family grew up in urban isolation and our mother was left with the hard job of teaching what knowledge she had of her heritage. Few relatives lived nearby so mum spent a lot of time alone. In those days, the early 1960s, we saw few of our people living in the city. It was a lonely experience but we were carried through by our mother's sense of humour and skills in theatrics. I draw on those skills to survive, it's a gift.

There are other mothers in my life. In our way, our family life is extended, and a number of other Aboriginal women took on, for me, that mother-figure role. They were there for me when I needed them. That wealth is the basis of our survival. Not all teachers were women. The men in my family were staunch, a mixture of intellectuals, performers, singers and philosophers, in the Aboriginal mould. One of the greatest visionaries I ever came across was Uncle John; he foresaw much of what is happening in the world and gave me many of those insights, helping me to survive.

I endured the torturous course of learning law because I wanted to understand a language that baffled me. It was about the time when both the federal and the South Australian government were negotiating Land Rights legislation; there was much discussion about what form of title to confer upon the people. The process was disempowering. I didn't understand a great deal of what the lawyers were talking about. Resistance to feeling disempowered surfaced, and I knew I couldn't be dependent upon the advice of other lawyers. Once I acquired the knowledge of how the anglo-Australian legal system worked, I had a detailed insight into how the law had justified one of the greatest land thefts in legal history.

My family may have been a bit daunted by my pursuit of legal studies.

However, generally they were encouraging and have been my greatest allies. Others suggested it may be too difficult for an Aboriginal woman, a sole parent and poor as well to take on such a difficult task. One person commented once (and ironically it was a well-respected educationalist) that he was concerned I may not be able to cope with the inevitable failure. The remark made me more determined. A similar comment came from a white male lawyer: 'The experience may be too stressful.'

I am now teaching at the University of South Australia a course titled 'Aborigines and the Law', which I wrote. I enjoy the freedom and balance of teaching legal issues affecting Aboriginal people with the day-to-day involvement I have with the Legal Service and the community. Prior to studying law the only lawyers I knew were the one or two who had worked for the Aboriginal Legal Rights Movement. Isolation from other lawyers has made my entry into the profession a great deal more difficult. A lawyer needs to be in contact with other lawyers.

I have not modelled myself on any perceived image of a 'lawyer'. I have been strong about reflecting or imaging Aboriginality. I saw an American Indian woman lawyer in a film acting in a land claim and in her address to the court she spoke as an Indian woman, but with the knowledge of the American legal system. In the unenviable position of negotiating on behalf of her people, her manner was powerful and strong. Rather than adopt the style and presentation of other American lawyers she presented as an Indian woman. It was perhaps one of the strongest influences in my life.

Rather than adopt the style and presentation of other American lawyers she presented as an Indian woman. It was perhaps one of the strongest influences in my life.

Schooldays were not happy days. I left school in Year 12, at 16 years of age. The education system failed me. It had little relevance to my life; my lessons were endlessly meaningless. I had lengthy arguments with my lecturer in Australian history on a number of important issues. I was taught that Aboriginal resistance to the invasion of Australia did not exist and that there were no reported massacres of Aboriginal people. For me this was a clear conflict of information — an absolute lie. The history I had been told by family and friends was a different story — a story of poisoned water holes, concentration camps (politely referred to as missions), homelessness, sickness, death, rape and murder. At 16 I had less patience and ability to endure so I left.

I was told to apply for a clerical position with the government and was sent to do a vocational guidance test based on IQ testing. On completion I was advised secretarial employment was an appropriate career path for me. The guy who told me of my results was glowing, as if I should have been over the moon, really pleased that my results had come up secretarial duties and not cleaning. I wasn't at all satisfied with the procedure; the interview seemed controlled and contrived. I decided to ignore the advice and do whatever it was that interested me.

It was 1970, and I was employed for the first and only time by the public service. An impatient person, I like things to happen quickly. Working for the government was an exercise in frustration. Following my exit from the Department of Aboriginal Affairs, I spent a number of years working at any available employment: cleaning, waitressing, cooking, shelling prawns, packing tomatoes, taking jobs wherever I happened to land. I lived a nomadic existence, travelling a lot and enjoying a range of experiences and knowledge. It was a happy, creative period. This was how education should be, real, relevant and dynamic. In this time I learnt most about life.

In 1979 I decided to give formal education another try. A sole parent in receipt of social security, I was living a lifestyle familiar to many Aboriginal and poor people throughout Australia. I enrolled in the Associate Diploma of Aboriginal Studies. The course was never regarded with any degree of academic esteem, but it was about my life and that's what I had the greatest motivation to understand more fully. Even then I was advised that the course may be too difficult and was cautioned about my enrolment. It was as though the white man was always there advising and controlling our destiny. I completed the diploma without any major obstacles, and had some input through criticism of the course content. Unfortunately many of my ideas were never recognised or supported.

Becoming a student again, the greatest challenge for me was to express myself through writing. I had grown accustomed to expressing ideas orally. It was difficult to translate all that thinking into a written form. (Aboriginal culture was and still is predominantly an oral society.) The transition into the written word is about a different style of communication and education. As a child and as an adult student I had no assistance. There seemed to be an assumption that urbanised Aboriginal people didn't experience educational and cultural differences when attending school. Yet we are not dissimilar in tradition to people living in remote bush communities. In both situations information is passed on by word of mouth, children are taught by the telling of stories, very few parents have an extensive education, and few communicate through writing.

After completing the diploma, I enrolled in law at Adelaide University. The Northern Territory *Land Rights Act* had been enacted with the Pitjatjantjara *Land Rights Act* to follow; there was discussion of a National Land Rights Act and everyone was talking about 'the Treaty'. I wanted to understand the process.

As a law student the greatest hurdle was convincing myself I needed to finish the degree. I had started it and wanted the satisfaction of finishing. During those four years of study, I became disenchanted with the legal system, seeing it as a long drawn out process of somewhere somehow someday a result may be achieved. The grinding slowness of it all was painful. Most difficult was my own constant analysis and questioning of the validity of what I was doing.

I am a strong woman. Aboriginal culture is about 'caring and sharing'. The strength of our women has been passed on from generation to generation, and women have a visible and strong place in all situations, we just do things differently from the men. Being a woman is central to anything I have ever done. Women need to be everywhere. There needs to be a balance between the male and the female energy, because when it's out of balance that's when problems arise; look at the world now. Those imbalances don't arise in traditional Aboriginal societies. Women must be involved at every level to share decision-making and the future in the same way. Aboriginal women have historically been a part of that process, in law, medicine, healing, economic survival, and the spiritual well-being of our communities.

What has happened to us as a people is similar to what all women have experienced; our disempowerment as a people is similar to the disempowerment of women. But there are major differences. The effects of racism on my life have been a greater blow than any experiences I have had through sexism. The combination keeps Aboriginal women's backs up against the wall.

I believe in one step at a time, taking each day as it comes. The thought of retreat, perfect peace, and harmony, is seductive. I could easily drift off into a lifestyle accommodating all that. I know what will not change about myself is the continuing struggle for truth and justice. What might change is the way I choose to achieve that lifelong commitment. My spirit is gladdened by the capacity for people to change for the better, and when those situations occur I feel a lot stronger. This affirms for me that one day we may become a humane society.

> **The effects of racism on my life have been a greater blow than any experiences I have had through sexism.**

I am proud of myself for becoming a lawyer. I got a lot of satisfaction finishing. The feeling that followed was self-empowering. The self-discipline I taught myself as a student has assisted in other areas of my life. Having a law degree has made it more difficult for people to identify me as simply a stirrer or a radical, and even though some may still hold that opinion, it's more difficult for them to dismiss me without listening. While they are listening there is an opportunity for change.

My aims for my children are simple. They are that my children have a future, that they learn the normal cycles of nature, of how the seasons change, and never see the sky darkened by the effects of war and pollution. I desire that they grow up in a healthy environment free of pressure and be fulfilled in their lives. My children are all girls and I want them to know and realise their roles as Aboriginal women.

The main differences arising for people when making decisions about their life's path relate to motivation, the choices we make and the availability of opportunities. If the opportunity doesn't arise—well you don't do the impossible. Recently an overseas visitor asked why I was the first Aboriginal person to graduate from Adelaide law school? Why had it taken so long, until 1985? Why? Opportunities were non-existent for my predecessors.

I don't ever see myself as 'retiring'— that's like retiring from life. I often want to stop and recently have done so. Some days I feel as though I've been fighting with everybody and it's at those times I stop and rest for the inevitable more 'fight'. I am a peaceful person and I hate to fight, but most of the time you have to, just to survive.

BORN IN A TOMATO HOTHOUSE

Irene Moss

Irene Moss graduated in arts and law from Sydney University, later taking a Masters degree in law from Harvard University in the United States of America. She is the Race Discrimination Commissioner with the Human Rights and Equal Opportunity Commission, a federal body having overall responsibility for administering the Racial Discrimination Act, the Sex Discrimination Act, the Human Rights and Equal Opportunity Commission Act *and the* Privacy Act.

Prior to her current appointment Irene Moss worked with the then newly established Anti-Discrimination Board (from 1977 to 1986). Irene Moss is presently chairing the Human Rights and Equal Opportunity's Commission's National Enquiry into Racist Violence.

Two critical issues dominate my thoughts as Federal Race Discrimination Commissioner. First, how to make the most effective use of my limited resources to reduce discrimination against Aborigines: this is an endless task but even modest improvements in government services (such as clean water and basic medical facilities) and modest reductions in private sector discrimination (for example, in the provision of rented accommodation) can transform the lives of thousands of Aboriginal people. Secondly is a recognition that Australia is inexorably and inevitably becoming a part of Asia, as a result of economic forces. The critical problem for the Australian society over the next 25 years is how we will adapt to Asian economies, Asian society and the Asian people.

When I embarked upon my career, some 13 years ago, fresh from two years gaining a Master's degree at Harvard, I considered my background and training suited me ideally, almost uniquely, to this field.

I was born in a tomato hothouse at 47 Dixon Street, in Sydney's Chinatown. The place is now a fun parlour, but when we lived there it was basic, spartan, and grey. Like our neighbours, we lived simply. The family ate and slept on the second floor, and packed tomatoes as a business on the ground. My experiences up to five years of age revolved around this old building in Dixon Street, as part of the closely knit community of working-class and small business people who spoke various simple village dialects of Chinese and potted English.

Mother could not speak English but, in her life, there was no need to. She played the role of supportive wife to an extremely hard working man who rose every morning at 3 am to go to the markets at the end of the street. Crime was almost unknown; we were free to wander around day and night talking to our neighbours and friends. I accompanied my mother to her regular evening mah jong games with shopkeepers up the road.

My father was proud and obstinate, although genuinely concerned for the welfare of his family. I often thought he was mainly concerned about 'saving face', putting forward a 'front' that we were a successful and normal family. His ability to work was cut down tragically by a stroke when I was six. He never recovered properly. Even then I realised that the stroke had a devastating effect on his pride and manhood. He had 'lost face'. His only capacity to earn money for the family, being purely of a physical nature, was taken from him. My mother spent the next 25 years nursing him day and night, until that wore her down.

I have recollections of my father (when he was well) being active in club activities, always in the company of other conservative Chinese men. They were social gatherings to discuss politics of the 'old days', the 'old country', and the two Chinas. They assisted in giving the participants an illusory sense of importance in a new land, an alien land. Women were seldom active in these club gatherings.

My father was 15 years older than my mother, who bore me at 42 years of age. Because of the nearly 60 years between him and me, I looked at him as a patriarch, or even a grandfather. We were never really very close, but cared for each other, although never with open shows of affection. The mere fact that he was almost continually present made his influence significant. My later interest in 'public affairs' originated, I think, from him.

Nevertheless my mother played the most important role in my life. She gave me unreserved support, comfort and love. My mother was a strong determined woman, but not in an imposing way. She was dominant without being domineering, and influential without interfering. She was kind and totally devoted to her family. She supported me whatever my aspirations.

I feel sad, reflecting upon the changes in our relationship as I grew up. In the very early years, there were warm communications, children's stories of mountainous villages in China, children being stalked by tigers and saved by heroes. I trailed after my mother as she wandered off to her mah jong games, or accompanied her to horror movies, a penchant for horror films being almost a cultural trait for Chinese. That all changed when I began at school.

My mother had never gone beyond a couple of years of primary education in China. Highly intelligent, and wise, she was still an immigrant woman, constrained by an alien culture and language difficulties, unable to express herself fully and unable to experience the Australian society. She bore that frustration philosophically. My Chinese was pretty limited and although she and I were extremely close, it was a quiet love and understanding that never bubbled overtly to the surface. The gap between us in formal education created communication problems which both she and I hated. It was hard to express the finer points of issues or situations. Yet my mother's support allowed me to develop the way I wanted, without pressure to conform or to accede to the expectations of others.

The gap between us in formal education created communication problems which both she and I hated.

I was fortunate as the last of five children in the family, with 10 years between me and the next oldest. My older brother and sisters helped to insulate me from my father's traditional attitude that 'women should know their place'. Thus, I never felt the inhibitions about achieving, which previous generations of Chinese women suffered. It became apparent at about six that I was doing well academically. My first year at school was devoted to learning to speak English. The next year I came second in the class, and thereafter first, through both primary and high school.

My father soon realised this could reflect favourably on him. He proudly boasted to his friends about my results, much to my embarrassment. I would say to him: 'Da-a-ad, please don't,' thinking it might hex me for the following year (another Chinese trait). However, in a way I was glad he was getting such a kick out of it because he had so little to celebrate in those years.

My father was a good man, an honest man, but a man conscious that we as a family were here at the munificence of this country and so we should not 'rock the boat', or owe money; we should be forever grateful and for God's sake fit in. His unwavering policy was to ignore the bad and make the best of the good. He never got into a fight with anyone except people in his own family. With outsiders he always gave in. I wanted to be many things my father was not. I wanted to support many things he did not. Most of all, I did not want any part of his humility. The development of my assertiveness was a direct response to his insecurity and grew more in rebellion than in accord with his values.

I didn't want a traditionally female role or job; there was a limit to gratitude. I didn't want to be a second-class citizen because I am Chinese. If justice demanded, I would 'rock the boat'. Observing my father and family live out a meek and mild role of continual gratitude fostered an anger and urgency in me to break loose. If my father were alive today, no doubt he would have been proud of my role, but I doubt he would fully appreciate the significance or urgency of equality for all. In retrospect, I understand him better than I did at the time — his life was dominated by the basic and immediate issues of survival.

Everyone majored in the same subject at Belmore Primary and Wiley Park Girls' High — 'self-reliance'. But even now I envy children who were given all the decent breaks that going to a top private or public school would have offered. In reminiscing with a high school friend we concluded that hardly a handful of people from our year had fulfilled their expressed aspirations. Few went on to complete tertiary studies. Most had not moved further than five to 10 miles from where they had been brought up. Many of our schoolmates were highly intelligent, yet somehow the system failed to support these potentially high achievers in attaining their goals.

Despite the good intentions of many a fine teacher at these schools, the deficiencies were too great, locking us into a belief that second best would do. The teachers, at times wrongly, second-guessed that kids would not have high ambitions anyway, so why try and why inspire? Thus, we got a basic education, but ambitions were watered down; creativity, individuality and (heaven forbid) difference were not encouraged. I vividly remember the barriers which I and my schoolmates encountered when wanting to attempt the highest levels in our favoured subjects. Teachers were either not available to teach at that level, or it was done most begrudgingly. Students soon got the message. Mediocrity was far more acceptable.

> Mediocrity was far more acceptable.

One of the most positive aspects about my primary and secondary school days was the overall perception that my Asian background did not disadvantage me, albeit for many years I was the only Chinese or Asian at the school. Later I found another 'ABC' (Australian-born Chinese) and later still a student from Hong Kong. (Now there is an extremely high percentage of Asian and Lebanese students in my old schools.) For some, my Chinese heritage was a curiosity — schoolmates queried my features and eating habits at home in a friendly fashion. Mostly I was one of the gang and enjoyed the company of my schoolmates immensely.

A few problems seemed important at the time. I don't know whether those incidents forged me into the person I am today, or whether I would be the same anyway. In primary school I did well in all the subjects, topping most of them; my teacher always separating me from the rest of the class at examination time; I couldn't understand why, was it to stop me from copying others' exam papers or vice versa? She never offered an explanation. The same teacher at history lessons ridiculed the Japanese for bidding against each other at wool auctions; in discussion of the ravages of the Second World War, she called me silly in front of the whole class, for saying that six million

Jews died: she said that was not possible, 'it was more likely to be six thousand'. Finally, in my last year of primary school, I remember her miscalculation of our final grades. I knew she was wrong. The prize for the dux of the primary school was a black leather briefcase with the victor's initials engraved in gold letters. I asked for a recount. The teacher was appalled and felt I was insolent, but I demanded. The miscalculation was corrected. The school had to scrape off the gold letters FD and put on IKC. In a funny way the victory felt sour.

The vanquished FD (I thought she would resent me) asked me home for lunch. Her mother picked me up one Saturday, and together we ate sausages and mash; afterwards, her mum took me back home. I'm sure that was to show me that there was no ill-feeling. How my spirits soared that there were such good, kind, and fine Australians!

I remember the encouragement of a special woman who was my science mistress at school — Mrs Waller — who said to me: 'He who aims for the stars shoots higher than he who aims for the treetops.' Those people, and I have encountered a few, who were generous to me in their advice were special; they gave me the confidence to go for more in life.

Very few of us, particularly those whose parents are not able to give guidance, form a definite view of what occupation we want to enter at an early age. We have inclinations and favourite subjects, but unless you spent your life at the dinner-table listening to what your parents do, much of it is pot-luck. I had one advantage — I listened to my father talking about packing tomatoes and I knew that I didn't want to do the same thing.

> 'He who aims for the stars shoots higher than he who aims for the treetops.'

My leaning was towards maths and sciences at school. I was rather proud at being chosen to be a Professor Julius Sumner Miller science student (invited to a special summer school lead by the professor), but I knew at university science was not my thing. I lurched towards the humanities (or inhumanities) and I took up arts/law.

At university I became really conscious of haves and the have-nots. I came across students who developed 'in-crowds', from private schools and nice smelling tree-lined suburbs, who lived in students' colleges where the fees must have cost their parents the earth. They laughed together and lived and how I envied their luck. I don't care anymore, but it was important then, as I thought they had all the advantages, all the breaks. Perhaps that made me more determined to do something important, whatever that was to be — something that would show to myself I was not powerless.

I took to student politics, becoming arts representative on the Students' Representative Council, member of the Women's Union Board, and later of the Amalgamated Union Board. Sydney University student politics in the 1960s were heady and exciting. Australian society was immersed in one of the most contentious episodes of our history — the Viet Nam war — and students felt strongly about the issue. Recently graduated colleagues were conscripted. Some died in battle. Others took a stand on conscription and did time in prison. Students demonstrated, had sit-ins, and police were called in to quell riots. A prominent judge's son was arrested for pouring sugar into the tank of a police sergeant's mini-minor. Another well known activist was arrested for biting the governor's wooden leg; one colleague avoided expulsion only by pleading temporary insanity (very convincingly).

Students also felt strongly about the Springbok tours, going out onto the streets to show it. It was a time of economic buoyancy, a 4 percent inflation rate and almost full employment. Students knew they would find jobs after graduation. All of that encouraged them to express their various political views more actively. Those times of dramatic social issues affected Sydney University immensely and forged interesting people. My contemporaries, many of whom were involved in student politics, were David Hill, Michael Kirby, Clare Petre, Deidre O'Connor, Robert Tickner, Meredith Burgmann (who landed herself in the back of paddy wagons on many occasions), John Aquilina, Peter Collins, Nick Greiner, Jim Spigelman, Geoff Robertson, Geoff Ferrow (now deceased), Nick Enright, Charlie Waterstreet, Fred Schepisi — a colourful pot-pourri of activists, self-made people, now successful professionals, members of parliament, judges, artists, academics, who have since 'made it'. I departed from the University of Sydney with some regret.

I will never know whether my difficulty in obtaining articles of clerkship, to become a solicitor, had anything to do with my race. My gender probably played a part. I saw others, mostly male and anglo who had not done as well as I had in the exams, obtaining clerkships reasonably easily. I wrote hundreds of letters, receiving hundreds of rejections. I typed my Chinese surname in bold print so that, should my ethnicity be a consideration, they could reject me out of hand. I did not want to go through the charade of an interview. I did not bother applying to the most prestigious law firms, thinking the combination of being Chinese, female, poor family, good but not brilliant university grades, would be considered a joke application.

After short stints in a Chinatown law firm, and then the Attorney-General's Department, I went to Harvard, obtaining a Master of laws degree. Just before my return from Harvard, the New South Wales government passed landmark legislation, the *Anti-Discrimination Act*. This was what I wanted — working with social justice legislation in a new organisation on the ground floor. The position of conciliator was a prized one. The controversial legislation was subject to intense debate and public interest. Both Alison Ziller and June Williams, who were appointed, had been active lobbyists for the legislation for years. I felt guilty that I had won the position over many others who had worked tirelessly in the area. However, I was the only lawyer on the team. That proved invaluable to the organisation and to its then head — Geoff Cahill. The 'gang of four' conciliators all moved on to senior positions. Alison Ziller became New South Wales' first Director for Equal Opportunity in Public Employment, June Williams is Western Australia's first Commissioner for Equal Opportunity and Les McGowan is Deputy Secretary of Environment and Planning. We were junior officers back in 1977, but the selection committee, which included Carmel Niland, must have had a smell for drive.

Carmel Niland, later my boss as the first female President of the Anti-Discrimination Board, and Geoff Cahill each possessed a streak of larrikinism. They encouraged a degree of individuality and creative thinking. Carmel's iconoclastic bent was something the bureaucracy found unmanageable. I found it refreshing. She taught me a great deal. Most importantly she taught me that we couldn't run for the popularity stakes in these jobs; that once you are at the helm it is more important to decide than to dither, and then be prepared to wear the consequences. Being her deputy, it was instructive to observe the workings of decision-making in government, and how politically sensitive and controversial issues were handled. Walking that fine line of independence (our statutory position) and recognition of political reality and political power was exciting enough to cause the occasional missed heartbeat. We had to get things done, we knew that. But, to get things done, we had to survive — we knew that too.

Having worked as a senior female bureaucrat for many years now, I sometimes wonder whether women will ever be a part of the inner sanctum of decision-making. Women in the main continue to work at the margins. Also, I still, too often, observe women resorting to playing silly female games to get their way with men. I suppose they think they have to because men, too, play silly games. Often the only alternative for those women who have aspirations is to be 'just like their male counterparts'. I hope that I am not deceiving myself when I say I fall into a third category of 'playing it straight but trying to play it smart as well'.

> **Women in the main continue to work at the margins.**

Although the area of my work has been similar over the 13 years, the nature of it has changed dramatically. It has been extremely exciting and gratifying, at times stressful and at times frustrating. Working as federal Race Discrimination Commissioner at the Human Rights and Equal Opportunity Commission, and prior to that at the Anti-Discrimination Board, has been working at the cutting-edge of social change, not only at the micro, complaint level, but at the macro level.

For the first five or so years I handled casework, embracing the frustration, losses, victories, and gratification of helping individuals. I worked hard on a particular sex discrimination case where the complainant was a female academic claiming lack of promotion because of her sex. An extremely complex matter, both legally and factually, it broke university resistance to submitting to jurisdiction in the area. The walls of academic autonomy were slightly chipped by what I regarded as a landmark decision (but it probably went unnoticed by almost everyone else). I worked day and night on this case, first as the conciliator in charge of it and later, when it went to a hearing, I represented the President where respondents were represented by Queen's Counsel assisted by juniors and solicitors.

There was a partial victory at the end for a pretty battered complainant. But I felt that much of her anger and frustration were directed at me and the Anti-Discrimination Board. She wrote profusely after the case, rankled about the injustices of the system and how impossible it was for complainants to achieve justice simply and cheaply. I don't argue with her on that, but I don't see a ready answer.

Many of our cases were like that: thankless, tiring and almost impossible. Nevertheless, there is a special gratification to conciliating complaints; like the time we finally, after several years, resolved the employment status of three Vietnamese female workers who had felt that physical criteria for admission to the workforce in a large semi-government body were discriminatory; like the time an Aboriginal worker had almost given up on lodging a complaint, but my examination and investigation showed a case to answer and the final settlement (unfortunately its terms were confidential) was substantial; like the time my intervention in a case of physical abuse of Aboriginal women brought the perpetrator to book.

Then there are the disappointments. I remember with pain one case which I handled for a disabled complainant; I really did try, but the complaint failed. His final letter to me expressed anger that I had ever raised his hopes. Fortunately, there have been many landmark cases that not only solved individual problems but also helped to educate the community.

Over the years I moved into management and had less client contact. In December 1986 I was appointed federal Race Discrimination Commissioner, as part of the Human Rights and Equal Opportunity Commission which reflects Australia's international obligations as signatory to conventions concerning race, sex, the rights of the child, the mentally ill, the physically disabled, privacy.

Individual complaints are important. Attempting to solve problems of discrimination at a broader level so that such complaints don't arise is more difficult. One project tackling this is the national stocktake on racist violence, where and how it occurs and what solutions are available. Other projects have included looking at water supply for remote Aboriginal communities and promoting good race relations in the workplace by developing training modules and marketing them to companies.

In 1988 the Commission released the Toomelah report (on conditions in the Aboriginal town of that name). We saw the report as having a public education role. I had hoped that Toomelah could be used as a model for reform for the nearly one thousand Aboriginal communities around Australia, but to a great extent the Toomelah reforms occurred because it was under the national spotlight. The report did not have as broad an impact as I had hoped. My 1990 report on the police raids in Redfern was met with resistance from the New South Wales police force.

My visit to Baryulgil in February 1990, followed by my report, prompted an immediate response from the state and federal governments with promises of action and resources. Time will tell. Baryulgil is an Aboriginal community where, in the 1940s, the workforce mined asbestos. Many of the town's buildings and roads were built from the asbestos fillings. The community has been fighting to have the area decontaminated amidst legal battles, general neglect and debate over how dangerous asbestos fibres can be.

> **My 1990 report on the police raids in Redfern was met with resistance from the New South Wales police force.**

Perseverance and commitment are vital prerequisites for the job, but I have learnt that making decisions on emotion, ideology, concern for popularity, being more concerned about your approval rating, being touched with an unreal sense of your own importance or influence, detract from effectiveness and efficiency. All must guard against such human frailties.

Integrity, strength, determination, a mind uncluttered of bias and at times a healthy distancing from personalities with vested interests are essential. Assertions must be armed with evidence or facts, and nothing less can do when attempting to achieve social change. But underlying everything must be an understanding, or 'savvy' of the political climate, how decisions are made, who are the power-brokers, and understanding and anticipating the eccentricities of the people with whom you work or those you are trying to persuade to your point of view. That appreciation must be accompanied by a good sense of timing: when to do things as well as when not to. You have to be innovative at times and try a little lateral thinking, not be squeezed by tunnel vision, and then get in there and play the game.

I recognise the assistance of colleagues, staff and friends in the contribution to achievements I claim. I look back at team effort and strong leadership which saw dramatic social changes achieved at the Anti-Discrimination Board, especially the innovation of sexual harassment laws and their infusion into personnel and industrial relations policies and practices; the introduction of legislation against racial vilification in New South Wales was another milestone.

I have saved till last to say that the single most influential person in my life is my husband. Allan is a highly compassionate human being, with a finely honed sense of social justice and integrity. He has given me all the support, comfort and love anyone could conceivably imagine. I have learnt some key characteristics from him — discipline, a good healthy reliance on cold hard logic, realism, rationalism, thoughtful decision making and thoughtfulness. Allan and I have been through a great deal together. Hopefully there are more exciting times to come. Who knows.

PIECES IN A CRAZY PATCHWORK

Fiona Tito

Fiona Tito (née Smyth) has worked mainly in law reform and government policy development, ranging from compensation and people with disabilities through to sustainable agriculture. She is married with two children and lives on a 100-acre farm at Michelago, south of Canberra. Her many other interests include patchwork, bottling, soap making and writing poetry. Fiona Tito and her husband Ron are developing their farm and lifestyle to become more sustainable.

My childhood, teen years and early adulthood were lived in Panania, a western suburb of Sydney. My mother returned to work as a school teacher when I was just five, though I was not aware of that being different. She continued to work as a teacher until retiring at age 60 and, even now, continues as a casual teacher. My mother did the household chores. She was constantly busy, between working full-time, caring for us and looking after my father. Dad sometimes mentioned that he 'let' my mum work, as if it was a concession on his part. I always knew I would work for a living.

My father's influence on my life was great as well: I had an earnest desire to please him, to prove that I could 'do my best' — most important in the family. Both my father and my mother had an interest in social justice and the environment, before either became 'trendy issues'. Consistently they tried to have us act in a socially responsible manner.

My childhood was extremely busy. We had some jobs at home but mainly it was other activities. Brownies then Girl Guides, Sea Rangers, and later I was a Cub leader. I started piano at five and later picked up flute and bagpipes. My mother taught the conventional 'female skills' — knitting, sewing,

197

crochet, fancy-work and cooking. Mum and dad encouraged us with art classes. I attended ballroom dancing and Scottish Highland dancing classes at different times. There was Sunday School and church, and homework was important too. I was never bored.

From an early age I was a performer — acting, singing and playing for people. At school in second grade I organised a play for the teacher every Friday afternoon. Later I played lead roles in school plays and musicals.

Toward the end of primary school I attended a special class in the public school system for children with above average IQs. Another boy and I put together a script of the *Wizard of Oz*. Later I wrote a Scottish spoof version, called the *Monster of Ness*; the kids in the band where I played bagpipes put it on. An enormous success, we were asked to perform it at an old people's home.

I loved writing and reading, and kept a composition book from first class until it was damaged in a household flood. Everyone had to write a composition about what they wanted to be when they grew up. I wrote that I wanted to be a flamingo; this confused the teacher no end. I simply thought the birds were beautiful and could do something which I could not yet manage: stand on one leg.

> I wrote that I wanted to be a flamingo; this confused the teacher no end.

Looking back now, my childhood was not conventional. Mum and dad gave us lots of opportunity for varied experiences. My younger brother Lionel and I both went to the special class, but mum and dad said that being clever or good at something didn't make you a good or pleasant person. They stressed equality, though they had some religious prejudices and saw significant differences between boys and girls.

I wanted to be very good at something, but I never did find anything at which I thought I could be the world's best. Nonetheless I gained skills and insights which make up the patchwork of my character. As a teenager, I hoped that my being alive would make a positive difference.

When it came to choosing a career, I was advised by vocational guidance to become a doctor because I did well in maths and science. I wanted to be a journalist because I like writing but they said there was no money in it. My mother and father, while encouraging me strongly to study and aim for university, advised me that medicine was a difficult career for a woman who would probably want to have a family sometime. My boyfriend, whom I met when I was 15 and subsequently married (at 20), also disapproved of this choice and I went through high school not being entirely sure what I would be but expecting to go to university. Then, about six weeks before we had to choose our degree course, I had an enormous argument with the English master. He said to me: 'I do not know why the hell you are thinking of doing medicine or pharmacy. You should do law — you would argue the back leg off a chair!' It struck me as perfect: I would be able to write, probably perform, and to make the world a better place. Here was the opportunity to do all I wanted. Mum and dad were keen. It also seemed a suitable career for a woman who would one day have a family.

My parents were not fanatical about my having a child. They had waited seven years after marriage to have me and then my brother. They had used contraception when it was considered almost immoral for a married woman to do so.

Sex always interested me. I became sexually active in my mid-teens and, for several months, the boy who later became my first husband and I played Russian roulette by using a combination of condoms and the rhythm method. Once my parents found out, dad was angry and mum concerned. I was hustled off for a pill prescription. I remember going into the doctor's surgery with my mother; she told the doctor that I was engaged. I was 17. This had a lasting effect on me: I believed I had made my bed and so must lie in it. The relationship with that boy was tinged with difficulties from the beginning. He was a manipulative man who knew how important it was to me not to disappoint my parents and to be seen as a 'good girl'. I was seriously interested in a number of men during our extended betrothal, and even broke off the official engagement once because of someone else.

In the end we married. It was a disaster. He was violent on a number of occasions while he was unemployed. I felt extreme guilt that I had not been supportive enough. I look back now, amazed. I understand how women stay with very violent men. It is partly out of fear and a sense of terrible shame that somehow it is your own failure. There is also the terror of: 'Where do I go?'

I was at university in the honours year of arts when the marriage ended. I went to marriage-guidance counselling. The psychiatrist told me I should give up foolish aspirations of completing my degree and look after the man who loved me desperately. However, having completed my honours year exams and the thesis, somewhat bruised and battered but surviving, I told both the psychiatrist and my first husband to take a flying leap and continued on to complete my studies. I had been actively involved in the Women's Movement for several years by then, but it took some bitter experiences before I integrated the theory into action in my own life. I still find it easier to tackle many feminist issues outside rather than inside myself.

> I told both the psychiatrist and my first husband to take a flying leap and continued on to complete my studies.

Never much for being alone, six months after separating from my first husband I met the man who became my second husband. My first husband was the right sort of man in the traditional fairytale sense: he was the right religion, from the same ethnic background as I, older, taller, blonde — and my girlfriends considered him handsome. I determined that the person I would marry next — I always intended to marry again — was to be a person

I liked. I wanted someone like a good pair of worn-in walking shoes — comfortable to be with.

I met Ron Tito at scout camp in Sydney. I was a leader trainer and he was on camp staff. I knew he was different. I remember in the flurry of first passion dragging him into my bedroom. As I was trying to undress him he asked me for a coat-hanger for his clothes!

I was at law school. There were men everywhere, but before going out, they wanted to know your grades — I found that irritating. It was like that ever since high school. At school I apologised for having done better than whichever boy I was keen on at the time. It didn't stop me from trying hard to do well, but was a real downer socially.

It didn't worry Ron. An apprentice fitter machinist when I met him, he was barely able to read or write. He never thought a second about asking me how to spell, and to write letters for him. He even seemed to think that these skills (which I valued so much) were not so important. He seemed strong and self-contained. Having been together now for almost 12 years, I think his attitude to my skills probably arose from his immensely practical nature. He saw them as skills, but not more important than his skills, of which he has many. I think I agree with him.

Ron's father is Italian, immigrated in the 1950s. Ron's mum died when he was 13. His family was Catholic and my being a separated and later a divorced woman raised eyebrows. We share a similar life-vision and are interested in the same issues, concerns and activities. From the beginning we determined to move to the country: we chose Canberra. Now we have two children. Daughter Anna was born in 1985; Patrick was a homebirth in 1988. They have enriched our lives and I believe I am a better policy-maker for their existence. I have learnt about human nature and the great emotional connections existing between parents and children.

> We live on a 100-acre farm at Michelago.

We live on a 100-acre farm at Michelago. Ron built virtually all the house, with some assistance from me. Solar cells and a wind generator make our power: the house is not connected to mains electricity. We grow an increasing proportion of our food and, in time, hope to be self-sufficient in most food production. Fifty acres of the farm is 'locked-up' to regenerate trees on the sloping area. We work hard since our garden is organic, and are hoping to produce a surplus to trade in the local area.

I have picked up many of the crafts learnt as a young girl including bottling, making preserves and making soap. I learnt to handle a gun; I used it once to kill a dog which was killing my geese. I have had to cope with understanding in all its gory detail how meat gets to the table. I have not yet killed for my own food though I have plucked, gutted and butchered many animals now. Taking responsibility for this has been important to me. In many ways these aspects are more real and empowering than so much else I have done. It's like taking responsibility for organising the homebirth of my second child. Birth, death, caring for the earth and the people around me and working in the community where I live are vital to me.

Many new skills have been learnt since we moved to the farm. I spin fleece from our sheep. I sew many of my and the children's clothes, and furnishings for our house. I quilt and do patchwork, particularly crazy patchwork. I even won 2nd prize for one of my crazy patchwork coats at Cooma Show. The training ground of being busy at home has stood me in good stead. I have tried on occasion to cut down parts of my life to focus myself on 'just' work or 'just' one other thing. However when I do, I feel out of balance. I need each facet to make me effective in the other areas.

After completing my law degree, I worked for six months with Professor Garth Nettheim, writing on 'Open Justice'. The environment at university was isolated. If I was to change the world that was not the place to do it. I therefore decided to practice law in a law firm. I attended the College of Law. This was not the way to change the world either. I redrafted the legal precedents, attempting to make them user-friendly and readable by clients, much to the chagrin of my tutors.

The sexism of the College of Law appalled me. The mythology of the helpless woman, coming to you only about family law matters was alive and strong! It incensed me so much I wrote to the board complaining about sexism in the instruction material. It also irked me that all firms of solicitors had to be addressed as 'Messrs so-and-so' even where the partners included a woman.

The sexism of the College of Law appalled me.

Finishing at the College of Law, students had to fill out forms saying what we wanted to achieve. Law firms selected those whom they wanted to interview after reading these forms. I was scrupulously honest, putting down that I 'wanted to overcome injustice, reduce social inequities and make the world a better place for my having a law degree'. I received no interview invitations from any of the large commercial law firms in Sydney. An interview request came from the New South Wales Law Reform Commission.

I commenced work there after marrying my second husband, and was set to work on the accident compensation reference. This was an ideal reference. It raised issues of fairness and the treatment of people with disabilities. I was privileged to work with Marcia Neave, research director (and now professor of law at Monash University). She has been the principal inspiration on my working life. She is a successful woman who has not sold out on her principles and I grew to respect and love her a great deal. I also had the privilege of working with another lawyer, Ronald Sackville — a hard task-master but open to young and eager input such as mine.

I gained useful experience dealing with people traditionally considered intrinsically worthy of respect, such as judges. I saw many of them with all their human frailties and prejudices and discovered that, just as there were pleasant and unpleasant tradesmen and fitters at Ron's work, so there were at my work. We also had a woman with a psychiatric disability who worked at the commission. I became interested in this area through watching the difficulties the commission had in dealing with her and the discomfort I felt personally.

Marcia Neave and I together worked up a case-study program. The best people to ask about how to improve the accident compensation system were the people who had been through it. This was a novel idea. On a number of occasions I had to explain to people who had had horrific experiences with the compensation system that I would not actually be able to fix their situation. What they were telling me would perhaps make it better for other people in the future. Without exception, people said: 'That's all I want. I want people not to have to go through what I went through.'

These people had the most profound effect on me. I saw in human terms the problems they had to endure. I became passionate in my eagerness to ensure new systems worked to assist injured people in a financial sense and in an empowering personal sense. With some people I recognised their overwhelming sense of powerlessness. I had worked as a volunteer at the Women's Legal Centre and there I had sensed the same powerlessness.

At the Women's Legal Centre the powerlessness related to the social security system and the *Family Law Act*. While I could give women advice about their legal rights, such rights hardly touched their lives. One could say: 'Yes, you can get a restraining order to stop your separated husband from harassing you and beating you.' But the terror the women experienced could not be supplanted by a feeble piece of paper. And the piece of paper was unlikely to stop a man intent upon harm.

I continued working up to the birth of my first child, and returned to work part-time when Anna was three months old. Adjusting to the role of motherhood was extremely difficult; I felt incompetent. The birth had not gone as I expected. I ended up in the most undignified, powerless position of stirrups, episiotomy and forceps lift out. I had difficulty getting breastfeeding established, though once it was, I continued to feed Anna until she was one-year-old. This, together with the enormous emotional turmoil one sometimes feels after giving birth, made my three months at home unhappy. There was an immense sense of loneliness and isolation in the four walls of my house with an extremely wakeful baby.

Before going on maternity leave I had enrolled in the Master of women's studies at the University of New South Wales and a number of other classes, since it was clear I would have so much time. I was to be working only part-time. The reality and constancy of child-rearing had not entered my psyche.

It came as a terrible jolt once Anna arrived. I returned from hospital and was sitting in the lounge, when I realised it was Friday night. I burst into tears. My husband said: 'What's wrong?' I said: 'It's the end of the week and we don't get tomorrow off!' I made it through busy weeks at work with the thought that we had the weekend off. Suddenly I had a 24-hour-a-day job where I was so tired and there was no break: the stark realisation of parenthood.

I had an immense sense of protection towards my daughter, but confusion about what I had taken on. At other activities I had felt extremely competent. I had mastered a broad range of skills enabling me to run the gamut from helping to build my own house, feeding myself and, by this stage, working as senior legal officer at the Law Reform Commission.

By contrast here I was with one small child, whom I loved desperately, but with no idea what to do. I had a number of unpleasant experiences with the local baby health centre nurse. On visiting day, I spent the morning in tears in anticipation, and the afternoon in tears after being told I was not doing it correctly. I began enjoying being a mother only when I returned to work part-time and felt in control of something — and being sure of getting it done. I worked two 4-hour days and two 10-hour days, with one day off. With Ron's rostered day off, we travelled to our Canberra farm every second weekend.

After a short secondment to the Workers Compensation Commission in 1985, I returned to the Law Reform Commission to act as Research Director for about six months. However, I had already decided it was time to move. I had begun applying for jobs in Canberra when a consultancy came up in the Northern Territory involving a review of the workers' compensation arrangements. Ron left his job and we went to Darwin with Anna who was nine months old. In three weeks, I finished the job I had been contracted for three months, so I asked what they wanted me to do next: 'You can help us devise the new no-fault scheme for workers.' Working in the Northern Territory on this project was very different from what it had been in New South Wales. There we had undertaken extensive consultation with the union movement. In the Northern Territory there was no union consultation and limited consultation with employing bodies, such as the Master Builders' Association. In that three-month period we went from nothing to a scheme put before Cabinet. It was amazing progress. This was the first jurisdiction where an integrated occupational health and safety, rehabilitation and compensation system had been organised in the one body. I christened it the Work Health Authority and the name stuck.

In Darwin we met some people who lived at the solar village at Humpty Doo. This was a saving grace for Ron. He had gone from a full-time job into full-time childminding on the seventh floor of an apartment block in Darwin. Like me, he had intended to do a million things while looking after the baby because 'there was only the baby to look after'. His experiences opened his eyes about the realities of being at home with a child.

Then the Department of Social Security in Canberra asked if I was interested in conducting a review of the Commonwealth government employees compensation system. I thought: 'Why not — at least I might be able to see the spread of improved no-fault systems to another jurisdiction.' I started work towards the end of December in 1985.

The change to Canberra was dramatic. We went from a fully furnished serviced apartment five minutes from work to a 15- by 20-foot wooden cabin with no running hot water and limited access to electricity, which came from one solar panel and some old batteries. In a little shed outside, we used a chip-heater to make hot water. The toilet facilities were an efficient composting toilet some distance from the house. I thought: 'What have we done?'

Simultaneously, I experienced pleasure at finally moving to our dream farm. We had owned it for three-and-a-half years by then and had spent many weekends commuting between Sydney and Canberra. It was great to stop travelling: it took us four hours each direction. But at first I missed these extended periods of sitting in the car reading or doing a craft activity.

With so much work to be done on the farm and then in my new job, I did not miss it for long. My first goat was a Christmas present from Ron. Christened Griselda, she is still alive and still milking. When I look back, the next 12 months were absolute hell. Brian Howe, then the Minister of Social Security, gave me an immense amount of support but I had great difficulties with the Office of the Commissioner for Employees Compensation and within some parts of my own department. I was considered a young upstart and too new to 'really understand' the bureaucracy.

> I was considered a young upstart and too new to 'really understand' the bureaucracy.

Eventually having eked some very small reforms in the first three months, I suggested to the Minister that a wholesale reform could not be more difficult than attempting to do it gradually, which had been the department's preferred position. He agreed. We proceeded. At about the six-month point the then commissioner said if I continued in my reforming zeal he would ensure I never had another job in Canberra. History shows I am still a bureaucrat and he is retired.

I spent that next nine months negotiating weekly with a committee of the Australian Council of Trade Unions (ACTU) and devising, with my small team, a series of 12 discussion papers on each of the issues. It was a rocky road, involving a number of interest groups, in particular the Department of Finance. I went to Cabinet with the Minister for the first and, later, second submission — it was great to experience this end of the process. Once we had that first submission endorsed, with work progressing, the Minister asked me to work on income support for people with disabilities with Bettina Cass (now associate professor at the University of New South Wales Social Policy Research Centre). The Social Security Review had been in train for sometime. The Minister wanted to bring about the same transformation to the social security system as in the compensation system. As the compensation reforms were still in a reasonably vulnerable stage I was to conduct both jobs. This was a difficult period. I was pulled between the two obligations, and I was pregnant with my second child. The second submission to establish Comcare passed through Cabinet with much debate. I completed the first draft of the disabilities issues paper about three weeks before Patrick's birth.

This second foray into parenthood was thoroughly enjoyable. I was far more aware and in control. Labour was an hour only, so it was intense, but I had friends around me. Anna slept through the birth, which was in the early morning, but she saw the baby when he was about an hour old. It was a community event — both midwives were local women. That was wonderful in giving me positive vibes about birth and parenting. We often talk about it — how it went and what happened; it's an affirming experience.

This second foray into parenthood was thoroughly enjoyable.

Ron and I worked part-time for a period. When Patrick was about six months, Ron's job finished, so I went back full-time. I joined Brian Howe's staff as a consultant on disability issues soon after. I had to give up breastfeeding because of the interstate travel required — and was disappointed, as I immensely enjoy feeding. It was a crazy life — certainly not designed for parenting or having any family commitments. I smocked and sewed on the plane to give me some feeling of connection. I became pregnant 'accidentally' during that period. Having convinced myself it was a good idea despite the negative views of work colleagues and some family members, I miscarried at 12 weeks. It was devastating.

After Pat's birth, I got strength to deal with another difficult problem. I had had an eating disorder, bulimia, since I was 14. I had told no one in all the 18 years. It hadn't even had a name for me, until I started reading feminist literature about it. Rather than eating vast quantities like bulimics, I used it to control my weight. A fat child, I had been on diets for as long as I could remember. Making myself sick meant I could eat normally and still maintain my weight.

Whenever I was pregnant, it had stopped and I generally lost weight then. However, once faced with the stresses of caring for a little baby, working and being all things to everybody, it began again. I was scared because I was no longer consciously in control of it. My doctor at the Women's Health Centre suggested a counsellor — it took me almost five months to decide to go.

I had not told Ron until just before I went — I thought he would be revolted. He just said: 'Well, I guess you'd better go and see someone — it can't be good for you.' The 12 months of counselling were difficult — I was working in a high-stress job, with two little kids, living on a farm in a half-finished house, having a miscarriage. The counselling addressed issues relating to women's self-image and my own desire never to disappoint and to please everyone. It touched very uncomfortable aspects of all my important relationships. To help me work it through I joined a supportive group of women addressing eating disorders from a feminist perspective.

In the end, I decided I couldn't deal with it properly while still working as I was. I did not renew my contract with Brian Howe. It was one of the most difficult decisions in my life. I was so personally involved in the disability issues. It is clear that the human rights of so many people with disabilities are compromised by our society's institutions. And yet I felt I had to leave in order to enable me time to deal with my own situation.

I moved to the Public Service Commission's Equal Employment Opportunity Unit to develop their strategy for the 1990s. I called it *Further Steps Forward*. There was a supportive environment and a lot less pressure. We launched the policy in December 1989 with a party in Parliament House. It was great fun and hopefully a good start to implementing the program.

I was then promoted to the Senior Executive Service in December 1990, into the Policy Projects Unit of Department of Primary Industries and Energy (DPIE). I have been a trouble-shooter, with five different jobs in 15 months. This has included work on a legal policy document on resource access in National Estate areas, drafting the DPIE *Sustainable Forest Use Issues Paper*, a detailed paper on fisheries management and cost recovery, and a major work on sustainable agriculture. I have come to understand the economic rationalist viewpoint, and have brought a different vision to all the work. I influenced the policy formulation to have a broader perspective than it otherwise would. There have been some terrible arguments, particularly about equity and social justice. Opportunities have arisen to try out my different staff management style.

I am now in my mid-30s. Many challenges remain, together with injustices to be addressed. I have had a fair measure of success in areas I have targeted so far, but even in these, I believe, there is still some distance to go.

I am trying to live more closely to what I want to achieve more generally. Ron used to say I was so busy trying to make the world a better place that I'd forgotten about my life. I now know the importance of this, as well as the difficulties in achieving a balance. I try to work fewer hours and have proper time for my kids and Ron. I try to manage my staff using co-operative, supportive, egalitarian models in a stiffly hierarchical bureaucracy. I try to find time for the other things I enjoy like sewing, gardening and playing music. I have my eating disorder licked. We both work regionally at a political level within the 'green' political spectrum. I have had another miscarriage and have not made up my mind about another child. I have space in my heart but we worry about the space in the world.

Once, I was a big planner, but each year has unfolded new options. I have some broad aims which haven't changed. I no longer feel as frustrated as I did when I was a teenager that I am not the world's 'best' at anything.

I need all the parts of my life. My life is like the crazy patchwork I so enjoy making. Every part has different and interesting interconnections but when you look at each piece you wonder how it will all fit together. I would like to think that, at the end of my life, I will look at the pieces in the finished article and it will have a wholeness of its own.

BEYOND THE LEGAL MYSTIQUE

Beth Wilson

Born in Hastings, Victoria, Beth Wilson left school at 15 years of age. After working in shops and factories, in 1971 she returned to formal education, being admitted to practice as a solicitor and barrister of the Supreme Court of Victoria in 1978. She has worked with Telecom, the Victoria Law Foundation, the Law Reform Commission, Victoria, and as senior research officer, Policy and Legislation Review, Department of Health in Victoria, and a legal member of the Social Security Appeals Tribunal (SSAT). She is a committee member of Feminist Lawyers and a senior member of the WorkCare Appeals Board.

When I left the Pict Frozen Foods factory in 1971 to study arts/law at Monash University some people told me I was merely exchanging one factory for another. No. A university education to me was a great privilege. The students who complained Monash was boring and factory-like had never worked on the process lines. I left school at the age of 15 because I had holes in my shoes. I went back to night school after saving some money. A university education was made possible by a Commonwealth Scholarship and later the abolition of university fees.

I was the first in our family's history to complete secondary education (let alone tertiary) so I was under no illusions as to what life was like without a formal education. While a university education may not have answered all my dreams, it gave me a far higher salary, a means of ordering the world within my own head and the potential to do something about injustice. For me a law degree was an end to personal impotence.

BETH WILSON

Why did I choose law? This was a question put to the first year tutorial in legal process in 1972. I blush to recall my answer. While the sons of stockbrokers explained they had chosen law because it gave you power and lots of money, I said: 'Because it is the father of the humanities.' The tute was stunned into an awkward embarrassed silence and I vowed to keep quiet in future.

A vow I was incapable of keeping. Many other faux pas were to follow: a polite tutor, eyes averted, told me the correct pronunciation of Descartes was not Dezcarties. During my moot court examination I gained no extra marks for citing Mr Justice Lopes (rhyming with Ropes) but worst of all was my literal pronunciation of Lord Cockburn's name. I probably chose law because it was the longest course available and the student life had far more appeal than factory work.

I was attracted to the mystique surrounding the law. I understood nothing of the extraordinary rules and procedures which ensured that we stayed poor while others got richer. The small town where I grew up had a very high crime rate. The only contact kids had with 'the law' was criminal law. The Magistrates' Court sat in the town hall where shopkeepers handed out three years of probation to the children of labourers for petty theft or driving cars too fast. The police administered their own form of justice at the end of a boot.

The local Rotary Club organised a 'careers day' to enable students to visit a workplace of their choice. I chose a lawyer with absolutely no hope of achieving such a goal and never dreamed I would. Along we went for a laugh, three 13-year-old girls visiting the law office of Alan Hunt in Mornington (he was later to become a member and more recently President of the Legislative Council). We spent a half hour or so consumed by giggles as he tried to get us to ask questions. The object of our mirth was a smallish man lying horizontal, his head propped against the wall, his bottom on the chair, a moderate pot belly (which looked huge to us) pointed to the ceiling and his legs and feet sprawled across the desk. I remember vividly his extraordinary posture, and the agony of trying to suppress laughter, but not a word of what he said.

After leaving school, I worked in various shops and factories, picked fruit and even worked on fishing boats. Opposition to the Viet Nam war was dominating the press. The forelady at the factory asked each worker if they were attending the big anti-Viet Nam 'moratorium'. I heard her tell the production manager: 'No one's going but Beth.' 'Beth!' he replied, dismayed. He liked me and I was a good worker. She responded with: 'Oh well, she's like that.' He must have done some thinking about it and came to see me on the process line. He expressed his fears for his sons but was very uncomfortable with the idea of public protest against government decisions. The war had a profound influence on so many people including me and it made me start asking questions and wanting answers.

I was 21, working in the frozen food factory during the day and waitressing at night when I decided to go back to school. My waitressing job was at Mannix College, a male-only university residential college. We were not allowed to talk to the students — 'No Fraternising' — so the boys wrote messages in sugar on the table: 'Hello Beth.' We met the boys at night and I soon realised I was every bit as bright as they were. Some of the other waitresses were students and encouraged me in this belief. It was they who gave me the confidence to do what I had long wanted — go back to school.

I telephoned the Education Department about night classes. The nearest were at Prahran High School, some 8 kilometres from my flat. A department bureaucrat told me I couldn't work full-time and do all four subjects in one year. This annoyed me so I did just that.

No car meant hitching rides to classes. Four nights a week after a hard day's work. I nearly gave up on one occasion when the teacher picked me up hitching in the winter rain and dark. When he gasped: 'Oh, you poor little wench' I burned with shame. **He was amazed someone would go to such lengths for an education and kindly gave me a lift** each Wednesday night to classes. Mr Shelton introduced me to his family and I met many people that year who remained an inspiration. Mary Owen was a member of my English literature class. I followed her career in the Women's Movement, the Working Women's Centre and Australian Council of Trade Unions (ACTU), and the Women's Electoral Lobby (WEL), with great interest. The topics she raised in the media influenced how I looked at the world.

When I completed my law training all prospective employers were men. All were middle class. At interviews I was questioned about which golf club my father belonged to. One asked me where my parents lived. They were divorced but when I replied: 'Bairnsdale and Hastings,' he responded: 'Oh we've got a summer house on the Peninsula too.'

Eventually I found employment with a large mining company. I hated the job. It was the most miserable time of my working life. I was completely alienated from the goals the corporation espoused. When demonstrators marched past and yelled abuse I was on the wrong side of the windows. At night I returned to a household dominated by 'greenie' values. I felt lost and confused.

By that time, 1978, the Women's Movement had made a significant impact. I was welcomed by the company into its legal department: not, however, as a solicitor (they were all men) but as a 'researcher/librarian'. I had never met a real life practising woman lawyer until I completed my law degree. A woman personnel officer determined to assist other women within the organisation. With her support I was soon promoted. I was, however, the typical 'token woman' in an all male department. They wanted me to do well but I felt I just didn't belong. I was full of guilt when I resigned, ostensibly to go overseas, but really to escape a work environment which made me feel I had been given a life sentence.

Overseas travel meant time to think about what I was to do with my life. As an unskilled factory worker I felt powerless but free. If I didn't like a job I'd just leave it and go elsewhere. In professional circles I felt trapped.

The worst thing about the law was that there seemed so little interest in, or remedies suited to, problems of ordinary people. In five years of law school domestic violence hardly rated a mention. Contract law seemed so remote and impotent, when I knew people 'ripped off' needed help. I recall the night a smooth-faced, fast talking salesman in a smart suit jollied his way into our house, all smiles and gallantry. This totally unexpected event disarmed mum (we rarely had such smart visitors). Kids were running every which way and Mr Smoothie even offered the eldest boy (14 years old) a cigarette. We could not have been more impressed.

> **The worst thing about the law was that there seemed so little interest in, or remedies suited to, problems of ordinary people.**

The pressure on mum, with hardly a bean to her name, to sign up for the three volume *Australian Encyclopaedia* was irresistible. It took her three years to pay those books off. That they were heavily used and adored objects (by me) doesn't remedy the reality: the hire purchase agreement ensured she paid far in excess of their market price.

Law in practice was far less appealing than in theory. In those days you completed a law degree without going anywhere near a court. In 1975 I went to have a look for myself and I didn't like what I saw.

At the Supreme Court of Victoria a jury was being empanelled. A woman about 50 years of age arrived late. She was hauled up in front of the bench. An old man sitting half way up the wall in red and white robes with an absurd wig on his head harshly demanded an explanation of why she had 'failed in her duty'. Trembling so much in her sad cardigan, the woman could barely speak. She had gone to the wrong courtroom (an easy mistake to make in the maze of courtrooms). The judge dressed her down, fining her $20. I couldn't believe it. That poor woman, humiliated and treated like a criminal. Such power in action was frightening.

I watched a criminal trial in the County Court. Two young men were on trial for throwing a hand grenade into the Burvale pub (it didn't explode). The trial was a circus. The huge judge practically bursting through his robes was cracking jokes, mostly at the expense of the prosecutor. Everyone in the courtroom was laughing with the exception of the prosecutor and the defendants. I couldn't stop looking at those boys. One had a tickle in his throat and was trying not to cough too loudly. At that moment he looked like a vulnerable little boy. He was Graeme Jensen, the man who was allegedly the reason for a deadly game later played out between 'the underworld' and the police. All these deaths later (of police and those classed by the media as the 'criminal underworld'), I wonder what might have happened if our courts and legal system functioned differently.

The Magistrates' Court in particular persuaded me to work in any profession other than law. The procession of pale faced young men looking sick and beaten being 'dealt with'; young women hauled to justice for shoplifting; a motley bunch of litterers and drunken drivers. These people looked as though they had stories to tell, explaining their behaviour. But there was no opportunity in these places for people to tell stories. One woman stood up for herself, giving a reasoned logical argument in response to a traffic charge. She got a far heavier fine than others. While some people would have been spurned into action by injustice, I was, at that time, scared off. I decided to work as far away from the courts as I could.

I did a post-graduate degree in librarianship, preparing myself for a happy, unhassled life of reading and looking up occasionally to stamp the odd book out on loan. I couldn't have been more wrong. Librarianship is a far more demanding (and rewarding) career than I could ever have thought. It taught me how to use a law library and to understand legal research methodology, a most empowering experience.

As Victoria Law Foundation and Law Reform Commission librarian, I undertook legal research as well as running the library. I was then appointed as part-time legal member of the Social Security Appeals Tribunal (SSAT). When the demand came from a woman friend: 'Quick, give me your CV. They need people at the SSAT,' I groaned: 'No, no, I couldn't do it, I don't know enough, I've never worked in that area of law.' 'Rubbish, give me your CV.'

> I'd always been interested in administrative law and alternative dispute resolution processes.

I'd always been interested in administrative law and alternative dispute resolution processes. Unlike the courts, boards and tribunals (or some of them) allow people to speak for themselves. To an extent (all too limited) people can raise issues they believe to be relevant, with decisions made on merit rather than by blind adherence to strict legal rules. My experience in the workforce outside the professions was a valuable background for SSAT work. After sitting as an observer and swatting over the almost incomprehensible language of the *Social Security Act* I soon gained confidence. Best of all was the opportunity to work with people from other disciplinary backgrounds, bureaucrats, welfare workers and doctors.

In 1991 the Victorian courts still had no women judges. Judge Lynette Shiften, appointed to the Victorian County Court in 1986, resigned after a short time to go into the private business sector. Women have, however, made an *important* contribution as magistrates and on the various administrative boards and tribunals. Women like Deidre Fitzgerald and Ann Coughlan know how to make things work at the SSAT. Deidre O'Connor has taken over as President of the federal Administrative Appeals Tribunal (AAT). She was the first woman appointed a judge of the Federal Court and, with other women like Rosemary Balmford and Joan Dwyer who sit as members of the AAT, and Cheryl Saunders at the Administrative Review Council (and now a professor of law at Melbourne University), gives cohesion to the Commonwealth administrative tribunals.

Making the boards function efficiently does not guarantee their ability to review decisions effectively nor to have an impact on the quality of the initial decision-making. Economic rationalisation has seriously eroded their ability to remedy injustices. They are sold to the public as venues where people may attain justice in an informal setting at minimal expense. Simultaneously amendments to legislation have removed important discretions which in the past enabled tribunals to make decisions which could ameliorate the harshness of bureaucratic decision making. The desire to save dollars — the order of the day — overrules other values like welfare rights and social justice. The independence of the boards is at risk as they are subject to ministerial directives and members are employed under short term contracts.

> **The desire to save dollars overrules other values like welfare rights and social justice.**

I moved on from the Law Reform Commission, retaining my position with the SSAT, to work as senior research officer in the law and policy unit of the Health Department, Victoria. I'd come across Bebe Loff, manager of the unit and convenor of Feminist Lawyers, before, but now she was my boss. We worked well together, becoming good friends. Bebe and I continue to work together through Feminist Lawyers, an organisation enabling women lawyers to use our collective strength to bring about change. These women lawyers, academics and students give each other strength and confidence through support at personal and professional levels. The best group of people I've ever worked with, they come from a range of class backgrounds. Our greatest success has been the campaign to obtain a pardon for Sandra and Tracey Collis, two sisters jailed for perjury when they were pressured into withdrawing complaints of incest against their father. We also succeeded in a professional misconduct action against the solicitor who had acted for both the sisters and their father, action seen by the Law Society to contravene the rules relating to conflict of interest.

People encouraging and supporting me have been important because I found the legal world so alienating. I survived only with the help of people like Yvonne Baker and Pana Dakos, the only other working-class women I met in law school. We remain friends. I felt less of a freak with Yvonne around. Her childhood was much harder than mine because she lost her mother but she battled on to become a practising lawyer.

Early role models were my parents. Mum, five kids, deserted by her husband and poor, was a strong, independent and resourceful woman who encouraged and felt pride in her youngest daughter's achievements. With no formal education, she understood the value of study and taught us to read on her knee using the *Women's Weekly*. Dad, when I saw him, was also an inspiration. Throw-away lines like 'you can forget about God for a start' proved influential and saved a lot of unnecessary soul-searching. His love of poetry (though he never completed primary school) and keen sense of humour are valued legacies.

My heroines were women like Zelda d'Aprano, Jean McLean (now member of the Victorian Legislative Council), Mary Owen. These were women, older than I, at the quarry front of change. When I read Zelda's book, *The Becoming of A Woman*, I stopped feeling lonely. She put into a book for everyone to see some of what I'd always felt most sensitive about— not being able to pronounce words well, not understanding middle-class social conventions and being working-class. Mary Owen showed me first-hand how much one woman could achieve. Jean McLean and Save Our Sons (opposing the slaughter of the Viet Nam war) gave us all a chance to march in the streets, demanding that our voices be heard. (More recently Chris Slattery of Feminist Lawyers has suggested we revive this movement renamed as Send Our Sons.)

Of course I have been supported by some men. Dave Me~:er and I have lived together for a long time now. He is interested in feminist literature and sometimes reads extracts to me while I'm cooking the roast. (He's not bad with spaghetti bolognese but hopeless with a roast.)

'Supportive' men say they agree that feminists are right about domestic violence, rape, inequalities between the sexes, but they never actually do anything on their own initiative. Stephen Foley's group Men Against Rape is a rare exception. Until the blokes in the pub start talking about rape being a problem it will continue. As with household management, men need to take the initiative without having to be given a shopping list. Women are taking on greater responsibilities in the workforce and in public life. Those of us living with men need their help; we don't need additional work at home. These old arguments are still not fully resolved in practice. Women in the paid workforce who also have children have my admiration — I just don't know how they manage.

It is, however, a difficult decision not to have children because this is not encouraged. I fear there is far more pressure on women to have babies now than at any time for many years. Recently a lawyer friend was offered $100 000 and a house, if she agreed to marry and have a child. The offer was made by her parents. For her, the worst thing about it was the realisation that her own parents could view her as no more than a vessel. Far better to have poor parents any day, than wealthy ones whose aspirations to grandparenthood leads them to place such pressure on their daughter. New artificial reproduction has deflected the debate about women's choices. The media, by concentrating on technological advances, ignores the possibility of women coming to terms with infertility or choosing not to have children.

The 'rights' of groups other than women in matters reproductive are being recognised by the law. In the past these rights were exerted through subtle pressures on women. Now the legal 'rights' of foetuses, husbands, grandfathers, and contracting fathers in surrogacy arrangements are threatening the hard-earned gains of the Women's Movement.

I used to think a woman should get a nice safe job before getting too old to attract employers. 'Too old' was later thirties. Now I see women who are changing their careers or continuing them successfully even into their seventies. This takes away the fear of growing older which many women have experienced. The fear was really one of being 'useless' or 'put out on the scrap heap'.

Hepzibah Menuhin, the musician, said the older she got the better she liked it. So far that has been true for me. At forty years of age I am far more 'free' than ever before. Economic independence remains incredibly important here. But also the older you get the easier it is to laugh at yourself and the things which separated you from other women in your youth. I saw a play once in which two old women were drinking tea together and having a good laugh about the time their friendship nearly faltered through having affairs with each other's husbands. How wonderful to arrive at an age, and state of wisdom, to find these things funny.

Of course no one wants to get too old. I'm certainly not looking forward to the time when bits and pieces of my anatomy start prolapsing and dropping out. Edith Morgan, a member of the Union of Australian Women (UAW) and welfare member of the Social Security Appeals Tribunal, once told me she had no fear at all of getting old, but the prospect of blindness troubled her. She's a marvellous example of a woman who continues to make a valuable contribution to the community in spite of losing her sight. I was pleased when they gave her a well earned medal: the Order of Australia. Sometimes, the right decisions are made, and recognition given, by honours committees.

I hope there will be some useful work for me as long as I'm able to do it. Even if they won't go on paying me I'm sure to find things to do. My greatest fear is not of old age but poverty. I worry about paidwork running out. Being wealthy may be ideologically suspect but having tasted poverty I know how demeaning that can be. I don't want to end up where I began.

GOLDEN GIRLS AND GOOD WOMEN

Jocelynne A. Scutt

Jocelynne A. Scutt *is a lawyer and a writer. Born on 8 June 1947 in Perth, Western Australia, since 1986 she has been in private practice in Melbourne.*

Her books include Women and the Law, The Baby Machine — The Commercialisation of Motherhood, Poor Nation of the Pacific — Australia's Future? *and* Even in the Best of Homes: Violence in the Family.

Until I was 12, I was determined to be a kindergarten teacher 'when I grew up'. My mother was a kindergarten teacher, a fact no doubt influencing this decision: until I was 6, and my younger sister Felicity was born, my mother ran her own kindergarten in Devon Road, Swanbourne, then taught at the kindergarten in Kalamunda on Western Australia's Darling Scarp. My sister Robin and I spent glorious days together with other children at the Swanbourne kindergarten, climbing naked in the mulberry tree at the bottom of my maternal grandmother's garden. The nakedness was dictated by my mother's prudent observation that clothes smothered in mulberry juice would not be welcomed by parents. She did not anticipate the outrage of several who objected to their young daughters and sons cavorting clothesless on the tree's broad branches. The foolishness of this response to child-nakedness has remained with me although I was only 3 years old at the time.

At 12, I decided on journalism. Like many children brought up on a nonstop diet of books, I had been churning out poetry ranging from crass romanticism to discourses on the tea-tree brown hills surrounding York, where we lived for several years. When we moved to Meckering, another wheat belt town in Western Australia, I produced newsletters together with my 'best friend' Margaret Carrig.

Law was my third choice, but once chosen, I didn't deviate. My family had a strong tradition of dinner table debate. Nor was debate limited to meal times. My maternal grandmother, Maud Helen Needham, and I engaged in just such a debate one afternoon when I was 13. Argument raged back and forth, and I won. 'Oh, well you'll just have to be a lawyer!' exclaimed nanna, pursing her lips. Fiona Tito had a similar experience when a teacher expostulated upon her winning a battle of words that law would be her forte. Yet, like Jennifer Coate, I did not express my ambition widely. Whether this was from female timidity, the thought that somebody might 'try to stop me' (although it certainly wouldn't have been my family), or that people might think I had 'uppity notions', I hugged this ambition close to my chest.

Later, my economics teacher suggested that, with my brains, I should apply for a teacher's scholarship. I did so out of deference to him, seeking to spare him the embarrassment of knowing my ambitions were 'higher'. My reaction was akin to that of Gay Davidson and Shirley Stott Despoja exclaiming 'not the women's pages' when they entered journalism. (Yet at various times, Melba Marginson, Janine Haines and Lariane Fonseca have found positive power in teaching. Today, Jane Cafarella edits a 'women's page' — an oasis of good feminist sense.) Had teaching been seen as an elevated profession for anyone, male or female, my view would have been different but my plans would not have changed. My attitude was dictated by a strong sense that intelligent girls were pointed towards teaching, without any appreciation of the many career paths girls could take, or which should have been open to us. No one suggested intelligent boys should apply for teacher's scholarships.

Commonwealth scholarships paid university fees. Like Irene Moss and Fiona Tito, I went straight to law school, not taking an alternative course as did Di Fingleton, Beth Wilson, Jennifer Coate and Irene Watson. One morning when out with my father, I asked him to stop by a red pillar box to return the teacher's scholarship offer. 'Are you quite sure you want to give it up?' 'Quite sure.' It was not that my father did not support me in my choice; it was, rather, he saw that teaching was 'easier' and perhaps 'more suitable' for a girl. Law was another matter altogether.

Throughout my childhood, the word 'career' was familiar. My mother continually emphasised the importance or 'careers' for us all, Robin, Felicity and myself. Not for her the notion that every girl should 'end up' married as the pinnacle of her existence. Like Jane Cafarella's mother, mine thought meeting the 'right' man and marrying was an extra. She was determined each of us would develop a long-term vision for a future of interesting, committed work. From an early age we learned women and girls had a right to participate in the world on equal terms with men and boys. But we had no artificial vision of this right to equality: we also knew that discrimination existed, not in those terms, but the existence of sexism was clear.

My mother wrote short stories, plays, songs. A song about a 'girl in a blue gingham gown' came high on a list of commendations in a songwriting competition. But much of her writing was for us. We performed her plays and sang her songs raising money for the Red Cross. My mother's reticence in putting forward her work for publication was a consequence of an all-too-female modesty: yet it motivated her to ensure her daughters would not be hobbled by a false humbleness inhibiting our desire to 'do things'.

Sexism hit full-on at law school. Two of the women in first year were obliged to enrol in arts rather than law, although taking all the first year law course subjects: legal history, constitutional law and two arts subjects (I took English and philosophy). It was apparently considered they must show themselves capable of 'doing law'. Myself and two other women (making up five women in first year amongst some 120 men) had no obstacle set against our entering law school directly: we had Commonwealth scholarships. Probably well over half the men did not have scholarships, yet were not obliged to enrol first in arts.

> Sexism hit full-on at law school.

Law school was extraordinarily machismo. Just as Patricia Brennan found sexism entrenched at medical school in New South Wales, and much later Irina Dunn and Janine Haines met it in federal parliament, and Fiona Tito at the College of Law, so too with law in Western Australia. First year students underwent ragging or indoctrination. All freshers had to attend to a law school assembly. The women students were derided publicly, before the whole student body, with comments on our physical attributes. Today, this is 'sexual harassment'. In 1965, the term was unknown, despite the Women's Movement's long awareness of the activity. Sophia Jex-Blake was harassed at Edinburgh University in 1859 by students bringing a sheep into the lecture theatre, a notice around its neck stating it would perform better than would Miss Jex-Blake. In the antipodes, women were being reviled 100 years later. Ironically, my legal training gave me access to law reports of the earlier battle.

Only in hindsight can the anti-woman nature of legal education at that time be properly appreciated. In the main I enjoyed law school, playing bridge with the boys in the common room (my family thought I was an avid studier; I was learning the finer points of contract bridge). I also learned to treat the male students as, in a sense, 'brothers'. This meant tolerating or ignoring some of the baser aspects of interaction between women and men students. A defence against sexism was to put any contemplation of romantic involvement to one side and concentrate on matters intellectual. It was 'too dangerous' for women students to become romantically or sexually involved with male law students. This led to derision, gossip in the common room, and general 'joking'. Rumours abounded that one woman was determined she would be the first St Hilda's girl to snaffle a man ('become engaged' was the way it was described in 'polite' company). According to rumour she made attempts at forging a romantic liaison with the most attractive men in fourth year, then third year, down to second year and finally her own year, first year, without success. Ultimately she settled upon a nice, but 'ordinary' third year student, becoming engaged after afternoons of 'snogging' in the carpark.

I had long been aware of social injustice and inequality, a consciousness that developed at home and at school. Like Patricia Brennan, Louise Liddy-Corpus, Gay Davidson and Lisa Bellear, I experienced a convent education for a time. (Mine was an all-boys school: girls were allowed up to eight-years-old.) The nuns at Mary's Mount in Gooseberry Hill impressed upon me firmly the horrors lepers suffered. In the 1950s, leprosy was the major ill in the sights of the Roman Catholic church — at least as far as Mary's Mount was concerned. The need to send money to support and comfort these people, and for compassion, became firmly fixed reference points. Later, class, race, economic and sexual inequality figured highly. In York, Aboriginal people lived on the outskirts in tin shanties. The children were forced to come to school, but were effectively separated off. Just as in Townsville Gracelyn Smallwood's uniform had to be whiter than white, in Brisbane Jackie Huggins was told 'you couldn't possibly', and in Adelaide, Darwin and Melbourne Irene Watson, Louise Liddy-Corpus and Lisa Bellear felt the barbs of discrimination, the Aboriginal children in York were trammelled by racism. Distinction was made by the school system between 'us' and 'them'. Then in Meckering, a white family lived in a shanty down by the railway lines. It was accepted by us school children that Joan was not only the sister of Junie, but also Junie's mother. Joan's mother was occasionally seen in the streets of the town, hair straggled, clothes ragged and obviously suffering physical abuse. We knew this, and if we did, then so did our parents. Yet nothing was done until many years later, when the father was charged and imprisoned for incest. (In Canberra, Adelaide and Melbourne, Shirley Stott Despoja, Dawn Rowan and Lisa Bellear came up against this problem in various ways.)

Law was a way of gaining power to fight.

Law was a way of gaining power to fight.

University in the 1960s meant being swept up in the Viet Nam war protests: this was the political issue galvanising Dawn Rowan, Irene Moss, Beth Wilson and Lariane Fonseca too. It also meant debating against the annual 'Miss University' contest — and its competitor, the 'Mr Hairy Legs' contest. A *Daily News* journalist interviewed myself and another woman on this parody of the Miss University quest, publishing the story alongside a photograph of us with 'Mr University', a pleasant red-cheeked young man who might have been assisted by a course in aerobics or regular jogging workouts.

After four years at law school, a further two years' articles was necessary to qualify as a lawyer. In Victoria, Greta Bird found an amenable law firm — at least for articles. Irene Moss came up against discrimination in Sydney. I, disinclined to remain in Perth despite family, the glorious weather and practically everything I knew about the world, removed to the eastern states. I commenced working in the public service as a graduate clerk but was invited to apply for a senior research assistant position at the University of Sydney law school. My good sense and practicality surprise me even now: at the conclusion of the interview I said I would accept the position only if my salary were set at or above my public service salary. It was only later that I discovered another research assistant's wage was well below mine, although she assumed hers was much higher than mine due to her earlier appointment and longer experience. I was (foolishly) too embarrassed to tell her of the discrepancy. Subsequently, two (male) law graduates from England were employed on my salary level. Thenceforth, all senior research assistants received the same wage.

I decided to do a higher degree, fixing upon the diploma of criminology. 'Why not do a Master's?' said Stephen Abadee, the assistant registrar, looking shocked at where I set my sights. (Other women have found men helpful, too. Gay Davidson was 'egged on' by David Solomon into radio journalism. Carolyn Watts found two male mentors at the ABC. Sue Schmolke took job opportunities offered by male colleagues. Clive Evatt was a role model for Patricia Brennan, Robin Millhouse for Janine Haines. Bill Hayden encouraged Di Fingleton.) On finishing the course, I applied to foreign universities—but not Yale or Harvard, assuming (unlike Irene Moss) that, as a woman, I would not be accepted. (This shocks me now.) I was accepted at Virginia, Michigan, Toronto and Cambridge, choosing Michigan, having worked as research assistant to Professor Peter Nygh (now judge of the Family Court of Australia) who had studied there; I admired his legal acumen.

With a year to fill before going to the United States, I completed a diploma of jurisprudence, then set off for Southern Methodist University in Dallas, Texas, for an introductory course for foreign lawyers. I stayed on at SMU, working at one of the halls of residency for three months. (Earlier, during my university holidays in Melbourne, I'd sold stockings at Myers, frocks at Moores in Prahran, and kept computer records at MacRobertsons. For a week I worked as a drinks waiter. Irina Dunn did likewise at university, as did Jennifer Coate at the swimming pool, and Greta Bird, Beth Wilson, Gay Davidson, Carolyn Watts.) I learned about sororities and fraternities, and pom-pom girls. The colleges operated commercially in vacation, hired out for conferences and courses. A group of bankers turned up in vivid red plaid slacks and luminous shirts. The cheerleading squads arrived, with their brightly coloured streamers. One team did a Black minstrel show routine, wearing black top hats and white gloves. None of the

Earlier, during my holidays in Melbourne, I'd sold stockings at Myers.

pom-pom girls or cheerleaders was Black. But Dallas magazines appeared in two versions — one for the white population, one for the Black. The white version carried advertisements featuring white models; the Black contained precisely the same advertisements — with Black models.

Despite rampant competition, assertiveness and overt materialism, the United States was impressive. There was no meek acceptance (the Australian approach) that 'that is how the law is'. Law existed to be used innovatively. Just as Melba Marginson found at the University of the Philippines, in 1973 the spirit of student rebellion of the late 1960s and early 1970s was still coursing through Michigan University. Women law students had won non-sexist language in courses, action against sexual harassment, and a course on women and the law (taught by Professor Virginia Blomer Nordby, principal drafter of the innovative Michigan sexual assault law). When law firms coming onto campus refused to interview women students, the university authorities banned them until they revised their policy. They immediately did so: not gaining access meant missing out on the brightest law students. They came to realise that many of the brightest law students were women.

Like Carolyn Watts in Perugia, Di Fingleton in England and later the United States, Greta Bird at Cambridge, and Sue Schmolke, Gracelyn Smallwood and Lariane Fonseca who combined travel with paidwork and learning, I was appreciative of my opportunities in America. Yet I lay awake some nights wondering 'what on earth am I doing here?' and hankering after home. It was now that I realised even more clearly the importance of my family to my career aspirations. (Janine Haines had always understood this, and Irina Dunn, Irene Watson, Irene Moss, Fiona Tito, Gracelyn Smallwood and others recognise the strengths of family supports.) I understood how strong my mother's indoctrination into the importance of career had been, and how substantial was my father's support. When I had fixed on journalism, he recalled a famous wartime woman journalist from the frontlines: 'You could do that, Joce,' he said. I grew up with the surety that 'if Joce is doing it, then it must be good'. Despite the homesickness, upon completing my degree at Michigan, I moved on to Cambridge University.

> I lay awake some nights wondering 'what on earth am I doing here?' and hankering after home.

Perhaps I should have gone to Cambridge first, Michigan second. After the enlivening intellectual experience at the University of Michigan, Cambridge was devastating. Studying jurisprudence with one of the doyens, Professor Glanville Williams, I felt stultified. Seminars commenced with a reiteration of Jeremy Bentham's utilitarian theory (Jeremy Bentham was once a student at Cambridge). Other philosophies were secondary — or ignored. In a class on 'consent', one student made reference to a recent Michigan case. A prisoner having been convicted of aggravated sexual offences was incarcerated indeterminately. He agreed to undergo castration.

A case was launched (and won) against the constitutional validity of the Act under which he was held. The man then withdrew his consent to the operation. The authorities would not accept this, making clear their intention to go ahead with the surgery. The court then held that the original 'consent' was no consent at all: obtained under coercion, it was not a free and informed agreement to the operation. Glanville William's response? What happens there, across the Atlantic, is of no moment; such peculiarities are not to be endorsed in England. So ended the discussion.

Cambridge was beautiful: mists in autumn, the bright and subtle greens of spring and summer, white-flaked snow at easter. To be a student at Girton College was to learn more completely of the brave history of Emily Davies' and her colleagues' fight for the right of women to a university education. An all-women institution was new for me. My mother believed in co-education. All my schooling had been co-educational. Now, I was together with women students, wonderful for their self-confidence. They claimed a presence in the dining-room, swathed in exotic gowns of glorious colour, bandanna around the head and cummerbund slung low at the waist—some slim, some rotund. Peacock blues, reds and yellows mingled with the more modest attire of the American students.

Completing a year at Cambridge (and it was in England that I, like Dawn Rowan, read Erin Pizzey's now classic *Scream Quietly or the Neighbours Will Hear*), I applied for a scholarship to Germany, to continue my comparative study of rape law. The interview was to be conducted in German; I spent each morning at the Cambridge language lab listening to records intoning: 'Das grosse silberne flugzeug wie ein vogel flog über die gelbe weizenfelder.' The German Constitutional Court had recently set the limits of access to abortion. Questioned on the decision, already primed by discussion with a German friend, I was able to answer in what must have been acceptable German. I won the scholarship.

I learnt more German in Germany at the Goethe Institut than I had ever learnt at school and realised that at school we had mostly done written translations. At the Institut, there were no English speakers in my class: French, Mexican, Spanish, Yugoslavian, the only common language was German. We devised pidgin German to communicate when hoch Deutsch evaded us, and I spent the afternoons walking around the shops reading notices, listening and doing my best to speak in German. The centrality of language to the maintenance of power was impressed on me, in a foreign country. For Irene Watson and Jackie Huggins language and power stood out in their own country, imposed through colonisation. Irene Moss, as a consequence of her English-language schooling and her mother's clear grasp of Chinese rather than the dominant language spoken in Australia, understood the power of language too.

I continued on with German lessons at Freiburg University whilst studying rape law at the Max-Planck-Institut and contributing to an institut project on the fine as a penal measure.

Mid-year a telegram arrived from the Australian Law Reform Commission inviting me to be a senior law reform officer. I had applied for a lectureship at the University of Sydney and gained it. But the Australian Law Reform Commission had only recently been established and was taking on exciting new work. Fiona Tito, too, some years later, choosing law reform at the New South Wales Commission, found that the innovative path beckoned. I renounced the lectureship.

Back in Sydney, I worked in the main on the privacy reference, together with a colleague, Sandra McCallum. We made a number of forays into various federal departments, first in Canberra, then Melbourne, discussing with departmental heads or deputies how privacy requirements affected their department. The logistics of our departmental research were instructive. Federal public service officers communicate with others at the same level. Because we were classed as 'senior law reform officers', a term unknown to the departments, they were unable to gauge our precise level. Thus we got through to the top!

The commission, headed by Justice Michael Kirby, was shaking up the legal profession. Members of the public accepted they had a right to demand changes to unjust laws. The judiciary and profession were sometimes affronted by the notion that the community could have anything relevant or intelligent to say on the matter; law was for lawyers, they held. But the commission had strong support from within its own ranks, and from more forward looking professionals.

Completing a 12-month term I returned to Michigan to finish my doctorate. Then it was back to Australia in March 1978, in time for International Women's Day. I completed writing up my thesis at the University of New South Wales, where Rob Brian the librarian provided me with a carrel in the law school library. In June I joined the Australian Institute of Criminology in Canberra, taking a contract for three years. (Permanent positions are not for me.) My time at the institute included the first national conference on women and crime in 1978, and in 1979 the first national conference on criminal assault at home. Rumblings emanated from the directorate when monies were used to fly women in for the 1978 conference. These grew louder at the family violence conference, accompanied as it was by stormy newspaper coverage. Women from women's refuges and rape crisis centres, and police attended. For the first time these two 'sides' came together in conference format. As was to be expected, exchange of views led to fireworks, reaching the front pages of the *Canberra Times*. The director, returning from overseas, was met by newspaper headlines. 'We'll never have those women at the institute again' was his apoplectic response (reported to me by his driver). Besides, he had intended to earmark the money used for the conference for a new institute motor vehicle.

I had, by then, determined that the next national conference would be on rape law reform. In the upshot, the conference was held away from the institute, in Tasmania under the aegis of the Tasmanian Law Reform Commission, the Tasmanian law school and the Institute of Criminology. It was a landmark for rape law reform. Most recommendations were supported unanimously by 300 or so participants from police, legal profession, social work, women's refuges, rape crisis centres, Women's Movement, the church and associated religious bodies, together with politicians and attorneys-general. The principles outlined in the *Women's Electoral Lobby Draft Bill on Rape* were central to the discussion. The Rape Law Reform conference and the Draft Bill have since formed the basis for rape law reform around Australia.

After the institute, I went into private practice. Then I was invited to be associate to the Hon. Justice Lionel Murphy of the High Court of Australia. That year, January 1982 to January 1983, was an important watershed for me, and I looked much more deeply into economic and commercial aspects of the law. At law school, I had done well in company law, but my subsequent work had concentrated on criminal law, constitutional law and human rights. On the board of the Australian Institute of Political Science from 1978, I had already begun bringing myself back into corporate matters.

> **I was invited to be associate to the Hon. Justice Lionel Murphy of the High Court of Australia.**

Lionel Murphy had a prevailing concern about the imperialistic policies of the International Monetary Fund (IMF) and the World Bank. He was adamant that their interference in finance and the world economy augured ill for 'third world' countries. Their machinations and manipulation led to and intensified the gross disparities between rich and poor—on a worldwide scale. We discussed this and the power of language (vide Noam Chomsky, Casey Miller and Kate Swift). His sense of humour was real, as was his comprehension of women's rights: though after long bouts of talking solidly about women's issues, he occasionally said to me: 'Jocelynne, you're taking it all a bit too far.' I kept talking. He kept listening.

After the year with Justice Murphy, I had another scholarship, back to Germany and the Max-Planck-Institut which wanted me to write the Australian contribution for an abortion law project. I relinquished the scholarship to become director of research with the Victorian Parliamentary Legal and Constitutional Committee in Melbourne, completing the work on abortion law without travelling to Germany. The March 1983 federal election loomed and I didn't want to miss the chance of living under a Labor government. (I was out of Australia for most of the Whitlam era—May 1973 to September 1976.) Labor won.

The committee comprised six members from the upper house and six from the lower, with representation from the Liberal, National and Labor parties. The chairperson, Milton Whiting, was National Party. This was one of the most satisfying positions I held and, despite the mix of political views, the committee worked constructively, producing five substantial reports in the 18 months I was there. The *Deregulation Bill Report* was one landmark, dealing with regulatory impact statements. (Alan Hunt, whom Beth Wilson had met so many years before, when she was thinking of becoming a lawyer, drafted the bill. I appreciated his strong support of my work on it.) The *Interpretation Bill Report* was another major contribution. The committee unanimously decided that all legislation should be non-sexist, including replacing 'chairman' with 'chairperson', 'president' or 'convenor'. The *Law Reform Commission Act* of 1984 followed this recommendation, as has other legislation.

Upon the setting up of the Law Reform Commission, Victoria, I became commissioner and deputy chairperson. (Later, Beth Wilson came as librarian, and later still she joined the Social Security Appeals Tribunal (SSAT) of which I was a member.) I headed the commercial sales and leases of goods reference, which required revision of Australian contract law. With governments advocating foreign trade, together with Britain's entry into the common market and British law changing anyway, it is uncommercial for Australia to cling to British contract law. Adopting United Nations contract law principles and standards, ratified by many countries including those in our immediate region—potentially great markets for Australia—makes better sense. Overseas commerce would be facilitated. English contract law is irrelevant to China or Japan, Germany or South America. As for state and interstate trade, making laws governing foreign trade and domestic trade identical would simplify trade relations.

Law Reform Commission, Victoria: I became commissioner and deputy chairperson.

I was disappointed not to bring the reference to fruition, but it was time to move out of committee. Like Jennifer Coate selling up her practice, Jackie Huggins leaving the public service, Jane Cafarella and Shirley Stott Despoja moving from one newspaper to another and Lisa Bellear recognising it was 'right' to leave local government behind her, I knew it was time to move from research to application. The independence of private practice was a breath of fresh air.

The continuing support of the Women's Movement has been essential to me. Conferences all over Australia have kept me in touch with women. A woman isolated in a male dominated profession needs discussion of issues and goals articulated outside male forums. And at the conferences I have met such good women — Gracelyn Smallwood, initially in 1981 at the first women's conference held in Townsville (where I first met and was interviewed by Louise Liddy-Corpus, at the ABC, too) and again in 1988 at the second; Jackie Huggins and Melba Marginson at the 1990 Women's Studies Summer Institute at Deakin University; Dawn Rowan at women's shelter discussions and conferences in Adelaide and Canberra; Sue Schmolke at the women and politics conference in Darwin in 1986; Janine Haines at a Zonta conference in Adelaide.

Just as Gracelyn Smallwood and Patricia Brennan recognise that 'mainstream' medicine misses out by paying no mind to 'alternative' systems, the lack of attention mainstream law pays to feminist jurisprudence damages the whole community. Whilst writing on 'straight' legal issues (where I have always injected feminist thought anyway), I have also endeavoured to publish in areas of particular concern to women, articulating a feminist position and ensuring women a voice. *Even in the Best of Homes* provided this for women bashed, beaten, abused, raped and brutalised in their own homes. In *Different Lives* 22 women speak of becoming a part of the Women's Movement, what it meant for them, and how they envisage the future. Now, the telephone rings at late at night: the woman at the other end tells me how closely she identifies with one or other or several contributors whose pieces she has just read. It is exhilarating to know the book has struck a chord. So too with *Growing Up Feminist* and *As A Woman*, books giving voice to women of diverse age and background.

The lack of attention mainstream law pays to feminist jurisprudence damages the whole community.

I am fortunate to be doing 'real' work — my legal work— and giving it top priority whilst also doing public speaking: students at Preston TAFE, Korowa Girls School, St Michaels Parents' Club, Wattle Glen Secondary College, Melbourne Grammar, the Tasmanian SAAP Conference, Business and Professional Women's meetings, the Victorian Women's Ethnic Communities Council, the Enid Russell Women Law Students' Society at Murdoch University, WEL and the Northern Territory Women's Advisory Council. There are many humbling experiences, like the call from Alyson Concannon of Northcote High, requesting that the school 'be allowed to name a prize for the top graduate girl at the school' after me. Initially overwhelmed, I agreed: far better for the prize to be named while the holder of the name is alive. Too often we remember our women by accolades only when they are discreetly underground.

What stands out in the cut and thrust, hillocks, peaks, deeps and denes of women's work and careers is an ability to make the most of 'what is', to be flexible and to have an eye on the horizon. None of the women here was born with a silver-spooned advantage. Yet each has made her life, and the life of others, golden. Although many of them had no early defined ideas of a precise career progression, all have a strong commitment to ensuring that their work is not selfishly self-centred. There is a clear sense of themselves as workers with careers, and as important in themselves. Truly golden girls, they are all 'good' women, women who have committed themselves to the moment, to the future and to the making of a better world.

Louise Liddy-Corpus doesn't put a time on it, but she intends eventually to be living in a little cottage writing *Gravel Patch* and a non-fiction history of the Northern Territory. Melba Marginson and Lariane Fonseca will continue their work for women and for themselves. Jackie Huggins is devoting five years of her life to her people's and her mother's history. Lisa Bellear is committed to her people. Sue Schmolke's setting out to do law. Jennifer Coate is poised for a new direction. Carolyn Watts contemplates a future, writing. Shirley Stott Despoja lost her column, yet retains her literary editorship and wonderful spirit. Fiona Tito miraculously moves the bureaucracy. Jane Cafarella has her cartoons. And me? In the 1960s I wrote a screenplay for the Beatles, somehow involving President Sukarno, the political strife in Indonesia, and the Sputnik. How these disparate identities and issues related, I cannot now say. A lively screenplay, it didn't come to the screen. But it set a direction for me, and in the 1970s I decided feminist soap-opera would change the world. (This would replace the television which Irene Watson deplores: what a positive impetus for the ratings a good injection of feminism would have for *Chances* and *Neighbours*!) In the 1980s I decided it was time for the Women's Movement to have a television station — fully controlled, run, committed to, by and for women. Patricia Brennan, Irene Watson, Lisa Bellear, Melba Marginson, Louise Liddy-Corpus see the media as central to the feminist millennium; so do I. In the 1990s, I am saving up for Channel Isis. In the year 2000 — who knows?

INDEX

Abadee, Stephen 221
Aboriginal
  family 25, 71, 76, 124–5
  identity 30, 124, 125, 126, 129, 177, 180, 183, 185
  Invasion Day 127
  land rights 125, 182, 184
  pride 29, 57, 60, 63, 74, 78, 124, 125, 127
  self-determination 79, 180, 181
  system of law 107
  tent embassy 24, 28, 30, 60
  values 79, 80, 129, 180, 185
  see also Aborigines; women
Aboriginal and Islanders Health Service 72
Aboriginal and Torres Strait Islanders Commission 127, 181
  see also Department of Aboriginal Affairs
Aboriginal Development Corporation 26, 27
Aboriginal Protection Act 72, 78
Aborigines and Torres Strait Islanders
  and discrimination 22, 23, 24, 78, 126, 187, 220
  assimilation 57, 58, 177
  citizenship 24, 124
  comparisons with other indigenous people 72, 73
  injustice against 57–8, 79, 80, 124, 177, 178, 179
  perception of 26, 47, 49, 60, 72, 78, 79–80, 107, 126, 183
  political activism 60, 125, 129, 130
  see also Aboriginal; domination, white; education; health; racism; work
abortion 99, 225
Abortion Law Reform Act 67
Ackland, WJ 145
Adelaide Advertiser 50, 53, 144, 145, 146, 147
Age 15, 16, 19, 37, 102
  'Accent' 19, 20
aging 122, 157, 176, 186, 207, 214, 215
AIDS 75–7, 78
alcohol 25, 32, 33, 76, 78
Ananda Marga 95
Anglican 49
Anti-Discrimination Act 192
Anything But Love 1
Arditti, Rita 156
articles (law) 101, 103, 174–5, 192, 201, 220–1
As A Woman 227
Associations Incorporation Act 145

229

INDEX

Austen, Jane 3, 5, 6
Australia, part of Asia 187, 226
Australian Broadcasting Corp./Comm. 26, 39, 42, 43, 44, 45, 140, 226
Australian Democrats 5, 67, 69, 97, 99
Australian Journalists' Association 26, 38
Australian Labor Party 68, 94, 95, 96, 99, 173, 226

Baker, Yvonne 213
balance, search for 2, 87, 88, 105, 172, 206, 207, 214
  see also motherhood; career
Balmford, Rosemary 213, 213
Barbayannis, Maria 107
Becoming of A Woman, The 214
Bell, Janet 27
Bellear, Lisa 5, 57–63, 220, 226, 228
Bellear, Sol 60
Belling, Kylie 63
bereavement 29, 40
Berry Street Babies Home 58, 59
Bird, Greta 5, 101–11, 221, 222
Bishop, Bronwyn 69
Bjelke-Petersen, Joh 96, 126
'Blackbirding' 21, 63
Bond, Carolyn 18
Bongcodin, Gene 102, 120, 121
Book of the City of Ladies, The 3
Brennan, Patricia 5, 81–90, 219, 220, 221, 227, 228
Brian, Rob 224
bulimia 205–06

Cafarella, Jane 4, 11–20, 218, 226, 228
Caffin, Jim 35, 36
Cahill, Geoff 193
Cain, Maureen 107
Call to Australia Party 94
Cambridge University 106, 107, 110, 222–3

Canberra Times 37, 38, 49, 224
Cant, Roly 35
career 3, 44, 92, 93, 105, 136, 172, 218
  oriented towards 1, 2, 11, 41, 44, 64, 65, 84, 92, 131, 137, 138, 151, 162, 173, 175, 177, 179, 198, 218, 222
Carrig, Margaret 218
Carter, Fay 63
cartoons 15, 16, 17, 18, 19, 20
Cass, Bettina 204
censorship 52
Cerni, Pat 14
childcare 18–19, 53, 65, 66, 69, 98, 105, 137, 173
Chipp, Don 69
Chomsky, Noam 225
Christchurch Press 35, 40
Christchurch Star 35, 36, 37
Coate, Jennifer 6, 121, 161–70, 218, 221, 226, 228
College of Law 201, 219
Commonwealth Bank 23, 24
Commonwealth Scholarship 48, 102, 208, 218
Cornwall, John 144
Coughlan, Ann 212
Cowell, Monica 176
Cox, Eva 98
Created Second 89
cross-cultural studies 72–5, 107–10
Cyclone Tracy 29, 133–4

Dakos, Pana 213
Daly River 27, 30
d'Aprano, Zelda 214
Damned Whores and God's Police 137
Daniels, Kay 107
Davidson, Gay 4, 32–40, 218, 219, 221
Davidson, Ken 37
Davies, Emily 223
Deacon, Destiny 57, 60
Denborough, Michael 94

230

Department of Aboriginal Affairs 28, 31, 127–8, 181, 184
De Pizan, Christine 3, 4, 5, 6
Deregulation Bill Report 226
Devereux, John 96
Different Lives 227
discrimination *see* Aboriginal; Aborigines; domination, male; domination, white; education; racism; sexism; working-class
divorce 15, 32, 68, 83, 200
domestic violence 120, 141, 142, 143, 148, 152, 156, 199, 211, 214
domination, male 1, 2, 3, 6, 28, 38, 39, 40, 51, 53, 54, 68, 69, 85, 86, 89, 90, 97, 98, 104, 107, 108, 109, 120, 122, 123, 131, 134, 137, 140, 141, 142, 144, 148, 152–3, 170, 193, 214
domination, white 5, 25, 27, 28, 31, 51, 58, 60, 63, 66, 78, 79, 85, 88, 93, 125, 128, 129, 149, 150, 181
Duck, Colin 19
Dunn, Irina 5, 91–100, 219, 221, 222
Dwyer, Joan 213

education 39–40, 83, 116, 189, 191, 223
  access to 5, 24–5, 27, 42, 47, 48, 61, 63, 71, 72, 85, 165, 186, 210, 220
  and financial problems 28, 34–5, 165, 208
  importance of 102, 163, 208, 210
  opportunities from 47, 48, 49, 65
  primary 11, 13, 21–2, 47–8, 72, 84, 102, 164, 190
  secondary 13, 14–15, 22–3, 33, 48, 59, 61, 66, 72, 84, 92, 102, 126, 150, 151, 164–5, 183, 190, 208, 210, 220

tertiary 27, 33, 34, 42, 48, 61, 65, 66, 84–5, 93, 117, 118, 126, 132, 140, 153, 154, 155, 165, 166, 184, 191, 199, 208, 212, 219, 220, 221, 222–3
Eggleston, Elizabeth 106
Electoral Act 95, 96
employment *see* career; work
epilepsy 13
equal opportunity 2, 28, 68, 170, 173, 193
Evatt, Clive 84, 221
Evatt, Elizabeth 176
Even in the Best of Homes 227

Family Law Act 202
father 12, 15, 21, 64, 78, 84, 91, 93, 94, 101, 102, 116, 124, 125, 151, 157, 161, 165, 188, 189, 197, 198, 214, 218, 222
Fear, Favour or Affection 106
Female Eunuch, The 165
feminism 4, 68, 84, 87, 88, 91, 96, 98, 121, 122, 141, 142, 144, 149, 163, 168, 218, 219
Ferris, Bob 37
Fesl, Eve 63, 109
Fett, Ione 88
Fighting for Peace 95
film 91, 95, 178
financial pressures 5, 37, 48, 49
Fingleton, Diane 6, 171–6, 218, 221
Fingleton, Philippa 95
Fitchett, Ian 38
Fitzgerald, Deidre 212
Foley, Gary 60
Foley, Stephen 214
Fonseca, Lariane 6, 149–57, 218, 220, 222, 228
Foumaini, Heather 44
Fraser, Dawn 163, 164
Fraser, Virginia 63

Garrett, Peter 94
Gaudron, Mary 176
gender 1, 50, 66, 104, 107, 117,

INDEX

122, 162–3
  images 82, 139, 140
Gillespie, Christine 63
Goethe Institut 223
Goss, Roisin (Hirschfeld) 174
Goward, Pru 46
Greer, Germaine 165
Growing Up Feminist 227
Guilfoyle, Des 43

Haines, Ian 67
Haines, Janine 5, 64–70, 97, 218, 219, 221, 222, 227
Harding, Eleanor 63
Harding, Janina 63
Harding, Johnny 63
Harvard University 188, 192, 221
Hawes, Elizabeth 1, 7
Hayden, Bill 173, 221
health 5, 63, 72–5, 78, 79, 80, 154
  services 72, 73, 74, 77, 79, 80, 142, 155, 156, 157
  see also AIDS
Herald 15, 16, 17
Hetti Perkins Home 74
Higson, Eve 95, 100
Hoey, Bill 15
Hoffman, Liz 63
Holt, Lillian 125
House of Representatives 68, 97, 98
Howe, Brian 205, 206
Huggins, Jack 124, 125
Huggins, Jackie 6, 124–30, 220, 223, 226, 227, 228
Huggins, Rita 124, 125, 126
Hunt, Alan 209, 226
Hutchinson, Ivan 14

I Can Jump Puddles 14
ILO Convention 156 2
immigrant 6, 149, 150, 189, 190, 192, 200
incest *see* sexual abuse
intellectuals 102
Interpretation Bill Report 226
Intruders on the Rights of Men 3

IQ tests 48, 65, 66, 162, 183, 198
isolation 132–3

Jackomos, Merle 63
Jackson, Sharryn 43–4
James, Clive 47
Jans, Jessie 14
Jex-Blake, Sophia 219
Johns, Brian 39
Johnson, Eva 63
journalism 4, 11–20 *passim*, 28, 35–9, 41, 49, 51–4, 98, 217, 222
  risks 20, 45, 51, 52

Kenny, SJ 145
Kirby, Michael 192, 224
Klein, Renate 156

Labor Party *see* Australian Labor Party
Land Rights Act 184
law 5, 6, 103, 138, 162, 163, 166–7, 168–9, 171, 172, 175–6, 178, 179, 182, 183, 185, 198, 201, 208, 209, 218, 220, 226, 227
  academia 103, 104, 106, 183, 221
  access to 103–4, 211
  and social justice 174, 192, 211, 212
  reform 201, 203, 213, 224, 225, 226
  tribunals 212, 213, 226
Law Reform Commission Act 226
law school 103, 167–8, 182, 184, 200, 209, 211, 219, 220
Lawrence, Carmen 46
legal centres 104, 174, 175, 180, 202
Liberal Party 67, 69, 97, 226
Liddy-Corpus, Louise 4, 21–31, 220, 226, 228
local government 62, 134, 135–6
Loff, Bebe 213
Lovett, Iris 63
Lymburner, Bessie 72

INDEX

Lymburner, Eric 71
lymphodemia 13

Macklin, Michael 69
mail-order brides 120, 122
Mansell, Michael 63
Marginson, Melba 6, 115–23, 218, 222, 227, 228
Marginson, Simon 120
marriage 5, 6, 17, 33, 171, 199, 218, 220
   see also motherhood; women
Marshall, Alan 14
Matrimonial Property Acts 3
Max-Planck-Institut 224, 225
McCallum, Sandra 224
McGauran, Julian 97
McGowan, Les 193
McLean, Jean 214
McQueen, Humphrey 107
measles 40, 101
medicine 85, 155
   training 85–6, 88
Men Against Rape 214
Menuhin, Hepzibah 214
Mercer, Dave 214
Miller, Casey 225
Millhouse, Robin 67, 221
Millington, Bob 19
Minden, Shelly 156
mission 22, 29
Morgan, Edith 215
Morgan, Paul 63
Moss, Allan 195–6
Moss, Irene 6, 187–96, 220, 221, 222, 223
mother 11, 12, 15, 16, 18, 21, 25–6, 27, 29, 41, 48, 58–9, 64, 67, 78, 82, 83, 91, 93, 99, 101, 116, 124, 125, 151, 157, 161, 163, 167, 170, 171, 172, 177, 182, 188–9, 197, 198, 213, 217, 218, 222
motherhood 4, 18, 19, 53, 65, 78–9, 87, 89–90, 103, 104–5, 130, 152, 184, 199, 200, 205, 214

and stress 18, 87, 105, 133, 152, 202–03, 214–15
and work 38, 19–20
   see also balance, search for; career
Ms 173
multicultural studies, law 109
   see also cross-cultural studies
Murphy, Lionel 173, 225
music 49, 103, 140, 219

National Companies and Securities Commission 38
National Party 94, 97, 100, 226
Naylor, Hillary 36
Neave, Marcia 201, 202
Needham, Maud Helen 217, 218
Nettheim, Garth 201
New Zealand Broadcasting Commission 37
New Zealand Journalists' Association 36
Niland, Carmel 193
Nile, Elaine 94
Nordby, Virginia Blomer 222
Northern Territory 21, 24, 131, 133, 135
Northern Territory News 26
Nuclear Disarmament Party 94, 95, 96
nursing, as career 12, 41, 72, 73, 83, 92, 152, 162
Nygh, Peter 221

O'Connor, Deidre 192, 212
O'Shaugnessy, Pieta 42
Owen, Mary 210, 214

Palm Island 71, 72
Papago Indians 72
Parliament House 39, 98
parliament, member of 5, 67, 96, 97, 148, 163
parliamentary privilege 144, 148
patriarchy *see* domination, male; sexism; women

233

INDEX

Perkins, Charles 27
Pettman, Jan 121
Philippines 115–20
Pilger, John 80
Pizzey, Erin 142, 223
PMG 24, 58
political awareness 5, 12, 49, 50, 53, 88, 116, 117, 118, 121, 122, 125, 129, 152, 154, 155, 167, 173, 220
Political Prisoners No. 1 178
poverty 78, 80, 177, 178, 215
powerlessness 150, 182, 185, 202
Prineas, Peter 99
Puplick, Chris 68

racism 23, 26, 62, 63, 78, 79, 130, 150, 151, 153, 177, 185, 193, 194, 220, 221–2
  see also Aborigines; domination, white
Radford, Gail 28
radio 4, 26, 31, 39, 42, 43, 45
Raine, June 87
rape see sexual abuse
Rathus, Zoe 176
Rayner, Moira 46
Recher, Harry 100
Reid, Alison 23
religion 82, 88, 89, 151
reproductive technologies 155–6, 214
Reynolds, Margaret 30, 68
Role of Law as it Operates in a Multicultural Society, The 108
role models 12, 29, 30, 42, 43, 67, 70, 78, 82, 91, 104, 124, 125, 156, 157, 163, 167, 182, 188, 213
  see also mother; father
Rosales, Etta 121
Rose, Danny 28
Rose, Miriam 30
Rowan, Dawn 6, 139–48, 220, 223, 227
Rowland, Robyn 46, 121, 155

Royal Commission into Aboriginal Deaths in Custody 60
rural environment 33, 41, 46, 64, 200–01, 204
Ryan, Susan 60, 107

Sackville, Ronald 201
Saunders, Cheryl 213
Schembri, Charles 121
Schmolke, Sue 6, 131–8, 221, 222, 227, 228
Scream Quietly or the Neighbours Will Hear 142, 223
Scutt, Felicity Beth 217, 218
Scutt, Jocelynne A. 1–7, 217–28
Scutt (now Joyce), Robin 217, 218
secretary 173
Senate 68, 94, 95, 96, 97, 100
Sense and Sensibility 5
sex 53, 199
Sex Discrimination Act 68, 69
sexism 53, 62, 79, 86, 98, 105, 131, 150, 153, 169, 185, 194, 212, 214, 219, 220, 222
  in academia 105, 106, 107, 108–10, 111, 193
  in the church 88, 89, 90
  in journalism 37, 38–9, 45, 53, 54
  in law 6, 103, 104, 169, 170, 176, 201, 219, 226, 227
  in medicine 85, 86, 88, 90, 219, 227
  in politics 39, 67, 69, 97, 219
  in teaching 66, 218
  see also domination, male
sexual abuse 32, 59, 76, 141, 214, 220, 225
sexual harassment 105, 153, 195, 219
Shankleton, Laelie 22, 29
Shellard, David 99
Shelters in the Storm 144
Shiften, Lynette 212
Simons, Pam 98
Singleton, Jane 46

INDEX

Smallwood, Gracelyn 5, 71–80, 220, 222, 226, 227
Smith, Murray 15
social work 61
Social Security Act 212
Solomon, David 38, 39, 221
Southern Times Messenger 145, 146, 147
Spender, Dale 143
Spender, Lynne 3
sport 151, 163, 164
Standard Newspapers 15, 16
Standing Orders 97
Stanley, Alf 72
Stott Despoja, Shirley 4, 47–54, 218, 220, 226, 228
Street, Jessie 99
student politics 117–18, 191, 192, 222
Sullivan, Kathy 97–8
Summers, Anne 137
Sun 102
Sunday Press 19
Sutherland, Narelle 176
Swift, Kate 225
swimming 163, 164
Swinstead, Dallas 16
Sykes, Roberta (Bobbi) 30, 60

Tate, Michael 97
teachers' college 102, 106, 165
teaching 70, 101, 106, 119, 151, 155, 156, 197
  as career 12, 64, 65, 66, 92, 118–19, 121, 140, 152, 162, 217, 218
television 4, 31, 179, 228
Teppitt, Veronica 28
Test Tube Women 156
Thiering, Barbara 89
Tito, Fiona 6, 197–207, 218, 219, 222, 224, 228
Tjululuk 30
toilet, unisex 39
Toomelah report 195
trade unions 23, 119–20, 155, 204

travel 12, 42, 46, 62, 72, 73, 74, 87, 88, 105, 106, 126–7, 132, 154, 167, 172, 173, 211
Truth 36
Turner, Pat 30

Ungunmerr 30
University of Michigan 222, 224
urban environment 178, 182, 184

Vallentine, Jo 94, 97, 99
Viet Nam war 140, 141, 153, 167, 191, 209, 214, 220

Warnock, Diana 46
Watson, Irene 6, 177–86, 218, 220, 223, 228
Watts, Carolyn 4, 41–6, 221, 222, 228
Webster, Alasdair 99
West, Rosemary 19, 20
Western Times 17
White, Carol 176
Whiting, Milton 226
Whitlam government 96, 225
Williams, Glanville 222–3
Williams, June 192
Willessee, Geraldine 30
Wilson, Beth 7, 208–15, 218, 220, 221, 226
women
  and achievement 5, 11, 12, 14, 20, 23, 46, 54, 89, 227
  and discrimination 4, 35, 37, 50, 65, 66, 85, 89, 110, 111
  and economic independence 7, 31, 34, 44, 53, 132, 173, 214
  and law 6, 169, 170, 174
  and marriage 17, 86, 152
  and oppression 170
  and payment for work 5, 38, 66, 152
  and relationships 15, 44, 199
  and self-image 11, 82, 136, 137, 152, 154
  and social justice 40, 220

INDEX

and threat of violence 49, 50, 152
appropriate roles 12, 92, 139, 140, 154
'dangerous' 1, 3, 7
see also career; domination, male; education; law; mother-hood; sexism; work
Women of Ideas 144
women's advisory council 137
women's conferences 75, 129, 155, 224, 225, 226, 227
Women's Electoral Lobby Draft Bill on Rape 225
Women's Movement 1, 6, 121, 129, 130, 141, 154, 173, 199, 210, 215, 226, 228
women's pages 35, 50, 218
women's shelters 6, 142, 143
Christie's Beach 142, 143, 144–7, 148
women's units 127, 128, 129
Wood, Robert 94, 95, 96, 97
work 2, 7, 18, 24, 25, 40, 41, 42, 43, 44, 50, 53, 54, 64, 69, 72, 83, 101, 132–3, 136, 137, 151, 153, 154, 165, 166, 175, 179, 180, 184, 197, 209, 210, 214, 215, 221
see also career; education; sexism; women
working-class 49, 85, 104, 110, 163, 213
writers 3, 4, 5, 29, 31, 107, 108, 228
see also journalism

Ziller, Alison 192

As a Woman – Writing Women's Lives
edited by Jocelynne A. Scutt

In her book *Silences*, the United States' feminist Tillie Olsen writes of the 'unnatural silences' of those who have never been able to write, or who have never been able to find the time to do so. In Australia in 1888, some eighty years earlier, Louise Lawson wrote: 'Compared to the countless centuries of the silence of women, compared to the century preceding ours — the first in which women wrote in any noticeable numbers — ours has been a favourable one.'

The silences that abound *about* women's lives, and *in* women's lives must continue to be broken. Compared with Louise Lawson's century, *our* century has favoured women. But women's voices, though heard and read well by many women, have not yet gained the same foothold in writing and publishing as the words of men.

With an introduction and epilogue by Jocelynne A. Scutt, *As a Woman — Writing Women's Lives* brings into the broader public arena the words and voices of twenty-two women with divergent hopes, aims and opinions. Their lives have been shaped by race, ethnic origin, geography, family constellation, socio-economic status, and as women. Each has an immeasurable capacity for laughter, for life, for achievement and success.

These women have stepped out, into the world, as political and social beings. They are 'ordinary' and 'extraordinary' women.

Contributors: Robin Joyce, Pamela Ditton, Sandra Shotlander, Judy Small, Lynne Spender, Kay Setches, Moira Rayner, Marie Andrews, Edith Hall, Irene Greenwood, Betty Olle, Lenore Manderson, Merrin Hartrick, Katie Ball, Julie Reiter, Faith Bandler, Anne Thacker, Michelle Schwarz, Rebecca Maxwell, Gail Warman, Renate Klein, Patmalar Ambikapathy.

Published by Artemis Publishing

Breaking Through – Women, Work and Careers
What the critics say...

'Women of all ages will find some special messages in *Breaking Through*, a worthwhile contribution to the Australian feminist debate.'
Corrie Perkins, *Sunday Age*

'This book makes me glad to be an Australian woman.'
Lenore Coltheart, *Adelaide Advertiser*

'... refreshing in its willingness to see that careers succeed for many reasons, not all of them found in textbooks.'
Penelope Nelson, *Weekend Australian*

'... moving writing, pointing to real and creative differences in the ways women approach the world of work.'
Margaret Simons, *Age*